Egan, Clifford L.

Neither peace nor
war

Neither Peace nor War

NEITHER
PEACE
NOR
WAR

*Franco-American
Relations, 1803–1812*

CLIFFORD L. EGAN

Louisiana State University Press

Baton Rouge and London

Designer: Barbara Werden
Typeface: Linotron Garamond
Typesetter: G & S Typesetters, Inc.
Printer and binder: Thomson-Shore, Inc.

Library of Congress Cataloging in Publication Data

Egan, Clifford L.
    Neither peace nor war.

    Bibliography: p.
    Includes index.
    1. United States—Foreign relations—France.
2. France—Foreign relations—United States.   3. United
States—Foreign relations—1801–1815.   4. France—
Foreign relations—1792–1815.   5. United States—History
—War of 1812—Causes.   I. Title.
E183.8.F8E43   1983   973.5'22   82-17272
ISBN 0-8071-1076-0

Chapter Three is a revised version of "The United States,
France and West Florida, 1803–1807," which was published
in the January, 1969, issue of *Florida Historical Quarterly*.

Publication of this book has been assisted by a grant from the
Andrew W. Mellon Foundation.

To the memory of
my mother and father,

EDITH *and* DANIEL EGAN, SR.

In the course of its history, which is now some two hundred years long, this is not the first time [that Franco-American relations have been strained]. For it really seems that as between our two countries there is always one whose instinct carries it toward moderation while the other tends to depart from it. At the different periods when France chose to lead an adventurous life, she did not find the permanent support of the United States. Today, when the latter in turn is particularly susceptible to the impulses of power, it is true that France does not constantly approve of them.

—CHARLES DE GAULLE
Paris, January 30, 1968

Contents

Preface xv
Acknowledgments xvii

ONE *Jeffersonian America* 1
TWO *Napoleonic France* 23
THREE *West Florida* 46
FOUR *Economic Coercion* 67
FIVE *From the Coles Mission
to the Cadore Letter* 103
SIX *Interregnum* 125
SEVEN *Neither Peace nor War* 147
Epilogue 186

Appendix: A Chronology 193
Bibliography 199
Index 219

Illustrations

following page 78

Thomas Jefferson
James Madison
James Monroe
John Armstrong
James Bowdoin
Jonathan Russell
Joel Barlow
William Lee
David Bailie Warden

following page 156

Augustus John Foster
Napoleon
Talleyrand
Duc de Bassano
Turreau

Maps

Napoleon's Europe in 1812,
   showing   154

   chief French ports and major
      European cities
   battlefields: 1805 – 1809
   Napoleon's Russian campaign
   Joel Barlow's route to Vilna and
      Zarnowiec

The United States in 1812,
   showing   155

   chief seaports and cities
   the West Florida claims

Preface

Chronologically, this study of Franco-American relations from after the Louisiana Purchase to the death of the American minister to France, Joel Barlow, in December, 1812, fits between Alexander De Conde, *This Affair of Louisiana* (New York, 1976), and Lawrence S. Kaplan, "France and the War of 1812," *Journal of American History*, LVII (1970), 36–47. Other historians ranging from Henry Adams to Marvin Zahniser have written about the subject and, as my footnotes indicate, I am indebted to many of them. Most of these historians have been Americans, because in the early diplomatic history of the United States, France was a great power while the United States was a minor nation. Thus, Americans were keenly aware of Napoleonic France's awesome strength while few Frenchmen appreciated the significance or the potential of the transatlantic republic.

Since no narrative of Franco-American relations can be understood without some knowledge of the troubled state of Great Britain's relations with her former colonies, my treatment of Anglo-American relations is necessary but peripheral. Those wishing more information on the subject should read Reginald Horsman, *The Causes of the War of 1812* (Philadelphia, 1962), and Bradford Perkins, *Prologue to War: Great Britain and the United States, 1805–1812* (Berkeley, 1961).

I have tried also to explain the often confusing story of commercial warfare prior to 1812. If relatively few Americans understood the economic restrictions imposed by their government between 1806 and 1812, even fewer citizens of the First Empire comprehended the maze of Napoleonic decrees created during the Anglo-French war beginning in 1803. It is not surprising that few historians have mastered the complicated economic restrictions of the period; consequently, I have tried to clarify the more important coercive measures as they affected Franco-American relations.

Given the complexities of the narrative, some of my more important points should be mentioned: Napoleonic France had an American policy after 1807, and that policy was to involve the United States in a war with Great Britain. The French pursued their goal in a most peculiar fashion because of the quixotic nature of the Emperor Napoleon. As I point out, the French ruler was served by a dedicated corps of individuals, some of them knowledgeable about America, who offered sound but largely unheeded advice. Thus, the War of 1812 came in 1812 and not at an earlier and perhaps more opportune date for France and the United States; and the Anglo-American war started not because of but despite France's duplicity and contradictory actions.

Thomas Jefferson and James Madison believed that, after the Louisiana Purchase bargain, the United States and France could coexist amicably. This does not mean that the two Americans were innocent children of the Enlightenment; both could be hardheaded, merciless men. What the Virginia leaders failed to understand properly was that neutral America's prosperity disturbed and infuriated the warring rivals, Britain and France; the longer Anglo-French hostilities endured, the greater the risk became for America because the cross-channel foes would enforce ever more Draconian and confusing economic measures to crush each other.

Looking back at the events following 1803, it is easy to censure the policies formulated by the Jeffersonians and to criticize their reasoning on the issues of the day. It should be remembered that these men sincerely desired peace, and in quest of it they experimented with a variety of economic weapons over a period of years. These measures may appear in retrospect ill-conceived or even stupid; but, as the international scene darkened and the screws of English and French commercial warfare tightened, economic coercion seemed a valid alternative to war. Despite the advent of war in the summer of 1812, few critics could claim that the government had not sincerely tried to maintain American neutrality.

France played an important part in the causation of the War of 1812. It was not that Napoleon had tricked a naïve Madison with the Cadore letter; nor was it, as some of the antiwar men believed, because the United States was fulfilling a secret understanding with the Emperor, who was then poised in Eastern Europe about to launch his invasion of Russia. Rather, French actions—the destruction of American shipping on the high seas, the capriciousness with which the French enforced their Continental System, the erratic treatment accorded American vessels in French ports— bewildered Americans and contributed to the intensification of nationalism in the young republic. Finally, in 1812, a majority of congressmen and citizens could bear belligerent insults no longer, and the most obvious, the most provocative, great power—Britain—was selected as the object of American wrath. With this national anger in mind, Joel Barlow journeyed to Napoleon's winter headquarters, determined to secure a long-promised but elusive settlement. Unsuccessful in his quest, Barlow died in Poland in late December, 1812. Napoleon's defeat in Russia, however, led to the Emperor's abdication in April, 1814; the collapse of the First Empire lessened Franco-American friction and led ultimately to the resolution of some of the outstanding disputes between the two nations.

Acknowledgments

I want to thank a number of people and institutions for their support and help over the years. The late Daniel M. Smith supervised my work as a doctoral candidate at the University of Colorado. I am most grateful to Professor Smith for his assistance and encouragement; I hope this book measures up to his high standards. Although Julian Boyd did not live to see the publication of this study, I like to think that he would have found it a worthwhile contribution to the historiography of Jeffersonian America. Other individuals who lent their support, their help, or inspired me include the Aldrich family of Barrytown-on-Hudson, New York, Madame Ulane Bonnel, Thomas Camfield, Edward Feasel, Victor Mote, James Poteet, C. Edward Skeen, Mrs. Aladeen Smith, and William R. Townsend. I want to express my appreciation also to the staffs of the John Hay Library at Brown University, the William L. Clements Library at the University of Michigan, the New-York Historical Society, the New York Public Library, and the Manuscript Division of the Library of Congress; men and women at these facilities went beyond the call of duty helping me in my quest for information. The American Philosophical Society and the University of Houston have provided material support.

More than anyone, my wife, Margaret Townsend Egan, has contributed to the completion of this manuscript. She has subsidized research costs, tolerated my scholarly eccentricities, and suffered through my involvements with such people as John Armstrong, Joel and Ruth Barlow, Robert Fulton, Daniel Parker, and Louis Turreau. Most important, she has, to the profit of readers, improved the organization and readability of the manuscript. A quote from a letter written by Ruth Barlow expresses my sentiments about my wife very well: "God bless and preserve my dearest and best beloved friend in whom I live and breathe." My sons Gregory, Richard, and Mark Adams Egan have delayed completion of "the book," probably to the benefit of readers also.

Neither Peace nor War

ONE

Jeffersonian America

For the second time in a decade, war erupted between Great Britain and France in May, 1803. Destined to continue for eleven years, this latest conflict between long-standing foes engulfed all Europe, and eventually the infant United States of America, as the two great adversaries tirelessly maneuvered for victory. Only with Napoleon exiled to the distant South Atlantic island of St. Helena and France occupied by the triumphant powers did lasting peace come.

[I]

During this period, America was a weak power, unrespected by and largely unknown to France. Ironically, France had served as midwife at the birth of the unwieldy band of states only a quarter-century before. As the French embarked on their greatest war to date, however, the United States eagerly embraced neutrality, encouraged by an overwhelming number of Americans desiring to escape European embroilments. "I trust . . . that everything will be carefully avoided which may tend to increase our European connextions," ran a typical comment. Some talked of curtailing commerce; others spoke with great fervor about changing the Atlantic Ocean into "a gulf of fire" once all Americans had returned to their native shores.[1]

President Thomas Jefferson shared these sentiments, and both publicly and privately he frequently expressed the hope that America would be

1. Thomas Sumter to Fulwar Skipwith, May 10, 1803, in Miscellaneous Manuscripts T., New-York Historical Society; William Wirt to James Monroe, June 10, 1806, in James Monroe Papers, Library of Congress.

spared involvement in Europe's war. Jefferson directed diplomats in London and Paris to report the dismay felt in Washington at the outbreak of hostilities. Further, the emissaries were to state that the United States would fulfill its obligations as a neutral and would anxiously await the return of peace.[2] This American position remained unchanged until the War of 1812.

Ample reasons justified this policy. In the first place, Americans harbored deep suspicions of Europe in general and France in particular. Travelers to the continent repeatedly stressed Old World immorality. Invariably visitors to France cited the improper attire of women as proof that France and Europe were decaying. At a theatrical performance in Bordeaux, one yankee described how "elegant dancers" wore a "silk net [which] covered part of their arms, their breasts, and the lower part of their bodies, of a flesh color, so that at a distance I thought they were half naked; for this cobweb covering was drawn over them so tight that you could discover every muscle." Since the dancers displayed "their hips at every move," the American maintained that "such indecent representations can never lead the mind to virtue. All the exhibition I have been at," he added, "appeared to me to be calculated only to inspire libidinous thoughts."[3] Young Washington Irving, witnessing an equally scandalous display, "felt my American blood mounting to my cheeks on their [the actresses'] account." Irving was even more disturbed at the indifference of the audience: "These lascivious exhibitions are strong evidences of the depraved morals and licentiousness of the public," he generalized. Another traveler, Victor Marie Du Pont, was shocked at a celebration honoring Napoleon Bonaparte's great victories in Italy, where the ladies did not compete to see "who will dress the most, but rather who will undress. I have never seen such display of human flesh." The nude statues in the gardens of the Tuileries and at the Luxembourg Palace distressed William H. Crawford, who represented the United States in France amidst Napoleon's downfall. Given the authority, he vowed, "I would prohibit the importation and even the manufacture, of naked people, in marble, plaster, or paper."[4] Not all Americans were as disturbed by what

2. Robert R. Livingston to Charles Maurice du Talleyrand-Périgord, in Archives du Ministère des Affaires Étrangères, Correspondance Politique, États-Unis, LVI, photostats in Library of Congress (hereafter cited as AMAE, with the appropriate volume number).

3. Entry of February 18, 1796, in Mary Lee Mann (ed.), *A Yankee Jeffersonian: Selections from the Diary and Letters of William Lee of Massachusetts, Written from 1796–1840* (Cambridge, 1958), 13. Another time, crying "Give me America," Lee described English women as "all very awkward & dress[ing] like the devil." William Lee to Susan Lee, April 16, 1802, in Lee-Palfrey Family Papers, Library of Congress.

4. Entry of September 8, 1804, in William P. Trent (ed.), *Mr. Irving's Notes and Journal of Travel in Europe, 1804–1805* (3 vols.; New York, 1920), I, 77–78; entry of February

they saw as Crawford, but many noted their alarm at the prevailing moral tone and indicated they wished to preserve the much sterner and correct code existing across the Atlantic.

A striking contrast existed between monarchical Europe and the republican United States. In the former, one often inherited status or, as in Napoleonic France, had rank conferred for service to the First Empire. In the latter, individuals were accorded rank commensurate with accomplishment. The difference between the two was especially noticeable at diplomatic functions where a devout democrat saw "many of the diplomatic corps from the different powers of Europe, bespangled with stars, crosses and other insignia of monarchy. With all their ornaments and ridiculous trappings none of them appeared as well to my eye as our plain-dressed ministers." In another instance, an American diplomat described the intricate social procedures he encountered visiting various dignitaries. After exchanging pleasantries with lower echelon figures, he finally reached a "saloon of reception," where he was announced successively as "the American Colonel," "the Consul," "the American General," and as "the Consul from Malaga." Shortly after, the same envoy cynically remarked that Paris had as many kings "as can be found in two packs of cards," and speculated that Napoleon might turn one of the drones into a coachman.[5] A recollection of these views partially explains the popular desire to remain apart from Europe.

Overseas venturers were perturbed by the incredible poverty they found. Massachusetts merchant Thomas Handasyd Perkins toured a lead mine in Brittany that employed 1,200 workers (including many women) who labored for the equivalent of twenty cents daily. Brittany had always been a poor section, but in other parts of France observers noted destitution and constantly complained of being accosted by hordes of beggars. In Marseilles, Irving claimed that Americans were "generally considered the patrons of beggars[,] shoe blacks[,] fiddlers & pedlars." In the Mediterranean port, the New Yorker was pursued by shoe blacks currying favor by crying the only English they knew, "monsieur, monsieur, G-d dam son de bish son de bish." Between Bordeaux and Bayonne in extreme southwest France, an

16–17, 1801, in Victor Marie Du Pont, *Journey to France and Spain, 1801*, ed. Charles W. David (Ithaca, 1961), 27–28; entry of August 26, 1813, in Daniel Chauncey Knowlton (ed.), *The Journal of William H. Crawford* (Northampton, Mass., 1925), 39.

5. Joseph C. Cabell to St. George Tucker, June 29, 1803, in Tucker-Coleman Papers, College of William and Mary; Lee to Susan Lee, December 27, 1809, in Mann (ed.), *A Yankee Jeffersonian*, 100–101. According to Lee, after his introduction as a Malagan someone replied that he was "too white to be a Spaniard"; Lee to Susan Lee, December 6, 1809, *ibid.*, 91.

American merchant captain was surprised to encounter penniless peasants unable to speak French; he was told that only the upper classes spoke the language. Astonished at the degradation of so many, Irving thought it was "impossible to conceive the various modes the lower classes in Europe have of getting a livelihood, unknown in America." Residents of early national American were appalled at the contrast between opulence and squalor. In America there was pauperism, but there was also opportunity. On returning home, one South Carolinian found "every thing flourishing. . . . This cannot fail to afford a charming prospect when contrasted to the appearances displayed in the Old World."[6]

Americans quickly realized that privileges and liberties they took for granted were nonexistent or abridged in wartime France. As early as 1793 Samuel Ward noted that residency in France strengthened his patriotism; in the United States, he wrote, "the only true liberty and equality exists—every man has the same personal rights of acquiring property—of having it preserved—of being in every respect protected and of choosing or in turn being chosen to all the [offices?] in the States."[7] A decade later, the French government was manned by a huge and powerful bureaucracy: theaters and museums were subsidized, the state ran schools, and domestic and foreign commerce was subjected to maddening delays because of excessive paperwork. The hiring of unneeded workers caused widespread corruption as employees solicited bribes to supplement low wages.[8]

Though generally respectful, and even intrigued by Europe, Americans developed an unflattering image of the Continent. Onetime affection for the homeland of their ancestors and appreciation for French military support that brought their revolution to a successful close were overtaken by the suspicion that Europe was debased, devoted forever to principles of elitism, closed to opportunity and individual freedom, and chronically at war. "What the world has pleased to call refinement," one disillusioned

6. Thomas H. Perkins to Sarah L. Perkins, June 2, 1812, in Thomas G. Cary (ed.), *Memoir of Thomas Handasyd Perkins* (Boston, 1856), 213; entry of August 27, 1804, in Trent (ed.), *Mr. Irving's Notes and Journals*, I, 73–74; George Coggeshall to his superiors, February 9, 1814, in George Coggeshall, *Voyages to Various Parts of the World Made Between the Years 1799 and 1844* (New York, 1851), 42, 44–46; entry of July 28, 1804, in Trent (ed.), *Mr. Irving's Notes and Journals*, I, 25–28; Thomas Sumter to Monroe, December 11, 1803, in James Monroe Papers, New York Public Library.

7. Samuel Ward to William Constable, January 3, 1793, in William Constable Papers, New York Public Library Annex.

8. "There are more custom house officers in one port of France where no trade is carried on, than there are in the whole of the United States." Underpaid, "these poor wretches . . . must starve or steal, and consequently, do the last." Entry of February [?], 1801, in Victor Marie Du Pont, *Journey to France and Spain*, 14–15.

young man wrote, "appears to me quite the opposite and instead of thinking the U.S. in a state of barbarism with relation to Europe I think them perfectly civilized."[9]

An outgrowth of this disenchantment with the Old World was the effort to eradicate European influence in America. Far more than France, Britain bore the brunt of nationalist wrath. "It is England who with a sure but silent hand saps the foundations of our real independence," a Rhode Islander complained. Another New Englander was convinced that Britain aimed "to reduce us to the situation of Colonies." Men who held such beliefs were enthusiastic backers of Jefferson's bid for the presidency; the Virginian appeared "determined to promote the internal resources of our Country, in order to render us a truly independent nation."[10] Thus, with the support of the opponents of foreign influence, Jefferson's embargo went into effect late in 1807. These nationalists argued that reducing foreign trade was advantageous because it diverted capital to domestic ventures and promoted self-sufficiency. Similarly, they opposed the rechartering of the First Bank of the United States in 1811 because foreigners owned most of the bank's stock (52 percent in 1798, 72 percent in 1809). Ignoring the fact that foreign investors could not vote their shares, the Senate narrowly defeated a bill to amend and extend the original charter.[11] Several factors figured in the bank's untimely demise, but Representative Erastus Root of New York emphasized that the "prejudice of the Republicans [supporters of Jefferson and James Madison] was very strong against Great Britain and everything British or in any way connected with her. The Bank was called a British bank, and its supposed influence in this country was dreaded."[12] As the financial history of the War of 1812 demonstrated, destruction of the

9. Charles Carter to St. George Tucker, January 18, 1807, in Tucker-Coleman Papers.

10. Jonathan Russell to Gilbert du Motier, Marquis de Lafayette, August 23, 1798, in Jonathan Russell Papers, Brown University, Providence, R.I.; Jacob Crowninshield to William Bentley, December 14, 1805, in Crowninshield Family Papers, Peabody Museum, Salem, Massachusetts; George Logan to Russell, May 20, 1801, in Russell Papers, Brown University.

11. Bray Hammond, *Banks and Politics in America from the Revolution to the Civil War* (Princeton, 1957), 209–22. Hammond downgrades the idea of an agrarian-mercantile clash, writing that "the way representatives of business enterprise worked against the Bank, and the way numerous agrarians worked for it, one finds it hard to ascribe the Bank's discontinuance to agrarian opposition" (212).

12. Quoted *ibid.*, 223–24. Former senator William Plumer heard "that a large portion of the shares of the present bank are owned by British subjects. That circumstance operates injuriously & with great force against us" because money was drained from America for interest payments. Besides, "our own monied men have sufficient capital to fill the subscription to the bank." William Plumer to Charles Cutts, December 15, 1810, in William Plumer Papers, Library of Congress.

bank proved a hollow victory. Nevertheless, it was considered a positive step because it represented an attack on alien control. This thrust at foreign influence was a harbinger of more vigorous action by the Twelfth Congress.

America's enviable commercial position between the warring powers also promoted neutrality. The conflict that ravaged Europe in the 1790s undeniably stimulated American commerce, as men like Samuel Ward predicted. Cut off from their tropical colonies, the French allowed colonial produce to enter their country in American vessels; the British, too, relaxed controls on American shipping in the Jay Treaty of 1794. The figures are revealing: in the early years of Washington's administration, exports were about $20 million annually; by 1801 yearly sales overseas were approaching $100 million. Imports, which were higher, followed a comparable course. The war-born prosperity ended when peace was restored in 1801. Prices declined immediately, business failures increased, and idle ships and unemployed seamen filled ports. The slump between late 1801 and early 1803 was the severest downturn business had experienced up to that time; but with the resumption of war, economic growth resumed. Exports climbed immediately from $56 million in the year ending September 30, 1803, to $77 million in 1804, to $95 million in 1805, and exceeded the $100 million mark for the first time in 1806.[13] "The renewal of the war in Europe must infallibly tend to increase the commerce and of course the revenue of the United States," English chargé d'affaires Edward Thornton predicted.[14] The Englishman proved to be accurate, and the Americans anticipated harvesting the fruits of neutrality.

A weak military establishment was a major reason for remaining noninvolved. "I know of no government which would be so embarassing [*sic*] in a war as ours," Jefferson wrote after his retirement.[15] Although the former president did not list military feebleness as an explanation for governmental discomfort, he knew the nation's weakness. At a time when European ar-

13. Timothy Pitkin, *A Statistical View of the Commerce of the United States of America* (Hartford, 1816), 38, 154; Walter B. Smith and Arthur H. Cole, *Fluctuations in American Business, 1790–1860* (Cambridge, 1935), 17. From 1799 to 1806, despite the jolt occasioned by the Peace of Amiens, the United States enjoyed a level of prosperity not to be attained again for several decades. George Rogers Taylor, "American Economic Growth Before 1840: An Exploratory Essay," *Journal of Economic History*, XXIV (1964), 440; and Douglass C. North, "Early National Income Estimates of the U.S.," *Economic Development and Cultural Change*, IX (1961), 389–96.

14. Edward Thornton to Lord Hawkesbury, July 4, 1803, Foreign Office Archives, Public Record Office, 5:38, photostats, Library of Congress (hereafter cited as FOA 5 with the appropriate volume number).

15. Thomas Jefferson to James Madison, March 17, 1809, in James Madison Papers, Library of Congress.

mies contained hundreds of thousands of men, the United States Army, with approximately 3,500 volunteers, was deployed defending far-flung frontiers. The navy was in somewhat better position because, though small, it had seen action in the recent Quasi-War with France and was occupied in a police action against the Barbary Corsairs of North Africa. Nonetheless, against a first-class opponent it would be as ineffectual as the army.

The origins of this martial weakness were complex. War was viewed as "foolish" and "wicked." Since years would elapse before the United States could match the resources available to European states, pouring money into a military structure seemed unwise when the fledgling nation had other priorities. Washington spoke of the nation's being ready to meet an attack by 1815; Secretary of State Madison accepted 1812 as the dividing line. In both men's opinion a rapidly growing population augured well for America's defensive potential.[16] Jefferson opposed funding a large defense establishment when revenue was needed for governmental operations and to scale down the national debt. Besides, naval expansion might provoke the British into a preemptive strike. The history-conscious Founding Fathers recalled that the army of Rome had been responsible for that ancient power's switch from republic to empire, and the American statesmen believed a minimal military organization would prevent the United States from suffering a similar fate. Finally, neither Britain nor France was considered physically able to endanger the United States while they remained at loggerheads. For these reasons, America's armed forces remained undermanned.

Also fostering the neutral spirit was a widespread conviction that the success of the United States meant mankind's salvation. While other nations were monarchical, undemocratic, and unitary in structure, America was a republic and a representative democracy organized on a federal basis.[17] Furthermore, black slaves excepted, individuals were accorded liberties the inhabitants of few nations enjoyed; this freedom guaranteed interest in and fidelity to the Union.[18] "The affairs of this country *cannot go amiss,*" Wash-

16. See Samuel Ward to William Constable, January 14, 1793, in Constable Papers; Washington told Gouverneur Morris, December 22, 1795, "If this country is preserved in tranquility twenty years longer, it may bid defiance, in a just cause, to any power whatever." See also his letter to Charles Carroll, May 1, 1796, both in John C. Fitzpatrick (ed.), *The Writings of George Washington from the Original Manuscript Sources, 1745–1799* (39 vols.; Washington, 1931–1944), XXXIV, 401 and XXXV, 30. Irving Brant, "James Madison and His Times," *American Historical Review,* LVII (1952), 868–69, contains Madison's forecast.

17. Joel Barlow, *Oration Delivered at Washington, July Fourth 1809; at the Request of the Democratic Citizens of the District of Columbia* (Washington City, 1809), 5–6.

18. Old Republican Nathaniel Macon phrased it another way: "As democracy is founded on truth, nothing can prevail against her, so long as any will do justice to the principle."

ington believed; because of the *"many watchful guardians of them . . .* one is at no loss for a direction at every turn."[19] In effect, an empire of liberty existed which "would be an example and a beacon, unsheltered and unafraid of the light of truth."[20]

The idealism of the young republic's citizens was well founded. Population growth had been phenomenal: in the mid-seventeenth century, colonial inhabitants numbered in the thousands; in 1800 there were 5.5 million Americans with the number increasing by 200,000 annually.[21] Equating population with power, many commentators concurred with Gouverneur Morris that "the proudest empire in Europe is but a bauble, compared to what America *will be, must be* in the course of two centuries, perhaps one."[22] As population soared, wilderness gave way to civilization and the trans-Appalachian West was peopled. Most spectacular had been the winning of independence from Britain. Racked by dissension, a group of disparate colonies had wrested their freedom from the premier world power. Thereafter, the American Revolution was transformed in the minds of the participants into a divinely ordained and glorious epoch. The newly created nation faced a precarious existence in a hostile environment, however; and since involvement in war threatened the very life of the sacred republic, the empire of liberty must avoid Europe's latest conflagration.

Sophisticated Americans recognized the subtleties of the balance of power concept. These individuals saw the United States receiving advantages from the Franco-British stalemate. Some believed that the English would moderate their disdainful treatment of James Monroe, then minister

---

Nathaniel Macon to Joseph H. Nicholson, May 1, 1805, in Joseph H. Nicholson Papers, Library of Congress.

19. George Washington to Gouverneur Morris, June 25, 1794, in Fitzpatrick (ed.), *Writings of Washington*, XXXIII, 414.

20. See Julian P. Boyd, "Thomas Jefferson's 'Empire of Liberty,'" *Virginia Quarterly Review*, XXIV (1948), 538–54. Washington informed a middle-aged Englishman that succees would lead to global imitation of the American experiment. John Bernard, *Retrospections of America, 1797–1811* (New York, 1887), 90; in 1789 Alexander Hamilton described the United States as "a young and a growing Empire, with much Enterprise and vigour." See "Conversation with George Beckwith" in Harold C. Syrett and Jacob E. Cooke (eds.), *The Papers of Alexander Hamilton* (26 vols.; New York, 1961–1979), V, 483.

21. In his *Voyages dans les deux Louisianes* published in Paris in 1805, François Marie Perrin Du Lac wrote that it was necessary to witness "the energy and industry of Americans, both in manufacturing and agriculture to have a true idea of what this new people are capable of becoming as a result of their population which will double three or four times in the course of the century." Cited in Durand Echeverria, *Mirage in the West: A History of the French Image of American Society to 1815* (Princeton, 1957), 240.

22. Morris to John Parish, January 20, 1801, in Jared Sparks, *The Life of Gouverneur Morris* (3 vols.; Boston, 1832), III, 144.

to the court of St. James, as a result of the great French victory at Austerlitz late in 1805. Others felt that a deadlock safeguarded America against conquest. "A balance of Power must be pursued," a Louisiana resident insisted, "or we shall be swallowed by the victor."[23] As a neutral, the United States might be able to exploit the balance of power for territorial expansion. This seemed probable in light of the Louisiana windfall that occurred when, under the threat of renewed war, Napoleon had ordered the sale of the vast territory around and above New Orleans to the United States. It seemed logical that Napoleon, realizing the value of America's neutral merchant fleet, would cooperate further by pressuring his Spanish ally into making a favorable boundary settlement in the disputed Floridas.[24] The United States had received dividends from exploiting the balance of power, and further rewards appeared imminent.

Finally, neutrality seemed a feasible policy because, by mid-1803, the United States had settled most major disputes with Britain and France. John Jay had negotiated a treaty late in 1794 with Britain that had unleashed prolonged violent debate in the United States between those who argued that he had accepted humiliating terms and others who considered the agreement the best possible under the circumstances. With Washington's support, the disputed treaty became effective in 1796; although Jeffersonians grumbled over its provisions, they accepted it. Jay's treaty ushered in a period of harmony in Anglo-American relations. The two nations, in effect, mutually agreed that compromise was better than war. Thereafter, as Franco-American relations eroded, the community of interests between the mother country and her former colonies expanded.

One cloud remained on the horizon. The Jay Treaty had not settled the impressment issue; that question plagued Anglo-American relations throughout the Franco-British conflict and ultimately was a major cause of the War of 1812. Even at the height of America's undeclared naval war with France, the British took seamen off United States merchant vessels. In one flagrant case in November, 1798, H.M.S. *Carnatic* took crewmen off the U.S.S. *Baltimore*. Strangely enough, most historians have overlooked or minimized impressment in these years and accepted the idea that there was

23. Seth Hunt to Monroe, February 20, 1808, in Monroe Papers, New York Public Library. Earlier Jefferson wrote that parity between Britain and France was essential "to hold in check the disposition of the other to tyrannize over other nations." Jefferson to Monroe, January 8, 1804, in Paul L. Ford (ed.), *The Works of Thomas Jefferson* (12 vols.; New York: 1905), X, 67. See also Lawrence S. Kaplan, "Jefferson, the Napoleonic Wars, and the Balance of Power," *William and Mary Quarterly*, Series 3, XIV (1957), 196–217.

24. See Fulwar Skipwith to Tucker, June 6, 1803, December 1, 1804, in Tucker-Coleman Papers.

an Anglo-American rapprochement.[25] If this were true, it was because the Adams administration preferred to ignore impressment. Jefferson did not, and relations with Britain worsened steadily following the outbreak of war in 1803.

Franco-American relations were more cordial in mid-1803 than they had been or would be for years afterwards. The undeclared hostilities styled the Quasi-War had been terminated with the signing of the Convention of Môrtefontaine in the early hours of October 1, 1800. Ironically, the same day France concluded a preliminary agreement with Spain providing for French control of the Louisiana country. Rumors of the transfer caused consternation in the United States and led to negotiations in which the American objective was the control of the lower Mississippi River through the purchase of the region around New Orleans.[26] Fate in the form of France's international frustrations smiled on the young republic and in late April, 1803, the French sold not only New Orleans and its environs but the enormous heartland of modern America. Thus, as the old Anglo-French rivalry flared anew, the possibility of another showdown with France disappeared. In the aftermath of the Louisiana transaction, Jefferson foresaw "nothing which need ever interrupt the friendship between France and this country."[27] Considering the understandings reached, this was a reasonable expectation.

In American minds, nothing need interrupt neutrality either. Why should the status quo be disturbed when prosperity reigned, the national domain was growing, and preoccupation with war precluded any European meddling in American affairs? Jefferson's resounding electoral victory in 1804 proved popular contentment. As the semiofficial *National Intelligencer* in Washington editorialized, the United States in its twenty-ninth year of independence basked in "PEACE, PLENTY, and HAPPINESS," whereas the Old World was gripped by "WAR, SCARCITY, and a widespread DISTRESS."[28] Whether the idyllic situation endured depended in part on the executive leadership and its agents overseas.

25. Bradford Perkins developed this concept in *The First Rapprochement: England and the United States, 1795–1805* (Philadelphia, 1955). Alexander De Conde, *The Quasi-War: The Politics and Diplomacy of the Undeclared War with France, 1797–1801* (New York, 1966), 120, 177, 200–201, discusses the impressment problem.

26. "I have scarcely met with a person under whatever party he may rank himself, who does not appear to dread this event, and would not prefer almost any neighbours to the French." Thornton to Hawkesbury, January 26, 1802, in FOA 5:35, LC.

27. Jefferson to Cabanis, July 12, 1803, in Gilbert Chinard, *Jefferson et les Idéologues d'après Sa Correspondance Inédite avec Destutt de Tracy, Cabanis, J. B. Say et Auguste Comte* (Baltimore and Paris, 1925), 25–26; Alexander De Conde, *This Affair of Louisiana* (New York, 1976), is the best treatment of the Louisiana Purchase.

28. *National Intelligencer*, November 5, 1804.

[II]

In death, as in life, Thomas Jefferson remains controversial. Nothing illustrates this point better than the dispute about Jefferson's libertarianism. His admirers believe the author of the Declaration of Independence was without peer; his detractors think otherwise. The critics cite his relationship with the press and argue that he paid lip service to the concept of a free press. In reality, however, Jefferson never trusted the press "and his distrust soon ripened into choler." Yet the definitive edition of the Virginian's correspondence, made possible initially by a subvention from one of America's leading newspapers, in the first volume quotes Jefferson on the press as "the best instrument for enlightening the mind of man, and improving him as a rational, moral, and social thing."[29]

An even sharper battle has raged concerning Jefferson and blacks. While acknowledging the immorality of slavery over a half-century span, Jefferson nonetheless held humans in bondage. Although he wrote that all men were created equal, Jefferson believed blacks to be generally inferior to whites. Finally, though he was a staunch opponent of miscegenation, circumstantial evidence points toward Jefferson's intimacy with a young quadroon slave named Sally Hemings.[30] The arguments about Jefferson's real attitudes toward the blacks and the press are a measure of the historical vitality of a man dead over a century and a half.

Few of Jefferson's contemporaries were neutral about him. His supporters and friends thought he exemplified the noblest human qualities; he was "so frank, so open, so unreserved," simple in dress and appearance, tolerant, intelligent, and possessed far-ranging interests.[31] His opponents found him a cunning infidel who affected simplicity for the sake of popularity.[32]

29. Leonard W. Levy, *Jefferson and Civil Liberties* (Cambridge, 1963), 48; Jefferson to Adamantios Coray, October 31, 1823, cited in Julian P. Boyd *et al.* (eds.), *The Papers of Thomas Jefferson* (19 vols.; Princeton, 1950–), I, xxi. See also Frank L. Mott, *Jefferson and the Press* (Baton Rouge, 1943).

30. Merrill D. Peterson, *The Jefferson Image in the American Mind* (New York, 1962), 164–89. Jefferson's major biographer, Dumas Malone, has felt constrained to discuss "The Miscegenation Legend" in *Jefferson the President: First Term, 1801–1805* (Boston, 1970), 494–98. Fawn M. Brodie, "Jefferson Biographers and the Psychology of Canonization," *Journal of Interdisciplinary History*, II (1971), 155–71, criticizes males who have written on Jefferson for their inability to admit that the Virginian might have had affairs with Sally Hemings or Maria Cosway, the latter a married woman he met in 1786. Brodie's book-length account of Jefferson and the "life of the heart" appeared as *Thomas Jefferson: An Intimate History* (New York, 1974); see my "How Not to Write a Biography: A Critical Look at Fawn Brodie's *Thomas Jefferson*," *Social Science Journal*, XIV, (1977), 129–36.

31. Isaac A. Coles to Cabell, November 10, 1806, in Joseph Carrington Cabell Papers, University of Virginia.

32. "Luckily for me I have been in Turkey, and am quite at home in this primeval

He was also "too timid—too irresolute—too fickle," and his reflective nature ill-suited the occupant of a high office.[33]

Jefferson's attitude toward France was misunderstood. His Federalist enemies charged that he was bewitched by the French and that his foreign policy was slanted in their favor. Circumstantial evidence existed to justify this assumption. The President had spent five years in prerevolutionary Paris. Although a diplomat, he associated with intellectuals who were involved in the approaching French Revolution, and he supported that upheaval enthusiastically. A contemporary said of Jefferson, "I look upon him to have been to this revolution what a key and a main spring are to a watch. He winds them up and then puts them into motion."[34]

Jefferson's Francophilia seemed confirmed by two acts during his presidency. First, working for a settlement of the boundary of the Floridas with Spain, he sought Napoleon's aid. Second, Jefferson employed an embargo on American exports when, according to adversaries, he knew that this measure discriminated against Britain. Looking at this record, political opponents saw an unwritten alliance linking France and America.

Nothing could have been more untrue. Jefferson had favored complete separation from Europe in the 1780s, but, fearing an English stranglehold on American trade, he revised his thinking and urged a close connection with France, "the only nation on earth on whom we can solidly rely for assistance till we can stand on our own legs."[35] Even as he recommended cooperation with America's ally, he worried about the morals of his countrymen exposed to Bourbon France's decadence. In a famous letter, he admitted that "the consequences of foreign education are alarming to me as an American" because a young man would be exposed to "drinking, horse racing, and boxing" and would acquire a "fondness for European luxury and dissipation and a contempt for the simplicity of his own country." Twenty

simplicity of manners," Englishman Augustus John Foster wrote Lady Elizabeth Foster, December 30, 1804, in Vere Foster (ed.), *The Two Duchesses* (London, 1898), 196–98.

33. Entry of March 15, 1806, in Everett S. Brown (ed.), *William Plumer's Memorandum of Proceedings in the United States Senate, 1803–1807* (New York, 1923), 453–55. Eventually Plumer became Jefferson's admirer; he admitted, however, that he never understood the Virginian. "His character baffles the pen of the historian," Plumer wrote in 1837. Lynn W. Turner, "Thomas Jefferson Through the Eyes of a New Hampshire Politician," *Mississippi Valley Historical Review*, XXX (1943), 214.

34. E. Haskell to William Constable, August 25, 1789, in Constable Papers. A short, book-length study is Lawrence S. Kaplan, *Jefferson and France: An Essay on Politics and Political Ideas* (New Haven, 1967), which is an outgrowth of "Jefferson and France: A Study in Political Opportunism" (Ph.D. dissertation, Yale University, 1951).

35. Jefferson to Ralph Izard, November 18, 1786, in Boyd *et al.* (eds.), *The Papers of Thomas Jefferson*, X, 541–42.

years later he showed the depths of this sentiment when he complained to Madison that John Armstrong, United States minister to France, was "already forgetful of [the] temper of his country & proves how readily we catch the hue of those around us."[36] The French recognized Jefferson for the nationalist he was in 1784 when one of them described him as "too philosophic and tranquil to hate or love any other nation unless it is for the interest of the United States."[37]

The English understood Jefferson's disposition. Shortly after taking office, he reminded Minister Thornton "there was nothing to which he had a greater repugnance than to establish distinctions in favour of one nation against another." Candidly confessing "some interest" in the French republic, Jefferson claimed "that was long over, and there was assuredly nothing in the present Government of that country, which could naturally incline him to show the smallest undue partiality to it at the expense of Great Britain or indeed of any other country."[38] Unhappily for Anglo-American diplomacy, the British ignored Jefferson. Perhaps he had been identified with the "French party" too long to be judged trustworthy. Perhaps the British placed excessive faith in the information they received from his enemies. Whatever the explanation, Britain's rulers dismissed Jefferson's assertion of impartiality. Thinking Jefferson was pro-French, the English rode roughshod over American rights. They had treated the United States in an arbitrary fashion before and remained unchallenged. There seemed no reason to change after 1803.

Consequently, Jefferson viewed France as a countervailing power. Napoleonic triumphs served a dual purpose: they made Britain more amenable to American demands, and they enhanced America's ability to expand

36. Jefferson to John Bannister, Jr., October 15, 1785, *ibid.*, VIII, 635–37. Compare William Lee's remarks: "I do not approve of my children being educated in a French pension. The manners & habits they will there acquire will be illy fitted for our country and their probable station in life." Lee to Susan Lee, November 1, 1806, in Lee-Palfrey Family Papers; Jefferson to Madison, March 29, 1805, in Madison Papers, LC.

37. Ann César, Chevalier de La Luzerne, to Charles Gravier, comte de Vergennes, [?], 1785, quoted in Samuel Flagg Bemis (ed.), *The American Secretaries of State and Their Diplomacy* (10 vols.; New York, 1927), II, 7. See also H. Hale Bellot, "Thomas Jefferson in American Historiography," Royal Historical Society *Transactions*, Series 5, IV (1954), 139.

38. Thornton to Lord Grenville, March 7, 1801, FOA 5:32, LC. Also Anthony Merry to Hawkesbury, December 6, 1803, in FOA 5:41. Soon after Jefferson took office, the French chargé wrote of him: "He will be like his predecessors very pacific and he will be as much so towards England as towards us; towards us, he will be so with the greatest sincerity." Louis André Pichon to Talleyrand, May 10, 1801, quoted in Albert H. Bowman, "Louis A. Pichon and the French Perception of the United States" (paper presented at the 41st Annual Meeting of the Southern Historical Association, Washington, D.C., November 15, 1975), 4.

territorially. Since he regarded Napoleon as a despot, the President was undeniably uncomfortable wishing success to French arms. He would do almost anything to escape a collision with the "great mad-house" Europe, however, since there was "no bravery fighting a Maniac."[39]

James Madison complemented Jefferson perfectly. Dedicated, loyal, and hardworking, Madison was stigmatized by foes as Jefferson's lackey, derogatorily called a "political pimp," and referred to as a slavish clerk rather than a secretary of state. Even administration supporters dismissed Madison as Jefferson's inferior. Certainly the contrast between the two was great: Madison seemed dull, provincial, and weak; Jefferson appeared to observers as flamboyant, worldly, and virile. The differences extended to their presidencies, also: Jefferson enjoyed six halcyon years before the embargo trouble; Madison's tenure was tranquil only at the end. Historically they have been treated quite diversely. Jefferson has been alternately praised and condemned, while until recently, Madison was ridiculed or simply ignored.[40] Some historians have, in fact, been content to link Madison's physical slightness with his performance, blinding themselves to his real role.[41] Rather than being an obsequious hack, Madison was inextricably involved in formulating policy. Because of the harmony between the two men, however, Jefferson has received much of the credit due Madison.

Jefferson and Madison shared many common ideas. Both were convinced that America had a great destiny; because an empire spanning the continent was an integral part of that future, the two were ardent expansionists. The acquisitive process Jefferson started in West Florida was completed by Madison in 1810 and 1813 when the area was occupied. Both believed in the efficacy of commercial warfare, and both utilized economic weapons during their terms in office. Since time was in America's favor, they felt war should be delayed until all alternatives had been exhausted;

39. Joseph I. Shulim, "Thomas Jefferson Views Napoleon," *Virginia Magazine of History and Biography*, LX (1952), 288–304; Jefferson to John Taylor, August 1, 1807, in H. A. Washington (ed.), *The Writings of Thomas Jefferson* (9 vols.; New York, 1854–1856), V, 149; Jefferson to David Bailie Warden, July 5, 1808, in Thomas Jefferson Papers, Library of Congress.

40. Irving Brant, *James Madison* (6 vols.; Indianapolis and New York, 1948–1961); "Madison and the War of 1812," *Virginia Magazine of History and Biography*, LXXIV (1966), 51–67; and "James Madison and His Times," are biased in Madison's favor. Ralph Ketcham, *James Madison: A Biography* (New York, 1971), is more impartial.

41. Madison was a "wizened little apple-john of a man." Raymond Walters, Jr., *Albert Gallatin: Jeffersonian Financier and Diplomat* (New York, 1957), 223; to Theodore Clarke Smith, "War Guilt in 1812," Massachusetts Historical Society *Proceedings*, LXIV (1930–1932), 345, Madison was a "small dried-up man." Anthony Steel, "Impressment in the Monroe-Pinkney Negotiation, 1806–1807," *American Historical Review*, LVII (1952), 369, thinks Madison had an "enfeebled constitution."

thus they sought to forestall hostilities for as long as possible. In retrospect, the continuity they brought to foreign policy was fortuitous.

Unfortunately, American diplomatists in France were not the equals of Jefferson or Madison. Robert R. Livingston, John Armstrong, Jonathan Russell, and consular officials including Fulwar Skipwith and David Bailie Warden were guilty of vanity, quarrelsomeness, and intrigue. Livingston, a partially deaf New Yorker known as the Chancellor, as minister to France was enmeshed in the settlement of spoliations from the Quasi-War.[42] A provision in the Louisiana agreement provided for the filing, judging, and paying of claims to those Americans who had sustained losses from French depredations.[43] Charges of corruption were inevitable because some aggrieved parties—who were not above inflating their losses—received less than they demanded. Inevitably, Livingston was attacked: "Mr. L," John Randolph asserted, "has been the dupe of a pack of unprincipled speculators, Gallo-Americans & foreigners, who will receive the money to the exclusion of bona fide American citizens." There is no evidence to indicate that the independently wealthy Livingston received graft.[44]

Another problem for Livingston was James Monroe, dispatched to France early in 1803 to aid in the negotiations that culminated in the purchase of the Louisiana region. The French decided to sell before Monroe arrived in Paris, thereby creating tension between the two men. Monroe felt cheated of potential glory; Livingston, in turn, believed the triumph his alone. A clash occurred and Monroe soon excoriated Livingston to Madison as "the man . . . whom you should avoid as most deserving the execrations of his country."[45] Encountering a roadblock when he tried to obtain

42. The standard biography is George Dangerfield, *Chancellor Robert R. Livingston of New York, 1746–1813* (New York, 1960).

43. There are enormous collections of papers relating to spoliations in the Manuscript Division, Library of Congress, and in the National Archives. Henry B. Cox, "To the Victor: A History of the French Spoliation Claims Controversy, 1793–1955" (Ph.D. dissertation, George Washington University, 1967).

44. John Randolph to Albert Gallatin, October 12, 1805, in Albert Gallatin Papers, New-York Historical Society; Livingston may not have been above land-jobbing, however. "I have some reason to believe that the family of Livingstons in New York wished to secure the government of Louisiana in the person of Edward Livingston the present Mayor of New York, probably with a view to the future land speculations in that country, and that an application which the latter made to the President some time ago was unsuccessful. I am told on pretty good authority that he has already sent surveyors and a confidential agent to take a view of the country; and these reports tend to confirm the former ones of the family having obtained large grants of land from France." Thornton to Hawkesbury, September 30, 1803, in FOA 5:38, LC; William B. Hatcher, *Edward Livingston: Jeffersonian Republican and Jacksonian Democrat* (Baton Rouge, 1940), 97, conjectures that economic opportunity drew Livingston to Louisiana.

45. Monroe to Madison, July 6, 1805, in Monroe Papers, New York Public Library.

Napoleon's approval to station American commercial agents in the West Indies, upset with Monroe, angered by charges of financial irregularities, and believing that he could no longer bear the extravagant living expenses in Paris, Livingston signaled Madison he wanted to come home. Noting that the New Yorker had become excessively irritable, Jefferson welcomed his resignation.[46]

Remarkably little speculation about Livingston's replacement ensued. In fact, only one candidate, Maryland senator Samuel Smith, had surfaced when Jefferson chose John Armstrong, Livingston's brother-in-law, as the next envoy to France. Though Smith was politically powerful, Jefferson was more impressed by the electoral strength of the Livingston faction in New York. Remembering that group's vital support for his candidacy in 1800, and wishing to continue the New York–Virginia political alliance, Jefferson selected Armstrong.

A native of Carlisle, Pennsylvania, Armstrong left the College of New Jersey (Princeton University) to serve in the American Revolution as an aide-de-camp to General Horatio Gates. A skilled writer, he authored the "Newburgh Letters," expressing discontent that the army's payroll was in arrears. After marrying Livingston's sister Alida in 1789, he moved to Red Hook, New York, and occupied himself with his family and his studies (he read Jefferson's book *Notes on Virginia*, which he faulted for containing "bad grammar" and poorly reasoned arguments), and served two brief stints in the United States Senate. Armstrong's fervent republican sentiments help explain why he undertook the French mission.[47]

Armstrong did not enjoy his six years in France, however. From the beginning, he was isolated because he could not speak French, and his lack of linguistic ability made him self-conscious. Furthermore, his stern republican philosophy was unwelcome in Napoleon's empire. Finally, Arm-

46. Jefferson to Madison, August 18, 1804, in Jefferson Papers, LC.

47. C. Edward Skeen, *John Armstrong, Jr., 1758–1843: A Biography* (Syracuse, 1981); Skeen has also written articles on various aspects of Armstrong's career, including "Monroe and Armstrong: A Study in Political Rivalry," *New-York Historical Society Quarterly*, LVII (1973), 121–47; "The Newburgh Conspiracy Reconsidered," *William and Mary Quarterly*, Series 3, XXXI (1974), 273–90; and "Mr. Madison's Secretary of War," *Pennsylvania Magazine of History and Biography*, C (1976), 336–55. An unpublished typescript biography by W. A. Chanler is housed in the New-York Historical Society. My sketch is based on Julius W. Pratt, "John Armstrong" in Dumas Malone, *et al.* (eds.), *Dictionary of American Biography* (22 vols.; New York, 1925–1958), I, 355–58; Pichon to Talleyrand, June 12, July 3, 1804, in AMAE, LVII, LC; and Julian Ursyn Niemcewicz, *Under Their Vine and Fig Tree: Travels Through America in 1797–1799*, ed. and trans. Metchie J. E. Budka (Elizabeth, N.J., 1965), 197–98. The quotations are from Armstrong's marginalia in his copy of *Notes on Virginia*, and Armstrong to Ambrose Spencer, June 8, 1807, both at Rokeby, the home of Richard Aldrich and others, Barrytown-on-Hudson, New York.

strong, who knew that the cost of living in Paris was prohibitive, had assured Jefferson that he and his family had "long since found out the secret of living within" their income;[48] but penny-pinching in the French capital curtailed Armstrong's social life, and he was seldom seen at the glittering gatherings of France's ruling circles. Thus, there was a shred of legitimacy in Napoleon's complaints later that there was no one from the United States with whom to negotiate.

There were other problems also. The constant bickering that had marred Livingston's stay continued with Armstrong as a new participant. Suspicious of those around him, Armstrong was certain that Madison maintained a spy in Paris in the person of Alexander McRae of Virginia. Jealous of Consul Warden's acceptance in Parisian intellectual groups, he exchanged recriminations with him. In a situation similar to the Livingston-Monroe feud, Armstrong became involved in a bitter dispute with James Bowdoin after this member of a prominent Massachusetts family arrived in Paris to aid in negotiations for the acquisition of West Florida. Finally, Armstrong was charged with being personally tainted by corruption.

Samuel Smith accused Armstrong of being unfit for his French mission because he lacked "the all-essential industry." Another observer felt otherwise, however, and claimed that Armstrong "was not deficient in energy and will succeed if anyone can."[49] The truth lay somewhere between these positions. Armstrong boldly asserted America's interests on occasion, but too often he was irascible. A more capable and tactful envoy might have had greater success. The very able Joel Barlow, who followed Armstrong as minister, was close to securing an important treaty when death intervened. If Armstrong was not a brilliant diplomat, neither was he an incompetent amateur.

[III]

Personal discord in Paris was accompanied by political discord at home. In the United States, the Federalist opponents of Jefferson and Republicanism were disturbed by the drift of events. In foreign affairs, as has been shown, they identified the Republicans with France; and France evoked images of a revolution "founded on infidelity, impiety, and atheism." France, they believed, was controlled by a power-mad despot bent on world domination. With France, the United States had nothing in common. Britain and America, however, were the "only nations who know and enjoy political

48. John Armstrong to Jefferson, June 2, 1804, in Jefferson Papers, LC.
49. Samuel Smith to Wilson Cary Nicholas, March 18, 1805, in Carter-Smith Family Papers, University of Virginia; Isaac A. Coles to Cabell, July 28, 1809, in Cabell Papers.

and civil liberty; our wants are reciprocal and we are peculiarly of one blood and one flesh."[50] To the Federalists, wooing Napoleon was senseless, and the only policy morally acceptable was the alignment of the United States with "one little Island . . . opposing all the world for her freedom."[51] As emotionally attached to England as they were, it must have seemed logical to the Federalists that their opponents were devotees of France.

The Federalists faulted their adversaries for numerous crimes domestically. They alleged that Jeffersonians were hostile to commerce, believing that eradicating commercial influence was part of a larger conspiracy seeking "the permanent elevation of the interests of the planting states over the commercial."[52] In their opinion, the Louisiana Purchase dealt another blow to New England, the stronghold of Federalism, because eventually new states would be carved out of the gigantic territory and dilute the power of the older ones.[53] Already Vermont, Kentucky, Tennessee, and Ohio had joined the Union, and the latter three were growing rapidly. Devout Federalists believed that not only would New England's strength diminish, but the people inhabiting the new states would be susceptible to Republican demagoguery and would swell the ranks of the Jeffersonians. Meanwhile, along the Atlantic seaboard, inhabitants of "low extraction" were dominant. Even the passage of the Twelfth Amendment, designed to prevent a repetition of the Jefferson–Aaron Burr electoral tie of 1800, was interpreted as an anti-Federalist stroke.[54] Altogether, things looked bleak through Federalist eyes.

Without realizing it, the Federalists were headed for self-destruction. Their earlier creativity gave way to obstructionism; they criticized Republican programs, but seldom offered feasible alternatives. The feeling of supe-

50. Entry of April 5, 1810, in William Henry Channing (ed.), *Memoir of William Ellery Channing* (3 vols.; Boston, 1851), 328–37; Timothy Pickering to Robert Liston, March 19, 1805, in Hervey Putnam Prentiss, "Pickering and the Embargo," *Essex Institute Historical Collections*, LXIX (1933), 98, *n*5.

51. Leverett Saltonstall, Jr., to Leverett Saltonstall, Sr., February 6, 1808, in Saltonstall Family Papers, Massachusetts Historical Society. A Virginian who felt like Saltonstall found people "among us who seem to contemplate the conquest of G. B. by France with great complacency, and to think that tho the Emperor were master of the sea as well as the land we should have nothing to fear—protected by our insignificance." Beverly Tucker to John Randolph, January 12, 1807, in Tucker-Coleman Papers.

52. Josiah Quincy to Harrison Gray Otis, November 8, 1811, in Harrison Gray Otis Papers, Massachusetts Historical Society. See also Samuel Tenney to Bartlett, January 25, 1802, in Josiah Bartlett Papers, Library of Congress.

53. Rabid Federalists claimed that the Louisiana Purchase was unneutral, reasoning that the money paid to France was bankrolling the French war effort. They overlooked Britain's financial involvement in the transaction.

54. Plumer to Jeremiah Mason, January 14, 1804, in Plumer Papers, LC.

riority exemplified in elitist statements such as that made by George Cabot—"*We are democratic altogether*, and I hold democracy in its natural operation to be *the government of the worst*"—antagonized potential voters. Their heretofore national appeal evaporated, and they became a sectional party. As their power waned, they became more shrill and alienated even more Americans.[55] Their major error, however, was in identifying themselves too closely to Britain.

The linkage was apparent to contemporaries. "It is true beyond all controversy that there is a dangerous British faction in the heart of some of these New England states," Benjamin Waterhouse told the famous English surgeon John Coakley Lettsom. Nonsupport of American foreign policy and overt sympathy for Britain combined with a blind, unreasoning hatred of Jefferson and Madison to suggest a loyalty to the former mother country rather than to the United States. Further proof of Federalist-British intimacy appeared when Massachusetts Federalists denounced President Madison after his dismissal of Francis James "Copenhagen" Jackson. Describing this as "matchless in the annals of anarchy," the enraged Armstrong asked, "Are these people determined to make themselves a colony of Old England?"[56] The Federalists fostered the image of a divided America when many citizens reasoned that unity alone ensured peace. "A belief on the part of Great Britain that she has many partisans in America who are able to divide and paralyze our councils," Pennsylvanian Jonathan Roberts replied to a dissenter, "has invited and encouraged her aggressions."[57]

55. George Cabot to Pickering, February 14, 1804, in Henry Cabot Lodge, *Life and Letters of George Cabot* (Boston, 1877), 341–44; see the analysis of Robert McColley, "Jefferson's Rivals: The Shifting Character of the Federalists," *Midcontinent American Studies Journal*, IX (1968), 23–24. In *The Revolution of American Conservatism: The Federalist Party in the Era of Jeffersonian Democracy* (New York, 1965), David Hackett Fischer writes that a new breed of Federalists ultimately displaced traditionalists like Pickering, Rufus King, and Charles Cotesworth Pinckney. In the period this book covers, however, the more visible Federalist spokesmen were the old wheelhorses.

56. Benjamin Waterhouse to John Coakley Lettsom, [?], 1810, in James J. Abraham, *Lettsom: His Life, Times, Friends and Descendants* (London, 1933), 364; Joseph B. Varnum to George Washington Campbell, March 19, 1810, in George Washington Campbell Papers, Library of Congress; Armstrong to Russell, April 5, 1810, in Russell Papers, Brown University.

57. Quoted in Victor A. Sapio, *Pennsylvania and the War of 1812* (Lexington, 1970), 150–51; also Ezekiel Bacon to Joseph Story, November 4, 1808, in Joseph Story Papers, Library of Congress. The English recognized the Federalists' friendliness: "Whoever may be the President, it is certain, that the next Congress will be composed of a large proportion if not a Majority of Federal Members, and therefore the Influence of a President of the Democratic [Republican] Party would be either opposed entirely or at any rate so far checked as to prevent a recurrence to very violent Measures [economic sanctions]." Erskine to Canning, October 5, 1808, in FOA 5:58, LC.

It may have been true that Jeffersonian Republicanism was simply not in the best interest of New England. Nevertheless, there can be no justification for the verbal support the Federalists rendered Britain in the years preceding the War of 1812. Rational and well-educated men forecasting degradation and doom at France's hands made a sorry spectacle. If the Federalists had really believed in the American Union they had helped create, they would have rid themselves of their despair and offered constructive criticisms of Republican programs. That they did not cease carping and submit solid alternatives proved their bankruptcy.[58] No wonder an exasperated Republican cried, "God damn their souls they do not see that it is their enmity to Mr. Jefferson that makes them in love with misdemeanors & treasons, provided they can bring his administration into contempt."[59]

The Republican-Federalist clash has obscured the divisions that existed among Jeffersonians. The neglect of these differences has been compounded by excessive attention paid to John Randolph of Roanoke, a caustic eccentric who among other things disagreed with Jefferson over appropriations to purchase West Florida and who led a small band of congressmen dubbed the Quids. Randolph's colorful personality lends itself to description, and few historians have been able to resist the impulse to sketch him. Studded with memorable barbs ("we have heard but one word—like the whip-poor-will, but one eternal monotonous tone—Canada! Canada! Canada!"), his speeches have been quoted frequently. Yet Randolph had little support and influence after his break with Jefferson.[60]

Among Republicans there were at least three identifiable factions harboring markedly different sentiments about American foreign policy during the Napoleonic Wars. One group was concerned with the safety of the unique American experiment in government. Including Nathaniel Macon and John Taylor of Caroline (both of whom were close to Randolph) and Thomas Cooper, this minority of Jeffersonians was considerably more dogmatic about Republican principles than either Jefferson or Madison. They dreaded possible involvement in war: Macon articulated their fear when he said "the war of killing, prepared the way for a war of taxes, which never end and the collectors are almost if not quite as destructive to the human race as so many Alexanders." They were disturbed by America's growing commer-

---

58. For contrary views, see James M. Banner, Jr., *To the Hartford Convention: The Federalists and the Origins of Party Politics in Massachusetts, 1789–1815* (New York, 1970); and Donald R. Hickey, "Federalist Defense Policy in the Age of Jefferson, 1801–1812," *Military Affairs*, XLV (1981), 63–70.

59. William H. Cabell to Joseph C. Cabell, April 9, 1807, in Cabell Papers.

60. Morton Borden, *Parties and Politics in the Early Republic, 1789–1815* (New York, 1967), 80–84.

cial stake in the Anglo-French war because they believed commerce to be corrupting and, more important, likely to involve the nation in hostilities. These men believed that if merchants wished to trade with belligerents, they should do so at their own risk. "No commerce . . . repays the *expence* of the hostility it includes," Cooper stressed. Castigating the "swinish multitude" of merchants, he implored Jefferson to check the drift toward a "mercantile war," which the President seemingly sanctioned. Cooper, Macon, and Taylor concurred that "neutrals will always in some degree be damaged," but felt war was only justified in defense of or to add to the national domain. They reasoned that the United States should remain aloof from Europe's catastrophe and husband its resources for any eventuality the future might bring. As Taylor asked, "Who should kill himself today, because he might die ten years hence?"[61]

Another group of Republicans, including Elbridge Gerry, William Plumer, Caesar A. Rodney, and William Short, criticized facets of Jeffersonian or Madisonian policy. Gerry, for example, reflecting his roots in maritime Massachusetts, disagreed with Jefferson's emphasis on gunboats for the defense of neutral rights; to rely on these vessels "to combat ships of War," he warned, "is like putting cock sparrows against game cocks." Plumer and Rodney agreed that a point was reached beyond which "injuries & insults must be avenged." By the middle of Jefferson's second term, the two men felt that the nation was arriving at that point. Short supported a policy designed to segregate America from Europe and the strengthening of national defenses.[62]

There was a third Republican faction composed of men united by a common dislike of James Madison and Albert Gallatin. These Republicans—Robert and Samuel Smith of Maryland, William Duane and Michael Leib of Pennsylvania, William Branch Giles and Wilson Cary Nicholas of Virginia—were disgusted by what they deemed the administration's craven surrender of neutral rights in 1809, 1810, and 1811. To these critics, Madison's devotion to diplomatic negotiations and Gallatin's control of the treasury had hamstrung United States foreign policy. They demanded vig-

61. Macon to Nicholson, January 31, 1806, in Nicholson Papers; Thomas Cooper to Jefferson, March 15, 1806, in Jefferson Papers, LC; Macon to Jefferson, September 2, 1804, *ibid.*; John Taylor to James M. Garnett, December 14, 1807, in Hans Hammond (ed.), "Letters of John Taylor of Caroline," *Virginia Magazine of History and Biography*, LII (1944), 124–25. See also Eugene Tenbroech Mudge, *The Social Philosophy of John Taylor of Caroline* (New York, 1939), 105–109.

62. Elbridge Gerry to Madison, February 18, 1806, in Madison Papers, LC; Plumer to Thomas Cogswell, January 27, 1806, in Plumer Papers, LC; Rodney to Jefferson, December 6, 1808, in Jefferson Papers, LC; William Short to Monroe, May 22, 1811, in Monroe Papers, LC.

orous action, even war, to vindicate the national honor, and in 1810 and 1811 these individuals exerted increasing pressure on Madison to act.[63]

Jefferson and Madison had to reckon with these varying outlooks. The two men realized that commerce could not be halted; indeed, with the passage of years, their tolerance of trade grew. Recognizing also that commerce deserved protection, they advocated resorting to economic coercion to uphold America's rights. While they desired peace for the young nation, they realized that a "love of peace" might mislead other powers into believing "our government is entirely in Quaker principles & will turn the left cheek when the right has been smitten." Such a misconception could lead to the country's becoming "plunder of all nations."[64] In 1812, with Jefferson in retirement, all attempts at peaceful solutions having failed, Madison led the nation into war.

63. See John S. Pancake, "The 'Invisibles': A Chapter in the Opposition to President Madison," *Journal of Southern History*, XXI (1955), 17–37; and J. C. A. Stagg, "James Madison and the 'Malcontents': The Political Origins of the War of 1812," *William and Mary Quarterly*, Series 3, XXXIII (1976), 557–85.

64. Jefferson to Cooper, February 18, 1806, in Jefferson Papers, LC.

TWO

Napoleonic France

Joseph Bonaparte's magnificent Môrte-
fontaine estate just north of Paris was the scene of a memorable fete cele-
brating the signing of the Franco-American Convention of 1800. Fes-
tivities seemed appropriate after seven months of trying negotiations, and
Napoleon's oldest brother outdid himself in making arrangements for the
gala event. A sumptuous dinner highlighted by toasts to Franco-American
friendship vied with a rain-dampened fireworks display and theatrical en-
tertainment for the diplomats' enjoyment. Only at three o'clock in the
morning did the grand party conclude.[1]

Both sides had ample cause for celebration. The Americans escaped
from the undeclared hostilities of the Quasi-War, and, more important, the
Franco-American treaty of 1778 no longer bound the nation. The French
obtained peace with yet another country. More significantly, they concurred with American maritime policy which emphasized neutral rights in
time of war, a philosophy compatible with America's weakness on the high
seas. A liberal concept of neutral rights had been embodied in John Adams'
plan of treaties drafted in 1776: nonmilitary goods, even if enemy owned,
were immune from seizure off neutral vessels; contraband goods were
strictly defined, and neutrals (a category expected to include the United
States in future conflicts) could trade with belligerents.[2] Since her naval

1. Peter P. Hill, *William Vans Murray, Federalist Diplomat: The Shaping of Peace with France, 1797–1801* (Syracuse, 1971), 194–96.

2. Compare Articles XII, XIII, and XIV of the Convention of Môrtefontaine available in David Hunter Miller (comp.), *Treaties and Other International Acts of the United States of America* (8 vols.; Washington, 1931–1948), 466–68; see also Gregg L. Lent, "The American

strength was inferior to Britain's, France had much to gain by accepting the American doctrine. She would appear sympathetic with the United States and other neutrals. Conceivably she would drive a wedge between Britain and America because the British would simply not tolerate lenient maritime codes when blockades and commercial warfare were key weapons in the island kingdom's arsenal.

Coupled with the Louisiana Purchase two and one half years later, the Convention of Môrtefontaine should have inaugurated a lengthy period of tranquillity in Franco-American relations. Unfortunately, this was not to be the case. In the coming months and years the onetime allies drifted apart until some Americans concluded that war alone would end the confiscation of American property in French ports, stop the discriminatory treatment accorded American goods in France, and curtail the generally capricious conduct of Napoleon's empire.

[I]

Napoleon Bonaparte was responsible for the deterioration of Franco-American relations. Although Corsican-born and a zealous Corsican patriot in his youth, Bonaparte eventually shifted his allegiance to France. After his rise to power he wasted neither time nor words outlining the new order placing France and its interests (as he interpreted them) above all other considerations. Where the United States was ranked in the Napoleonic world scheme is difficult to determine. Certainly the new republic was not the most hated country; Britain probably enjoyed this dubious distinction.[3]

Actually, there is little evidence that Napoleon thought of America at all.[4] Confronting hostile coalitions abroad and bearing responsibility for governing France, the French ruler lacked the time necessary to study and

---

Revolution and the Law of Nations, 1776–1789," *Diplomatic History*, I (1977), 20–34, and "John Adams and the Drafting of the Model Treaty Plan of 1776," *ibid.*, II (1978), 313–20.

3. Henry Adams, *History of the United States During the Administrations of Jefferson and Madison* (9 vols.; New York, 1889–1891), II, 52, asserts that Napoleon had "two rooted hatreds," Britain and America, but the "deeper" detestation was for "the organized democracy" called the United States. Baltimore merchant Robert Oliver said that the Emperor had "a greater hatred to, and contempt for the People of America than any People on the face of the Earth." Robert Oliver to Monroe, July 4, 1811, in Miscellaneous Letters of the Department of State, Department of State Archives, National Archives.

4. Napoleon's published correspondence proves this. America's insignificance during the Consulate and Empire is evident also in French historiography. In Louis Madelin, *Histoire du consulate et de l'empire* (16 vols.; Paris, 1937–1954), and André Fugier, *La révolution française et l'empire napoléonien* (Paris, 1954), the United States is infrequently mentioned. Harry Ammon, *The Genet Mission* (New York, 1973), 182, has written: "Although more books have been written about the French Revolution than any comparable epoch in Euro-

understand America and he generally ignored the impact of his actions on American opinion. To the degree that he did think of the distant country, he imagined the United States to be a land inhabited by greedy merchants with a weak government and an impotent army. His arrogant and condescending attitude was evident throughout his reign. Following the sale of Louisiana, for example, he proclaimed that the United States "are indebted to France for their independence; they will henceforth owe to us their strength and grandeur."[5] In 1810 he immodestly announced that "His Majesty loves the Americans." American prosperity and trade delighted him and favored his policies; helping America secure her independence had been one of France's immortal accomplishments, and it had been His Majesty's privilege to help the United States grow through the Louisiana transaction.[6]

Chargé d'affaires Jonathan Russell complained about Napoleon's temperament in 1811. "One day we are told that the Emperor has learnt that the non-intercourse law will be severely executed, that he is in good humor and that everything will go well—the next day it is stated that he has heard something which displeased him and the American property, lately arrived in this country is in the utmost jeopardy."[7] No particular malice motivated the Emperor. Nations were like men, merely objects to be manipulated.[8] Though America suffered from French actions, her plight was not unique. Denmark and Portugal were hurt much more severely. Both had been caught between Britain and France and both sustained grievous damage: Denmark's fleet was attacked by the British (who also bombarded the city of Copenhagen), while Portugal became the site of land warfare between French and British armies. At least geography put the United States beyond the range of Napoleon's legions.

An argument can be made that the neutral United States received gener-

---

pean history, there is almost nothing in French historical works about French policy toward the United States or the Genet mission." A study of a particular facet of Franco-American relations in the Napoleonic era has been done by a native Texan, Ulane Bonnel, *La France, les États-Unis et la guerre de course, 1797–1815* (Paris, 1961).

5. Quoted in the *National Intelligencer*, March 26, 1804. The original is in Napoleon to Talleyrand, January 16, 1804, in *Correspondance de Napoléon Ier publiée par ordre de l'empereur Napoléon III* (32 vols.; Paris, 1858–1870), IX, 209.

6. Napoleon to Jean-Baptiste Nompère de Champagny, August 2, 1810, *ibid.*, XXI, 2.

7. Russell to Smith, March 15, 1811, in Despatches from United States Ministers to France, Department of State Archives, National Archives.

8. Of Napoleon, Germaine Necker (Madame de Staël) said, "He regarded a human being as a fact or a theory, and not as a fellow creature. He did not hate anymore than he loved, there was only himself for himself." Cited in Harold T. Parker, "The Formation of Napoleon's Personality: An Exploratory Essay," *French Historical Studies*, VII (1971), 23.

ous treatment in the four years following the rupture of the Peace of Amiens. During the first half of this period the French faced Britain alone. An Army of England was constituted and invasion craft were constructed; with Britain's defenses at a low ebb it appeared that Napoleon might stage a successful invasion. In this environment France could afford to overlook the growing American trade with England and Europe.

In 1805 the situation changed. Fearful of Napoleon's insatiable ambition and supported by English subsidies, Austria, Prussia, and Russia formed the Third Coalition. Unaware of the new alignment, but filled with suspicion, Napoleon moved his armies east. Hostilities ensued and after difficult campaigning the French scored victories against their opponents at Ulm and Austerlitz. Again in 1806 Napoleon was engaged in campaigning in Central Europe, this time crushing Prussia. The following winter he pressed the Russians and, after inconclusive battle on the snow-covered field of Eylau in February, he smashed Alexander I's forces at Friedland the following June.

The victories of 1805, 1806, and 1807 added luster to French arms, but England remained unshaken. After wrecking the Third Coalition, Napoleon momentarily considered new invasion plans for Britain; the Emperor recognized, however, that a successful assault on the island kingdom hinged on French control of the English Channel. That possibility had been dashed by the defeat of Admiral Pierre Villeneuve's combined Franco-Spanish armada at Trafalgar in October, 1805.[9] Thus, for all of its power on the continent, Napoleonic France was unable to challenge Britain at sea. The English found themselves with the opposite dilemma: dominant at sea, they lacked the military strength to bring Napoleon to bay on the land; the best that Britain could do was to launch ineffectual amphibious operations on the continent and wait for Europe to revolt. To spur discontent in French-controlled lands and to damage France economically, the English resorted to commercial warfare, blockading part of Europe's coast and screening exports to the continent. This, of course, was a two-edged sword. A substantial percentage of England's exports went to Europe, and the French, if they chose, could exclude a significant proportion of these goods. The English also recognized that neutral powers would be displeased with restrictions imposed by His Majesty's government. Neither of these factors daunted them, however. The British were convinced that they would win

9. Virtually all historians agree that after Trafalgar the French ceased being a threat to British maritime supremacy. An exception is a Canadian scholar, Richard Glover, "The French Fleet, 1807–1814: Britain's Problem, and Madison's Opportunity," *Journal of Modern History*, XXXIX (1967), 233–52; and Glover, *Britain at Bay: Defence Against Bonaparte, 1803–1814* (London and New York: 1973).

any test of wartime economies with France. Domestic hardships would be experienced and unemployment would increase in industrial areas, but given the lack of political influence of the working classes, Great Britain could and would hold firm in its policies. As Britain's rulers ignored internal distress, so they shrugged off the complaints of neutrals hurt by English commercial controls. Britons perceived the struggle with France as a lonely effort to preserve Western Civilization. They recognized that sundry small nations would be inconvenienced in the course of the war, but that problem was dismissed with the assumption that minnows were always hurt when whales fought. Besides, the neutrals, notably America, were taking advantage of Britain's preoccupation with the war to expand their merchant marine and exploit traditional English markets. In light of these circumstances any thoughts of conciliation were rejected.

England's hardening attitude was recorded in the observations of two diplomats. James Monroe, United States minister to Britain, reported widespread disenchantment with America's rapid growth: "They seem to consider our prosperity not simply as a reproach to them, but as impairing or detracting from theirs." In contrast to Monroe, Augustus John Foster, a young member of the British staff in Washington, maintained that "there is not, thanks to our Tars, a single French or Spanish merchantman that now navigates these seas—&, these Jews want to navigate for them." If the aggressive yankees happened to suffer occasionally at the hands of the Royal Navy, Foster explained, "we want elbow room and these good neutrals won't give it to us, and therefore they get a few side pushes which makes them grumble."[10] These were the seeds of future conflict.

Not long after Monroe and Foster wrote, Great Britain ushered in the age of commercial decrees with the proclamation of Fox's blockade on May 16, 1806. Bearing the name of the prominent statesman Charles James Fox, this measure applied to the coastal strip of northwest Europe between the Brittany peninsula of France and the Elbe River, but it was to be enforced officially only in the zone between the Seine River and Ostend. Neutral vessels could visit French ports if they carried no contraband or French-owned merchandise and if they were not engaged in coastal trade between French ports. Fox's blockade was ostensibly designed to placate opinion in the United States by standardizing restrictions, but Americans interpreted it as yet another infringement on neutral rights because the Royal Navy was

---

10. Monroe to Madison, March 15, 1804, in Stanislaus M. Hamilton (ed.), *The Writings of James Monroe* (7 vols.; New York and London, 1898–1903), IV, 155; Augustus John Foster to Lady Elizabeth Foster, May 3, 1806, in Bradford Perkins, *Prologue to War: England and the United States, 1805–1812* (Berkeley, 1961), 28; Foster to Lady Elizabeth Foster, February 1, 1806, in Foster, *The Two Duchesses*, 271.

incapable of strictly enforcing Fox's blockade. As this form of warfare ran counter to the liberal maritime philosophy of the United States, Fox's blockade was denounced in the young republic; the semiofficial *National Intelligencer* in Washington reflected American unhappiness when it asked if six million Americans would accept passively what two million British colonials had scorned three decades previously.[11]

Ironically, Fox's blockade was not the first blow struck in the complicated and confusing battle of decrees. Scarcely a fortnight after the renewal of war the British issued an order in council dated June 3, 1803, that excluded neutral vessels carrying colonial produce of enemy origin from Britain. Then France closed her ports to all British colonial goods and merchandise carried on British vessels; in addition, neutral shipping without proper certification by French consuls or agents was also barred. States under Napoleonic domination followed the French lead, and portions of this act were soon enforced in the Netherlands.[12] Why the English did not vociferously object to these French maritime restrictions is an interesting question. Presumably in 1803 and 1804 they were biding their time until they themselves issued stringent trade controls; then existing French measures could be cited as the pretext for British actions. In the Anglo-French war that began in 1793, the English had justified their orders in council of that year as retaliation for alleged French maritime violations. English silence might also be explained by the fact that their trade was generally unhindered in the early days of the Napoleonic Wars. As controls developed, however, and orders in council followed decrees, Americans charged Britain with inaugurating commercial restrictions, in effect accepting the Napoleonic view that France was responding to British provocations.

In the months following Fox's blockade, Napoleon was winning victories over the Prussians at Jena and Auerstadt. On October 27, 1806, he entered Berlin, and less than a month later the Emperor issued a decree bearing the name of the Prussian capital. The British Isles were declared blockaded and all communications and trade with them were prohibited. Goods of British or British colonial origin were declared good prize. One provision excluded from continental harbors any vessel coming from British or British colonial ports. Napoleon claimed that the Berlin edict was "repugnant to our hearts," but retaliation was in order for Fox's blockade.

---

11. For a different view of Fox's blockade, see Adams, *History of the United States*, V, 277; *National Intelligencer*, June 16, 1806; Jacques Godechot, *L'Europe et l'Amérique à l'epoque napoléonienne, 1800–1815* (Paris, 1967), 167.

12. William Glenn Moore, "Economic Coercion as a Policy of the United States, 1794–1805" (Ph.D. dissertation, University of Alabama, 1960), 282; *National Intelligencer*, October 19, 1803, February 1, 1804.

"England forbade him the sea," the Emperor's private secretary Claude-François de Méneval wrote, so "he forbade her the Continent."[13]

Fox's blockade was a convenient pretext for action Napoleon would have taken anyway. Unable to destroy Britain on the battlefield, France would crush her economically. In Napoleon's mind, Britain had to trade or die; if Britain's commerce shrank, her ability to finance hostilities would be jeopardized and her powerful commercial classes would suffer. Enormous budget deficits would compound financial problems caused by a crushing national debt. In short, the English economy would collapse and commercial restriction would accomplish what the French war machine could not.[14] It seemed like a good plan. No one could contradict Napoleon in an age when economics was in its infancy and when few understood that a nation's manufacturing capability was more important than its supply of specie. In 1801, France had imposed a continental blockade with encouraging results; now in 1806 and 1807 there would be no Peace of Amiens to rescue England.[15]

It was unclear how the United States would be affected by the Napoleonic pronouncement. Technically the Môrtefontaine Convention was still effective and its provisions explicitly exempted America from the type of warfare the Emperor now pursued. Minister Armstrong knew that the agreement was still binding, but he immediately asked for clarification of the Berlin decree. Unfortunately, Napoleon and other ranking officials were not in Paris; therefore, Armstrong had to accept the opinion of Denis Decrès, the French navy minister, that the Convention of Môrtefontaine would be respected. Armstrong also secured "written assurances" from unidentified sources that the Berlin edict would not disturb existing relations between France and America. It was on this evidence that a notice appeared in the American press assuring the public that France would honor her Môrtefontaine commitments.[16]

---

13. "Decret," Berlin, November 21, 1806, in *Correspondance de Napoléon*, XIII, 555–57; "Message au Senat," November 19, 1806, *ibid.*, 552–54; Claude-François de Méneval, *Memoirs Illustrating the History of Napoleon I from 1802 to 1815* (3 vols.; New York, 1894), II, 64–65.

14. In addition to the articles and monographs cited below, I have relied on François Crouzet, *L'economie britannique et le blocus continental, 1806–1813* (2 vols.; Paris, 1958), for information on the Continental System.

15. Hugh Ragsdale, "A Continental System in 1801: Paul I and Bonaparte," *Journal of Modern History*, XLII (1970), 70–89; for a different view about the success of the 1801 blockade in the north, see A. N. Ryan, "The Defence of British Trade with the Baltic, 1808–1813," *English Historical Review*, LXXIV (1959), 445.

16. Armstrong to Madison, December 3, 1806, in Despatches from France, NA; Armstrong to William Lee, December 6, 1806, in Despatches from United States Consuls in

Napoleon had other ideas. He was dissatisfied with the chronic im-
balance in Franco-American trade—through peace and war France consistently imported more from the United States than she exported. Napoleon
was convinced that France's trade deficit with the United States damaged
the nation.[17] The Emperor was also keenly aware that Anglo-American
trade was booming: if the United States was profiting from its trade with
France, Great Britain was reaping a bonanza from American business. Plain
arithmetic indicated to Napoleon that France was subsidizing archenemy
England. The situation was simply intolerable. Regardless of the Convention of Môrtefontaine, despite Decrès' favorable interpretation, no matter
what Armstrong's anonymous informants believed, it was only a matter of
time before the Berlin decree was applied to America.

The Berlin decree's primary purpose was to damage Britain's capacity
for waging war with the corollary aim of making France Europe's dominant
economic power. Napoleon recognized that France could not abruptly halt
the importation of manufactured goods from England so he ingeniously
promoted the exchange of French goods for English wares through the
license trade. In other words, the French government sold permits for trading with the enemy. The Emperor believed that since France exported far

---

Bordeaux, Department of State Archives, National Archives; Denis Decrès to Armstrong,
December 24, 1806, in AMAE, LIX, LC; *National Intelligencer*, February 16, 1807.

17. French trade with the United States:

(in francs)

Year	Imports	Exports
1802	55,355,884	15,096,696
1803	44,769,083	17,199,426
1804	70,717,762	39,943,799
1805	107,751,504	32,226,546
1806	113,208,686	45,923,932
1807	98,744,358	43,159,886

These figures are from AMAE, LXIV, LC. See Bonnel, *La France, les États-Unis et la
guerre de course*, 263, n28; A. Chabert, *Essai sur les mouvements des revenus et de l'activité économique en France de 1798 à 1820* (Paris, n.d.), 324, 327; overall French commerce (p. 321):

(in francs)

Year	Imports	Exports
1802	492,692,856	339,120,607
1803	500,040,592	373,468,506
1804	510,538,773	411,067,287
1805	548,422,457	400,783,338
1806	531,558,442	464,810,280
1807	418,284,811	384,639,709

more to Britain than she imported, gold drained into French coffers; and gold everyone knew was essential to the management of the English economy.

In retrospect, Napoleon seriously miscalculated the effect of the license trade. A clever stroke to Frenchmen, the trade infuriated neutrals and French allies alike. Americans were confused and then enraged by this traffic which permitted the belligerents to engage in trade they denied to others. France's ally Russia initially accepted Napoleon's scheme, dubbed the Continental System, for exclusion of Britain's commerce from Europe, but as the volume of the license trade increased, so did Russian resentment. The license trade was an irritant in Franco-American relations; it was a cause for war between Russia and France in 1812.

Enforcement was another difficulty because European customs agents were as corrupt as their French counterparts. Consequently the Continental System was more like a sieve than a seal. If the English could not deliver goods by bribery, they employed ruses such as illegally using neutral flags. In the Baltic, for example, British vessels flying the flags of the United States or the Hanse cities found the port of Riga a convenient center of exchange.[18] At best the French diminished the flood of English manufactures to the continent.

There were other factors underlying the failure of Napoleonic economic warfare. Historically the French experience with paper currency had been disastrous. The Emperor was therefore unwilling to believe that another country could succeed where France had failed. Either from ignorance or because of hubris, France did not recognize that Britain was technologically far ahead of France. The evidence was obvious: with a much smaller population, Britain was able to maintain large armed forces, meet domestic economic requirements, and export sufficient quantities of merchandise to keep her war machine functioning. The performance was impressive, yet many Frenchmen joined Napoleon in refusing to acknowledge the accomplishment. In frustration, the Emperor contemptuously branded Britain a nation of shopkeepers, and although he later claimed the description was offered in admiration, the scornful remark has endured.

Underrating England's economic flexibility was another Napoleonic error. Faced by restrictions in Europe and an embargo in America, Great Britain's survival was effected by intensive exploitation of older outlets and

18. M. S. Anderson, "The Continental System and Russo-British Relations During the Napoleonic Wars," in K. Bourne and D. C. Watt (eds.), *Studies in International History* (Hamden, Conn., 1967), 67–80.

vigorous entrance into newer markets. France inadvertently aided England's quest for new business when Napoleon's interference in Spanish affairs provoked rebellion in 1808. Spain and her colonies, when joined by Portugal and its colonial possession, Brazil, absorbed significant quantities of British manufactures at a crucial moment. While England was certainly hurt by commercial warfare, especially in the months from 1810 to 1812, her economy survived the challenge.

Napoleon also misjudged the impact of this type of warfare on France. He expected the trading centers on the Atlantic and Mediterranean, including Bordeaux, Nantes, and Marseilles, already reeling from the impact of the Revolution, to be further damaged. This did not particularly concern the Emperor; agriculture was of paramount importance to Napoleon, with industrial production next and commerce last; in addition, he despised merchants, reportedly describing them as men "who would sell (their) country for a shilling."[19] If the port of Bordeaux is typical, however, the war did not especially impair trade. The chief reason was that neutral vessels, many of them American, offset the loss of French shipping. In the first nine months of 1803, for example, 68 American ships entered Bordeaux; between March and September 1804, 81 American ships arrived; and in 1805, 201 vessels put into the southwestern French port.[20] Only in 1806 did the number of neutral arrivals decline and only then did Bordeaux begin to suffer.[21]

Just as the Emperor erred in judging the effect of his measures on his

19. E. Tarlé, "L'Unité économique du continent européen sous Napoléon I", " *Revue Historique*, CLXVI (1931), 245; Vincent Nolte, *Fifty Years in Both Hemispheres or Reminiscences of the Life of a Former Merchant* (London, 1854), 78.

20. Paul Butel, "Crise et mutation de l'activité économique à Bordeaux sous le consulat et l'empire," *Revue d'histoire moderne et contemporaine*, XVII (1970), 540–42, 546–48. In other French ports American trade was more harassed by petty bureaucrats than English men-of-war. Nonetheless, vessels continued to arrive in appreciable numbers. See the following reports of American consuls: Stephen Cathalan, Jr., to Madison, July 13, August 18, 1803, June 30, December 31, 1806, in Despatches from United States Consuls in Marseilles, Department of State Archives, National Archives; W. D. Patterson to Madison, May 18, 1805, January 1, 1806, in Despatches from United States Consuls in Nantes, *ibid*. In a private letter Patterson complained, "I find my position here highly disagreable [*sic*] by the continual acts of unjust rapacity committed by the Custom House on our commerce." Patterson to Biddle, June 28, 1805, in Nicholas Biddle Papers, Library of Congress. A similar charge was made by Thomas Lovell to Madison, February 7, 1805, in Despatches from United States Consuls in La Rochelle, Department of State Archives, National Archives.

21. William Lee, trying to dispel notions that he was making a fortune from his office, instructed his wife to cite the decline in Bordeaux's trade to those who thought otherwise. Lee to Susan Lee, April 18, 1807, in Mann, *A Yankee Jeffersonian*, 69–70.

ports, he also underestimated the consequences of the Continental System on various segments of the French economy. French manufacturing costs soared as the prices of imported raw materials rose, and French goods were at a competitive disadvantage relative to Swiss, German, or English products. Exporters suffered as severely in certain instances as importers; the silk industry, which was concentrated around Lyons, was especially damaged.[22]

In 1810 and 1811 the French economy stagnated with inflation intensifying and unemployment worsening. Napoleon's solution was further restrictions; new tariffs were imposed, trade licenses were issued in huge numbers, and orders were enforced specifying the composition of export cargoes. Somehow the crisis in the imperial economy was weathered, but the maze of new regulations numbed Frenchmen and bewildered the neutral Americans. "We have the perfect liberty to go to France," Representative Burwell Bassett of Virginia explained, "provided we carry no cotton [and] no tobacco and pay for the unprofitable articles admited [*sic*] an enormous duty."[23] Bassett was not entirely accurate, but the situation was bad enough.

Since expediency was Napoleon's basic motivation, it is tempting to deny that he even had a formal American policy.[24] Actually, until midsummer 1807 the Emperor's attitude toward America was contingent on current problems between the two nations. With the implementation of full-scale commercial warfare against Britain, however, Napoleon determined that an Anglo-American war would be of considerable benefit to France. From late 1807 until the outbreak of the War of 1812, French efforts were directed towards achieving this goal. Thus France had an American policy, but Napoleon's quixotic actions obscured the fact.

The Emperor or his subordinates took advantage of every opportunity to remind American diplomats or indeed anyone visiting France of Britain's outrageous treatment of her former colony. In late 1807, for instance, Napoleon instructed Foreign Minister Jean-Baptiste Nompère de Champagny to discuss the boarding of American ships by the Royal Navy. Champagny was to declare that France recognized how unjust this practice was to

22. Richard J. Barker, "The Conseil Général des Manufactures under Napoleon (1810–1814)," *French Historical Studies*, VI (1969), 193–94.

23. Chabert, *Essai sur les mouvements des revenus et de l'activité économique en France*, 369–95; Burwell Bassett to St. George Tucker, January 1, 1811, in Tucker-Coleman Papers.

24. Perkins, *Prologue to War*, 68–69, writes that Napoleon "shifted his attitude—his actions scarcely had the continuity to be called policy—according to interests of the moment and particularly his estimate as to whether the carrot or the stick would prove most effective."

a sovereign nation and to emphasize that the American people must win respect for their flag by recourse to arms if less dramatic tactics failed. "The war that England is now waging is no ordinary war," Champagny subsequently wrote the French minister in Washington. "She attacks the independence of every flag; it is necessary that all the maritime states unite for their common defense." On March 24, 1811, annoyed by the continuing passiveness of the United States in the face of British aggression, Napoleon reiterated earlier pronouncements: "I regard the neutral flags as a territorial extension. But the power that allows them to be violated cannot be looked upon as neutral."[25] Quite simply either the United States resisted British encroachments or they would be treated as a hostile nation subject to French retaliation. Thus American ships were burned at sea and American property in France was confiscated; the United States was to be goaded into war with Britain.

Napoleon was not always so heavy-handed in practicing diplomacy. Sometimes he championed neutral rights. Occasionally he spoke of reviving a League of Armed Neutrality, a group of nonbelligerent sea powers banded together for safety against Britain, modeled on earlier armed neutralities assembled between 1780 and 1800. To Americans, however, actions spoke louder than words: France could claim to be a defender of neutral rights when she respected American shipping and property. If France wished American friendship, Napoleon need only assist the United States in obtaining West Florida from Spain.

Late in 1803 François de Marbois, a servant of the old regime who had transferred his allegiance to the new order, dispassionately appraised Napoleon. He recognized the French ruler's brilliance and abilities, but he noted these assets were offset by rashness. "If experience moderates his impetuosity, France will never have been governed by so great a man."[26] Experience did not cause Napoleon to alter his treatment of the United States or to moderate his conduct in Europe. In one situation his recklessness delayed the fulfillment of a goal; in the other it led to his downfall.

[II]

Napoleon was so powerful it is easy to dismiss most of the Emperor's underlings as ciphers, sycophants, and time servers, and to describe them as mere

---

25. Napoleon to Champagny, November 15, 1807, in *Correspondance de Napoléon*, XVI, 165; Champagny to Turreau, February 15, 1808, in AMAE, LXI, LC: and Georges Lefebvre, *Napoleon: From Tilsit to Waterloo, 1807–1815* (New York, 1969), 131.

26. Cited in E. Wilson Lyon, *The Man Who Sold Louisiana: The Career of François Barbé-Marbois* (Norman, 1942), 124.

echo chambers repeating Napoleon's thoughts. It was openly acknowledged that in the Emperor's absence no decisions of any importance could be made. Even Frenchmen downgraded Napoleon's subordinates. "The Emperor governs so much by himself, that a Minister is nothing more than the pen, and not the hand that guides it," the French ambassador in St. Petersburg told John Quincy Adams.[27]

French diplomats responsible for American affairs are usually included in the ranks of factotums. Charles Maurice de Talleyrand-Périgord, a man whose name became synonymous in America with intrigue and corruption because of his involvement in the notorious extortion attempt called the XYZ Affair in 1798, was the most well known of Napoleon's foreign ministers. Among the French representatives in the United States during the presidencies of Jefferson and Madison, one name was dominant: Louis Marie Turreau de Garambouville—or Turreau—a flamboyant figure who spent six years in Washington. The attention focused on Napoleon and Talleyrand and to a much lesser degree Turreau has obscured the fact that French diplomats and high-level Foreign Ministry personnel were well acquainted with America and sometimes offered valuable advice on Franco-American relations.

Louis André Pichon is an example. After serving as secretary for the French delegation in the delicate Môrtefontaine negotiations, Pichon became chargé d'affaires in Washington in March, 1801, and stayed until Turreau's arrival late in 1804. Pichon was recalled as consul general in Philadelphia in 1805 under a cloud because of alleged irregularities in his accounts. Actually, Pichon had angered General Charles Leclerc, Napoleon's brother-in-law and commander of the ill-fated expedition to subdue San Domingo (Haiti) in 1802. Pichon's major offenses appear to have been his representations on behalf of America and his criticisms of French colonial plans. Pichon's admiration of America had grown steadily while he spent more than a decade in residence in Philadelphia and Washington; during this period he served as secretary to two ministers, the famous Edmond Charles Genet and Jean Antoine Joseph Fauchet. Later, in the summer of 1798, it was Pichon who approached William Vans Murray, then America's representative at the Hague, with news that France desired peace following the XYZ episode.

Pichon's lack of zeal in serving France was noticed in several areas. He seemed too willing to attack the San Domingo undertaking, too ready to accept Secretary of State Madison's explanations about American policy

27. Entry of May 6, 1811, in Charles Francis Adams (ed.), *Memoirs of John Quincy Adams* (12 vols.; Philadelphia, 1874–1877), II, 259.

toward the rebellious colonial territory, and either unable or unwilling to stand up for France. Returning to his homeland, Pichon was reprimanded by the *Conseil d'Etat* and relieved of his duties. Yet in 1809, with Jerome Bonaparte's help, he reappeared as a *conseiller* working with the American consul in Paris to settle maritime prize cases and he took the opportunity to offer friendly advice about American policy toward France. Pichon even translated Jefferson's *Manual of Parliamentary Practice* into French.[28] Like many others filling offices under Napoleon, Pichon readily switched his loyalty to Louis XVIII following the Bourbon restoration.

Louis Marie Turreau, the first French minister in Washington since the 1790s, did not possess the friendly sentiments toward the United States that Pichon had. An unpolished former soldier, Turreau deserves special mention because he was France's representative in a crucial era and because his place in history has been affected by the repeating of erroneous tales that seem to have originated with unfriendly contemporaries who relished reporting what might be called Turreau stories, especially those featuring Turreau as wifebeater. According to Augustus Foster the "Bluebeard" beat his wife while the general's private secretary "played the violincello" to drown her screams. Senator William Plumer improved Foster's account with more details: Turreau was writing a dispatch when his wife "came by him with a smothing iron and struck him. He rose & beat her cruelly with a large cane. She cried murder—the children & servants came in crying— instantly the Secretary of Legation raised the windows & to drown the noise played furiously on the French horn."[29]

28. "I have reason to believe that his Disgrace has been occasioned by some Representation of his too great Partiality to this Government being prejudicial to the Interests of the Country whose affairs had been committed to his Charge." Anthony Merry to Harrowby, February 14, 1805, in FOA 5:45, LC; for details of Pichon's career, see *Grand Dictionnaire Universel de XIXe Siècle* (17 vols.; Paris, n.d.), XII, 944; Bonnel, *La France, les États-Unis et la guerre de course*, 152–53, 194 *n*17; M. Dunan, "Un adversaire du système continental," *Revue des études napoléoniennes*, VII (1915), 262–63; Frédéric Masson, *Le départment des affaires étrangères pendant le révolution, 1787–1804* (Paris, 1877), 459–60; Albert H. Bowman, "Louis A. Pichon and the French Perception of the United States"; Edward A. Whitcomb, *Napoleon's Diplomatic Service* (Durham, 1979), 61, 110; on Pichon's American connections, see Monroe to Fulwar Skipwith, January 2, June 30, 1807, in Monroe Papers, New York Public Library; and the nineteen communications from Pichon to David Bailie Warden dated from September 1, 1809, to January 10, 1810, in the David Bailie Warden Papers, Maryland Historical Society.

29. Richard Beale Davis (ed.), *Jeffersonian America: Notes on the United States of America Collected in the Years 1805–6–7 and 11–12 by Sir Augustus John Foster, Bart.* (San Marino, 1954), 158–59. Foster left behind other dubious stories. In his account of events preceding congressional approval of war in 1812 (in Augustus John Foster Diary, May 23, 1812, Library of Congress), for example, the Englishman described Virginia Senator Richard Brent

An examination of the wife beating episode reveals contradictions in the stories beside what instrument the secretary used to drown Madame Turreau's screams.[30] First, the general must have had some feelings about his wife; they came to America separately and, when his wife's vessel was overdue, Turreau was obviously disconcerted—the English minister Anthony Merry said he was living like a recluse. Moreover, the Turreaus were separated by death alone, and those who knew the couple well such as Albert Gallatin said nothing about their marital disharmony. Furthermore, Napoleon simply would not have tolerated such escapades. If the two did not get along, either Turreau would not have been appointed or Madame Turreau would have remained in France.[31] Second, Senator Plumer, whose diary contains several references to the Turreaus' disputes, did not witness any beatings of Madame Turreau. In late January, 1806, he dined at Turreau's and was pleasantly surprised to find the general a gracious host; Madame Turreau was absent, having had a baby boy on January 21. It is improbable that a pregnant woman, even a sturdy one springing from the bottom of French society as Madame Turreau supposedly did, could have taken the punishment alleged. Contrary to legend, also, Madame Turreau must have been a woman of some taste and refinement, for after the general's death she solicited Gallatin's opinion about opening a school for young girls. Finally, the accounts of Turreau's misbehavior come from English or Federalist sources; an exception are two Dolley Madison letters, but they are based on hearsay.[32] These discrepancies suggest that Turreau deserves a reassessment.

---

as an excessive drinker. Yet, on his elevation to the upper house, a contemporary wrote, "The election of Mr. Brent to the Senate has given great moral satisfaction here. His manners, character & talents have exerted general esteem & respect among the members of the [Virginia] assembly." Joseph C. Cabell to Nicholas, January 18, 1809, in Wilson Cary Nicholas Papers, *ibid.*; entry of January 18, 1806, in Brown, *William Plumer's Memorandum*, 383. Minister Merry gave a new twist to the Turreau tale: "His treatment of them [Madame Turreau and his family] was carried latterly to so barbarous an excess as to oblige them from his house, and only the Mediation of, as I believe, the Secretary of State, aided by the Necessity of the Case was sufficient to bring them again all together." Merry to Lord Mulgrave, June 30, 1805, in FOA 5:45, LC.

30. For an amusing discrepancy of accounts, see Frederick B. Tolles, "What Instrument Did the French Minister's Secretary Play?" *William and Mary Quarterly*, Series 3, XI (1954), 633–34.

31. Merry to Harrowby, December 26, 1804, in FOA 5:42, LC. There are several notes from Turreau or his wife to Gallatin between 1806 and 1817 in the Albert Gallatin Papers, New-York Historical Society; Whitcomb, *Napoleon's Diplomatic Service*, 89.

32. Entries of November 30, December 8, 1805, April 27, December 4, 1806, in Brown, *William Plumer's Memorandum*, 336–37, 345, 493–94, 521; entry of January 25, 1806, *ibid.*, 390–92; Plumer to Mrs. Plumer, January 26, 1806, in Plumer Papers, LC;

Turreau seems to have been a decent man, all things considered. Born July 4, 1756, in the small northwest town of Evreux, Department of Eure, Turreau joined the army and fought through the European phase of the American Revolution. He left active duty after the American war when his hopes for advancement were dashed, returning to Evreux. A partisan of the French Revolution, he answered the summons to arms when invading Prussian and Austrian forces seemed on the verge of victory over the embattled motherland. In the summer of 1793 he was posted to the west of France, to the Vendée, a battleground where no quarter was given between enraged peasants fighting for God and king and troops of the Convention, as the French government was called.

Although he distinguished himself in battle and was promoted to general late in 1793, the struggle in the Vendée blemished Turreau's career. Falling into disfavor, he was relieved of his command in May, 1794, and then arrested. Not until the Directory had replaced the Convention was Turreau released and returned to duty. Thereafter he served honorably in various campaigns as far afield as Switzerland and Italy; perhaps in Italy he caught Napoleon's eye. But Turreau never escaped the Vendée blot; in Britain and America Francophobes always noted his viciousness. "I *have dispatched* within three months, two hundred thousand individuals of both sexes and of all ages. *Vive la Republique!*" one yarn had Turreau boasting to the Convention. The truth was bad enough: perhaps one hundred thousand souls perished in the region, many in mass executions. Turreau, however, was but one of several high officers serving in that remote theater.[33] In any case, civil wars, as Americans learned, are the worst kinds of strife.

It is not altogether clear why Napoleon sent Turreau to America. The French army officer corps provided twenty-two ministerial rank diplomats; these were men that Napoleon liked and trusted. Army officers, the Emperor knew, were obedient. On the other hand, it is conceivable that Na-

---

Dolley Madison to Anna Cutts, June 5, 1805, to James Madison, November 15, 1805, in *Memoirs and Letters of Dolly Madison* (Boston and New York, 1886), 50–51, 61–62.

33. The quote is from [?] Stewarton, *The Secret History of the Court and Cabinet of St. Cloud* (New York, 1807), 234–35; Turreau's notoriety may have been due to an account he wrote of the campaign against the western insurgents while he was imprisoned. It was promptly translated into English and published as *Memoirs for the History of the War of La Vendée* in 1796. Nonetheless, a French historian with Republican sympathies, Jacques Godechot, has written: "General Turreau traversed the Vendée at the head of 'infernal columns' that pillaged and massacred so wantonly that the repression, rather than leading to the pacification of the Vendée, produced the opposite effect." Godechot, *The Counter-Revolution: Doctrine and Action, 1789–1804* (New York, 1971), 224. See also Ramsay Phipps, *The Armies of the First French Republic and the Rise of the Marshals of Napoleon I* (5 vols.; London, 1931), III, 30–34, 160.

poleon used distant Washington as a place of exile for Turreau. It is also true that employment in important positions (Washington was the sole French legation in the new world) was a way to reward faithful followers and to promote adherence to the new dynasty.[34] Whatever the reason, Turreau followed orders, and he won the title of baron—as one of six ministers given this rank—in 1811. He proved his loyalty to the new order again when he served the Emperor during the collapse of 1813–1814.[35]

Considering his background, it is not surprising that Turreau was sometimes an inept emissary, clumsy and heavy-handed in making demands on the American government or protesting situations of minor importance. The Bonaparte-Patterson marriage was an example. Shortly after landing in America late in July, 1803, Napoleon's brother, Jerome Bonaparte, was attracted to eighteen-year-old Elizabeth Patterson of Baltimore and early in November they were married. By all accounts the bride, who was related to the politically influential Smith family of Maryland, was proud of her acquisition; according to Foster, it was a matter of "veni, vidi, vici."[36] The French ruler took a dim view of his brother's trans-Atlantic nuptials; and Pichon voiced his master's displeasure to Jefferson, who felt he was powerless to intercede.[37] Aware of Napoleon's anger, Jefferson was extremely irri-

---

34. Whitcomb, *Napoleon's Diplomatic Service*, 32, 39, 93; Napoleon may also have sent officers with undesirable personal qualities on overseas assignments if Thomas Barclay, an English observer, is to be credited. Antoine Rey, consul general in New York, had a "ferocious disposition, violent temper, imperious manner, and [was] much addicted to Liquor." Napoleon ordered Rey to the United States "to get rid of him—He springs from the Dregs of the nation." Thomas Barclay to Anthony Merry, June 1, 1804, in George L. Rives (ed.), *Selections from the Correspondence of Thomas Barclay* (New York, 1894), 160–61.

35. See the *Grand Dictionnaire Universel du XIXe Siècle*, XV, 76–77. Other sources for Turreau's life include Adrien Carré's error-ridden and hostile "La Vendée, ses bourreaux et l'armée française," *Revue du Souvenir Vendéen*, n.v. (December, 1969), 3–22; *Biographie Universelle* (45 vols.; Paris and Leipsig, n.d.), XLII, 300–303; Georges Six, *Dictionnaire biographique des généraux & amiraux français de la révolution et l'empire, 1792–1814* (2 vols.; Paris, 1934), XX, 517–18; Whitcomb, *Napoleon's Diplomatic Service*, 84. Armstrong to Madison, October 20, 1804, in Despatches from France, NA. None of the French envoys who served in America left any private papers. Ulane Bonnel to the author, February 24, 1970; Jean Favier to the author, January 4, 1977; and Roger Pierrot to the author, January 19, 1977. Interview with Ulane Bonnel, Annapolis, Maryland, October 27, 1977.

36. Foster to Lady Elizabeth Foster, August 4, 1805, in Foster, *The Two Duchesses*, 234–35. Others corroborated Foster's statement: "The young lady is not a little proud of her new situation." Jacob Crowninshield to William Bentley, February 5, 1804, in Crowninshield Family Papers. John Quincy Adams claimed "it was really the young man who was seduced." Entry of January 7, 1804, in Adams (ed.), *Memoirs of John Quincy Adams*, I, 284–85.

37. Jefferson to Livingston, November 4, 1803, and Livingston to Jefferson, January 11, 1804, in Jefferson Papers, LC.

tated when Turreau tactlessly raised the issue anew; to the President the marriage was an accomplished fact and beyond his control regardless of Napoleon's fury. Jerome soon returned to Europe following his brother's orders. Betsy Patterson, after creating a sensation with her revealing dress, and causing endless speculation about the future of a child sired by Jerome, disappeared into obscurity and died in 1879.[38] A veteran diplomat would have handled the matter with greater tact, but Turreau was a novice in his position and he was literally following instructions when he delivered protests about the Patterson-Bonaparte union.

By the time of the Moreau affair, Turreau had been in America almost a year and he should have acquired some diplomatic finesse. One of Napoleon's more gifted commanders, General Jean Victor Moreau had been linked with but was actually innocent of involvement in a royalist conspiracy against Bonaparte. Arrested early in 1804, he was nonetheless found guilty by a rigged court and given a two year sentence which Napoleon commuted to banishment in the United States. Sailing from the Spanish port of Cadiz (his ship was twice boarded by the Royal Navy), Moreau arrived in Philadelphia late in August, 1805; he then journeyed to Morristown, New Jersey, where he settled.[39] The French wanted Jefferson to ignore Moreau and Turreau reminded Secretary of State Madison that the exiled officer had left France "under the shadow of an [unfavorable] legal judgement." Jefferson, who was aware that many of his countrymen believed Moreau was in America for ulterior reasons, was determined to avoid any embarrassing connection with the exiled officer, and he resented the tone of French protocol suggestions, at least as delivered by Turreau. "We are not," he told Madison angrily, "of those powers who will receive & execute mandates." Turreau probably meant no disrespect; he simply did not understand the etiquette associated with the art of diplomacy. A more skilled practitioner of the craft probably could have voiced Imperial com-

38. "Having married a Parissian she assumed the mode of dress in which it is said the Ladies of Paris are cloathed—if that may be called cloathing which leaves half of the body naked & the shape of the rest perfectly visible—Several of the Gent" who saw her say they could put all the cloaths she had on in their vest pockett—& it is said she did not appear at all abashed when the inquisitive Eyes of the young Galants led them to chat with her tete-a-tete." Simeon Baldwin to Mrs. Baldwin, January 12, 1804, in Simeon E. Baldwin, *Life and Letters of Simeon Baldwin* (New Haven, n.d.), 345.

39. See Maurice Garçot, *Le Duel Moreau-Napoléon* (Paris, 1951). Another French officer who fell into disfavor, General Charles Pichegru, was less fortunate, dying in his cell under mysterious circumstances. Before his death the *National Intelligencer*, October 19, 1803, commented that "Bonaparte says Pichegru is a royalist; Pichegru loves his country and mankind, and wishes therefore rather for a monarchy under a legal sovereign than a monarchical Republic, and republican tyranny under a Corsican Usurper."

mands in a more subtle manner knowing that Jefferson and the United States would be especially sensitive to any hint of foreign pressure. As Senator Plumer observed, Turreau's "manners have more of the soldier than the courtier."[40]

Turreau shared with most other Europeans an inability to understand the United States. With many observers, he concurred that America had a bleak future.[41] The major shortcoming of the sprawling nation was that the government was too weak. The president was powerless and congressmen were "slaves of their own popularity."[42] "When one treats with the United States," he noted contemptuously, "it is not with the Government it is [with] the people."[43] The sheer size of the country was a handicap; the polyglot population was another. He was convinced that the Constitution would soon prove too unwieldy to hold the enormous land and diverse population together.[44] Turreau was aghast at the rampant materialism of the new nation. Citing a Philadelphia editor, he agreed that "money constitutes every virtue, varnishes over or extinguishes every vice" and thus sapped the strength of the people. Blaming America's English heritage for this defect, Turreau deplored the survival of British influence in Jeffersonian America; to the Anglophobic former soldier, it was equally important for the United States to combat England's power at home and on the

40. Turreau to Madison, August 14, 1805, in Notes from the French Legation, Department of State Archives, National Archives; Jefferson to Madison, August 25, 1805, in Thomas Jefferson Papers, Massachusetts Historical Society; Madison to Jefferson, September 1, 1805, in Jefferson Papers, LC; entry of March 11, 1806, in Brown (ed.), *William Plumer's Memorandum*, 448.

41. See the commentary of Turreau's fellow diplomat, Louis Auguste Felix, baron de Beaujour, *Aperçu des États-Unis au commencement du XIXᵉ siècle, depuis 1800 jusqu'en 1810* (Paris, 1814), 68–69, 78–79, 122–23, 143–44, 170–71, 180, 187–88, 192, 195, 208–209, 222–23, 237, 247–48. Echeverria, *Mirage in the West*, 236, found French diplomats more critical of America than their fellow countrymen who remained in the United States for extended periods.

42. Turreau to Champagny, November 30, 1808, in AMAE, LXI, LC.

43. Turreau to Champagny, June 15, 1809, *ibid.*, LXII. In similar tones Britain's discredited envoy Jackson railed that he had come to America for negotiations with a conventional government, not "with a mob and mob leaders." Francis James Jackson to George Jackson, November 14, 1809, in Lady Jackson (ed.), *The Bath Archives: A Further Selection from the Diaries and Letters of Sir George Jackson, K.C.H., from 1809 to 1816* (2 vols.; London, 1873), I, 45.

44. Turreau to Talleyrand, March 9, 1805, in AMAE, LVIII, LC; Louis Marie Turreau, *Aperçu sur la situation politique des États-Unis d'Amérique* (Paris, 1815), 77. Turreau's book contains some interesting insights, but it must be used with caution. Much of it is made up of letters written by an individual styling himself Inchiquin, a Jesuit priest ostensibly touring the United States. See the *National Intelligencer*, June 22, 1811; and Robert E. Spiller, *The American in England During the First Half-Century of Independence* (New York, 1926), 301.

ocean.[45] Perhaps disturbed by the vitality American citizens displayed and frustrated because America tolerated British insults and restrictions, Turreau berated the United States as a "parasitic power" deserving inferior status.[46] Later, after America had redeemed itself in the War of 1812, Turreau modified his views and even praised the United States.[47]

Americans who disregarded Turreau's deportment and extravagant dress noted his abilities. John Quincy Adams, certainly a critical observer, described the Frenchman as an "Adonis in dress and manners," but the Massachusetts senator admitted that Turreau could converse intelligently on many subjects. Jefferson also thought highly of Turreau and claimed that only the delicate state of Franco-American relations prevented a "cordial manifestation" of the esteem with which he held Turreau.[48] Turreau certainly was not a great diplomat. The Patterson-Bonaparte marriage and the Moreau case revealed deficiencies in his knowledge and practice of diplomacy. On the other hand, there is no indication that the most suave or the most experienced of French emissaries could have calmed American anger over Napoleonic conduct any better than Turreau.[49] It should be remembered also that Turreau won the respect and friendship of many Americans. His English counterparts, Anthony Merry, Francis James Jackson, or even David M. Erskine could not say the same.

Pichon and Turreau reported to the minister of foreign relations, Talleyrand, who was himself acquainted with Americans and America.[50] Besides his role in the XYZ Affair, Talleyrand spent more than two years in the

45. Turreau, *Aperçu sur la situation politique des États-Unis*, 53 *n* and (quoting William Duane's *Aurora*), 42–46, 51, 57, 81–82; Turreau to Talleyrand, July 1, September 20, 1805, January 15, 20, 1806, in AMAE, LVIII, LIX, LC.

46. Turreau, *Aperçu sur la situation politique des États-Unis*, 91; Turreau to Talleyrand, January 27, 1805, in AMAE, LVIII, LC.

47. Entry of April 5, 1815, in Adams (ed.), *Memoirs of John Quincy Adams*, III, 182–83. See also René Rémond, *Les États-Unis devant l'opinion française* (2 vols.; Paris, 1962), I, 317–18.

48. Adams to John Adams, December 24, 1804, in Worthington C. Ford (ed.), *Writings of John Quincy Adams* (7 vols.; New York, 1913–1917), III, 102; Jefferson to Short, November 15, 1807, in Jefferson Papers, LC. Jefferson noticed Turreau's dress also; he told Senator Adams that the Frenchman would have to shed some of his gold lace or have "the boys in the streets . . . run after him as a sight." Entry of November 23, 1804, in Adams (ed.), *Memoirs of John Quincy Adams*, I, 316.

49. Carré, "La Vendée, ses bourreaux et l'armée française," 20, *n*24, claims that Turreau's conduct in the United States contributed to the delay of the Anglo-American war until 1812.

50. John L. Earl, "Talleyrand in Philadelphia, 1794–1796," *Pennsylvania Magazine of History and Biography*, XCI (1967), 282–96. Crane Brinton, *The Lives of Talleyrand* (New York, 1930), is an acceptable biography.

United States as a refugee in the mid-1790s. He apparently enjoyed his sojourn; shortly after landing he announced how happy he was to live in a peaceful country and he specifically noted the friendliness of Philadelphians. In his memoirs written decades later, however, Talleyrand could recall only the shortcomings of the nation that had sheltered him at a perilous moment in his life. He denounced Americans for their materialism, though he enjoyed the benefits of wealth and participated in various money-making land schemes, bank stock investments, and other commercial ventures.[51] He complained about America's cultural deficiencies, and Britain's influence annoyed him. "America," Talleyrand stated categorically in 1795 "is completely English."[52] Both complaints are understandable. Youthful America could not equal the splendors of mature and established France; it was true too that American society would appear common to one who had been a member of the Old World's elite. Minor personal slights might have prompted Talleyrand's caustic recollections more than the actual faults listed. Despite introductions from prominent personages, for example, President Washington refused to receive Talleyrand either officially or unofficially. Since this denial occurred at a time when Washington was actually a tourist attraction and was meeting scores of strangers, the Frenchman was offended. Talleyrand caused consternation by openly consorting with prostitutes and black women. A greater understanding of American sensibilities could have spared the Frenchman some awkward moments—if he cared. In 1796, with the Directory in power, he left the United States and never returned.

Theoretically Talleyrand could advise Napoleon about American affairs by drawing on firsthand knowledge about the trans-Atlantic republic. Unfortunately, Napoleon generally did not pay much attention to either Talleyrand or his successors in making foreign policy decisions, and although Talleyrand recognized the existence of a deeply rooted English prejudice against America, and although he knew that even a lukewarm regard for American rights would benefit France, there is little evidence that he bothered trying to modify Napoleon's American policy and much to

51. Hans Huth and Wilma J. Pugh (eds. and trans.), *Talleyrand in America as a Financial Promoter, 1794–96*, American Historical Association *Annual Report, 1941* (3 vols.; Washington, 1942), Volume III. Honoré Gabriel Riqueti, comte de Mirabeau, said of Talleyrand: "For money he has sold his honor and his friends. He would sell his very soul for money, and would be right too, for he would be bartering excrement for gold." Quoted in Echeverria, *Mirage in the West*, 196–97.

52. "Les États-Unis et L'Angleterre en 1795," quoted in Perkins, *The First Rapprochement*, 1. The United States was "a second edition of England, but reproduced on a much larger format than the original," wrote Constantin Chasseboeuf, comte de Volney in 1803. Quoted in Echeverria, *Mirage in the West*, 206.

indicate that he used his position to enhance his personal fortune.[53] Thus John Armstrong was wasting his time when he enlisted Talleyrand to awaken the Emperor to the advantages of a more liberal treatment of America in August, 1807.

Jean Baptiste Nompère, comte de Champagny and (after mid-1809) duc de Cadore, succeeded Talleyrand. Champagny had spent twelve years in the navy, and he had served in the Estates General as a deputy representing the nobility. His naval experience led Napoleon to appoint Champagny to the marine section of the Council of State. Thereafter he filled various posts ranging from an ambassadorship in Austria to head of Napoleon's Interior Ministry. Champagny shared his predecessor's susceptibility to corruption, but "he lacked the cunning slyness . . . and the duplicity of Talleyrand."[54] Champagny faithfully executed Napoleonic policies toward the early American republic.

Talleyrand and Champagny had an able assistant who was very knowledgeable about America, Alexander Maurice Blanc de la Nautte, comte d'Hauterive. D'Hauterive, after beginning his diplomatic career in Eastern Europe, served as French consul in New York in 1793–94. Frightened by revolutionary excesses, he stayed in America until 1797, forming friendships with prominent citizens including Albert Gallatin, then a rising figure in the ranks of Jeffersonian Republicans. It was also in the United States that d'Hauterive became friendly with Théophile Cazenove, a French land speculator, and where he renewed contact with Talleyrand whom he had known earlier; back in France, the middle-aged diplomat (like Cazenove) was employed by the Foreign Ministry and as Talleyrand's star rose so did d'Hauterive's. Thereafter d'Hauterive participated in crucial affairs: he drafted the Concordat of 1801 establishing tolerable relations between Paris and the Pope; he also figured in the Amiens and Tilsit negotiations of 1802 and 1807 respectively. In the absence of his superiors, d'Hauterive handled American affairs frequently; for example, in the summer of 1809, he effec-

---

53. "An entire generation and a new reign will have to pass before the Englishman will believe that the American is his equal." "Memoir sent to Mr. Casenove," June 23, 1794, in Huth and Pugh, *Talleyrand in America*, 37; for analyses of Talleyrand as foreign minister see Elaine Feifer, "Vergennes et Talleyrand," *Sciences Politiques*, LII (1937), 239–52, and Whitcomb, *Napoleon's Diplomatic Service*, 120, 126–27.

54. Whitcomb, *Napoleon's Diplomatic Service*, 135, and 27, 34, 50, 140. Whitcomb describes Champagny as "honest," but one observer declared Champagny's corruptness "as notorious as that of his predecessor Talleyrand." François Cottier to Dominique André, August 26, 1809, in Jean-Jacques Hémardinquer (ed.), "Une correspondance de banquiers Parisiens (1808–1815): aspects socio-politiques," *Revue d'histoire moderne et contemporaine*, XVII (1970), 518.

tively soothed the Americans during a particularly trying time in Franco-American relations.[55]

D'Hauterive symbolized the contradictions in the Franco-American connection. He remembered that in his hour of need the United States had been his home. "I have not changed, in opinion, in viewpoint, or in hopes for all that relates to the happiness of a country where I received so many evidences of goodwill and affection," he told Gallatin. In the same letter he speculated about the longevity of the weak, vacillating government he had held in contempt during the 1790s and that he still despised. In the 1790s the United States had followed policies favorable to Great Britain; under Jefferson America still seemed unwilling to force the English to respect neutral rights. "If God wants Liberty to win all the peoples of the earth, he has sown the first seeds on very damp ground," d'Hauterive concluded.[56]

Reflecting upon Franco-American relations in the Napoleonic era, it is clear that after 1807 a cardinal objective of France was an Anglo-American war. Given the complexities of American domestic politics, this goal would have been difficult to achieve in the best of circumstances. In this environment Napoleon should have followed a more enlightened American policy. But Napoleon believed that nations are motivated by self-interest and, as the Emperor interpreted the aims of France, America was of peripheral value. The French ruler was a victim of his own prejudices; his vision was narrowed because of his Continental bias. Surrounded by officials who reinforced his views, or had little influence, Napoleon was incapable of pursuing a consistently harmonious relationship with the United States. Thus the Anglo-American war he ardently desired was delayed to 1812.

55. For information on d'Hauterive's career, see Artaud de Montor, *Histoire de la vie et des travaux politiques du comte d'Hauterive* (Paris, 1839); Masson, *Le départment des affaires étrangères*, 409–11; Whitcomb, *Napoleon's Diplomatic Service*, 21–23, 76, 85; and three articles by Frances S. Childs, "A Secret Agent's Advice on America, 1797," in Edward M. Earle (ed.), *Nationalism and Internationalism: Essays Inscribed to Carlton J. H. Hayes* (New York, 1950), 18–44; "The Hauterive Journal," *New-York Historical Society Quarterly*, XXXIII (1949), 69–86; and "Citizen d'Hauterive's 'Questions on the United States,'" Institut Français de Washington *Bulletin*, nos. 5–6 (1957), 34–44. See also the introduction to John Adams' marginalia on d'Hauterive's *L'État de la France a la fin de l'an VIII* in Zoltan Harastzi, *John Adams and the Prophets of Progress* (Cambridge, 1952), 259–63.

56. D'Hauterive to Gallatin, July 3, 1809, in Childs, "The Hauterive Journal," 85; D'Hauterive to Adet, August 1, 1798, in Childs, "A Secret Agent's Advice on America, 1797," 38; entry of October 24, 1793, in Childs, "The Hauterive Journal," 73.

THREE

West Florida

Neutral rights dominated Franco-American diplomacy prior to 1812, but other difficulties certainly existed. Probably the most important of these secondary issues was the fate of West Florida, a Spanish-controlled territory encompassing portions of present-day Louisiana, Mississippi, Alabama, and Florida. In brief, the United States maintained that the coastal strip between the Mississippi and Perdido Rivers had been included in the Louisiana Purchase. The Spanish possessors insisted the land was theirs and both nations appealed to Napoleon to resolve the dilemma. Having sold the United States land with a dubious title, the French ruler wished to concentrate his attention on winning the war against Britain, employing Spain in the process. In other words, with Spain playing an important role in France's immediate future, Napoleon was unwilling to honor Talleyrand's 1803 assertion that the United States could draw on France's good offices to secure West Florida. Thus the American claim fell victim to Napoleonic expediency.

What Napoleon airily dismissed was of vital importance to the United States. Unfettered navigation of the Mississippi would be in jeopardy as long as another power's territory fronted on the river. Equally important, development of the Mississippi Territory hinged as much on freely navigating the rivers that flowed into the Gulf of Mexico as it did on settling the problem of marauding Indians. Jefferson therefore spent considerable time promoting a West Florida settlement with Spain. Cognizant of this, his adversaries flayed the President for his alleged complicity in an evil scheme to defraud Spain of West Florida using Napoleon as middleman. A nod from the Emperor, Jefferson's foes assumed, and the somnolent Spaniards would convey the desired real estate. Napoleon's cooperation, these critics were positive, was guaranteed because France was anxious to subdue the rebellious blacks of San Domingo who, aided by American supplies, had been successfully fending off all attempts by France to reimpose its authority. Certainly a reciprocal arrangement seemed plausible: termination of American trade would halt supplies which in black hands was hindering France's reconquest of what had been her richest colony; a grateful Napoleon would reward his friend Jefferson with West Florida. The only losers would be decadent Spain and the hapless insurgents of San Domingo.

Jefferson tried to utilize France in his quest for the remainder of Louisiana. His enemies erred, however, when they charged that he was involved in illegal and immoral acts to accomplish his goal. Equally wrong have been scholars such as John Bach McMaster and Charles Callan Tansill, who have portrayed Jefferson as a puppet doing Napoleon's bidding for the crumbs from the Emperor's table.[1] Jefferson solicited Napoleonic assistance because France had claimed that West Florida was part of Louisiana and because Spain for all practical purposes was a French-controlled state. From another perspective, Napoleon could have used the West Florida question to strengthen the Franco-American community of interest begun with the Convention of Môrtefontaine and given a mighty impetus by the Louisiana sale. Blinded by his Continental bias, the Emperor balked and allowed the Spanish chimera to damage Franco-American harmony. Coupled with his contemptuous treatment of neutrals, Napoleon's mishandling of the West Florida issue helped subvert his goal of an early Anglo-American war.

[I]

The quest for West Florida originated with the inexact wording of the Louisiana agreement. The United States purchased territory "with the same extent that it now has in the hands of Spain, and that it had when France possessed it."[2] Superficially this phrasing seemed unequivocal; in reality, the geographical limits of Louisiana were unknown. The United States, it might be recalled, had originally sought the acquisition of the Island of Orleans although New Orleans was not situated on an island. Minister

---

1. "There was no insult which Jefferson would not brook, no degradation to which he would not descend in order to please Napoleon and rescue the Floridas." John Bach McMaster, *A History of the People of the United States from the Revolution to the Civil War* (8 vols.; New York, 1883–1913), II, 219. Also Charles C. Tansill, *The United States and Santo Domingo, 1798–1873: A Chapter in Caribbean Diplomacy* (Baltimore, 1938), 109. A recent French article reflecting this view is Yves Auguste, "Jefferson et Haiti (1804–1810)," *Revue d'histoire diplomatique*, LXXXVI (1972), 333–48.

2. Miller, *Treaties and Other International Acts*, II, 498.

Livingston spent little time quizzing Talleyrand or Talleyrand's underling François de Marbois about boundaries. From Talleyrand he heard "you have made a noble bargain for your self, and I suppose you will make the most of it."[3] Marbois was more specific, fixing Mobile and the Perdido River as the eastern limits of Louisiana. No binding commitment on boundaries was forthcoming, however, and Livingston, having convinced himself and his superiors that the Louisiana Purchase extended to the Perdido, pressed the French to the extent that they assured the United States "of every aid that we can ask in case the business is set on foot at the Court of Madrid."[4]

While Livingston labored in Paris, Jefferson evaluated the options open to him concerning West Florida. He could have, as Livingston advised, ordered the miniscule American army to liberate the land from Spain's feeble grasp, ignoring Spanish outrage and possible French protests. Yet Jefferson felt Spain's impotence made her the ideal colonial power to share a border with the United States. Besides, the President was wary of using military force even for such an exalted purpose as liberation. The United States of course could have allowed the Floridas to remain in Spanish hands until some future date. This idea had merit in 1786 when Jefferson contemplated Spain's presence in North America, but by 1804 he and James Madison were convinced not only that the United States was sufficiently strong to incorporate the area into the American Union, but that the national security demanded expansion at Spain's expense lest a third power intervene.[5]

Therefore a third option was chosen. Negotiations for the Floridas—East and West—would commence in Madrid utilizing promised French support. The United States would be ready to forego acquisition of East Florida if West Florida's boundary was settled. Her negotiating position was buttressed by the Mobile Act, legislation creating a customs district for the Mobile area, a measure designed to intimidate the Spaniards by reminding them that the young republic was at Spain's gates on the Gulf of Mexico awaiting the transfer of West Florida. The Mobile Act was signed by the President in February and proclaimed in May.

In between the signing and proclamation, Jefferson and Madison asked their longtime friend and fellow Virginian, James Monroe, to join Charles Pinckney, United States minister to Spain in the negotiations. Monroe, Madison directed, should travel via Paris where he could "ascertain the views of the French government" before journeying to Madrid.[6] Slow com-

3. Livingston to Madison, May 20, 1803, in Despatches from France, NA.

4. Livingston to Monroe, December 10, 1803, in Monroe Papers, LC.

5. Concerning Spain's position in North America, see the important letter of Jefferson to Archibald Stuart, January 25, 1786, in Boyd (ed.), *The Papers of Thomas Jefferson*, IX, 218.

6. Madison to Monroe, April 15, 1804, in Gaillard Hunt (ed.), *The Writings of James Madison* (9 vols.; New York, 1900–1910), VII, 141.

munications and the press of diplomatic business in London where Monroe represented the United States delayed his departure until October. When he finally arrived in Paris, the forty-nine-year-old troubleshooter promptly requested the French aid Talleyrand had spoken of the previous year.

Five weeks later, not having received an official response, Monroe left Paris. Putting up a brave front, he said, "I shall pursue the object intrusted to me with zeal and diligence, and I trust with success," but Monroe must have harbored doubts about what he would accomplish. Talleyrand's failure to respond was certainly a sign that France had reassessed the situation from 1803. Even more ominous, however, when Monroe informed the French foreign minister he was leaving for Spain, Talleyrand had replied that he would experience "much difficulty" in Madrid. A counterthrust by Monroe referring to French support brought a "smile" to the Frenchman's face.[7] Meanwhile, both Livingston and Monroe had been approached separately by subordinates of Talleyrand, who spoke of money being necessary if America was to obtain any territory. "*France wishes to make our controversy favorable to her finances,*" Livingston reported the day after François de Marbois had hinted that the Floridas could be Americanized for sixty million francs. Marbois suggested a similar amount to Monroe while the comte d'Hauterive argued that "Spain must cede territory, and . . . the United States must pay money."[8]

On December 21 Talleyrand finally answered Monroe's appeal submitted six weeks before. His denial that West Florida was part of Louisiana must be seen in light of the international situation. The seizure of Spanish bullion vessels by British warships had brought Spain into the war as a French ally on December 14. On January 4, 1805, the two nations signed a treaty in which France guaranteed Spain's "territorial integrity" in Europe "and the return of colonies seized from Spain in the course of the current war."[9] The French, whose treasury was already theoretically being subsidized by Spain at an annual rate of sixty million francs, thus gained an ally and a substantial increment to French naval power. The United States could scarcely match these tangible results.

Not surprisingly, Monroe and Pinckney spent six months in Madrid

7. Monroe to Fulwar Skipwith, December 18, 1804, in Isaac J. Cox, *The West Florida Controversy, 1798–1813* (Baltimore, 1918), 116; Skipwith, however, doubted that Monroe would succeed in either Paris or Madrid. Skipwith to St. George Tucker, December 1, 1804, Tucker-Coleman Papers; Monroe to Madison, December 16, 1804, in Hamilton (ed.), *The Writings of James Monroe*, IV, 280.

8. Livingston to Madison, September 21, 1804, in Madison Papers, LC; Monroe to Madison, December 16, 1804, in Hamilton (ed.), *The Writings of James Monroe*, IV, 281–82.

9. Francis G. Davenport and Charles O. Paullin (eds.), *European Treaties Bearing on the History of the United States and Its Dependencies* (4 vols.; Washington, 1917–1937), IV, 180.

deadlocked in fruitless discussions about what was included in the Louisiana transfer. Armstrong was similarly frustrated in Paris when he sought French help for his colleagues in Madrid. Threats of an Anglo-American alliance drew the rejoinder "we can neither doubt nor hesitate,—we must take part with Spain," and the French ominously alluded to the vulnerability of valuable American properties in France and Holland.[10] Clearly, in the winter of 1804 a solid Franco-Spanish front had emerged against the United States.

Jefferson and Madison were not particularly perturbed at the rebuff suffered by their envoys. "All she [Spain] can expect is to have the pill wrapt up in the least nauseous disguise," Madison wrote Monroe.[11] The two leaders agreed that if the Spaniards were foolish enough to reject the opportunity for a mutually acceptable agreement the United States should consider other alternatives. Jefferson favored informing the French that a Spanish-American rupture would drive the United States into England's embrace. Before the Louisiana Purchase the supposedly Anglophobe Jefferson had contemplated alliance with Britain; two years later he again mulled over the possibility. Acquisition of Louisiana had forestalled an Anglo-American alliance in 1803; now cabinet opposition led by Madison caused the President to abandon the idea.[12] That Jefferson twice considered an Anglo-American alliance is a remarkable commentary on his statecraft as well as his determination to secure West Florida.

Instead of threatening Napoleon with an Anglo-American linkup, the administration decided to enlighten the French of their own self-interest: Britain stood to benefit most from Spanish-American troubles, and American vessels carried a considerable portion of France's commerce and were a significant factor in what prosperity wartime Bordeaux, L'Orient, Nantes, and other French ports knew. Presumably the hardheaded Napoleon would recognize the value of a neutral America and reconsider his stand on West Florida.

To awaken the French emperor further to the opportunity for mutual gratification, the Jeffersonians moved to regulate American trade with San Domingo in March, 1805. The United States had been trading with the black rebels of San Domingo since George Washington's presidency, and this traffic continued even as the Môrtefontaine settlement and Louisiana

10. Armstrong to Monroe, March 12, 1805, in Monroe Papers, New York Public Library.

11. Madison to Monroe, November 9, 1804, in *Letters and Other Writings of James Madison, Fourth President of the United States* (4 vols.; Philadelphia, 1865), II, 208–209.

12. *National Intelligencer*, February 6, 1805; and Clifford Egan, "The United States, France and West Florida, 1803–1807," *Florida Historical Quarterly*, XLVII (1969), 237.

sale brought tranquillity to Franco-American relations. The French were unhappy about the exchange, but in the early days of the attempted Napoleonic reconquest of Hispaniola they remained silent about American trade with the insurgents. As increasing resistance and yellow fever decimated the ranks of their invading army, the French attitude shifted. Napoleon insisted that victory was obtainable provided the Americans ceased supplying the blacks. Following his master's wishes, chargé d'affaires Pichon protested American trade with San Domingo during the winter of 1803 – 1804, emphasizing the potential threat of clashes between recently armed American merchantmen and French warships attempting to interdict the illicit commerce: it was conceivable that a ship captain could cause a serious confrontation between the two nations.

The French argued also that shipments from America were prolonging the rebellion. They labeled the trade "illegal," in violation of the rules of war, and they requested that the United States government halt it. To impress upon the Americans the gravity of the situation, Pichon raised the question of what effect a successful uprising by Haitian blacks would have on the million slaves in the United States. [13] Jefferson and Madison did not treat Pichon's protests lightly; being southerners they were especially sensitive about the potentially explosive black powder keg in their midst. [14] A *National Intelligencer* story, which the Virginians obviously saw, reported how "[white] women with children in their arms were seen flying through the streets [in a Haitian city] to avoid their pursuers; and being overtaken by them, one thrust of a bayonet pierced both mother and child!" With such an image before them, certainly the president and secretary of state were desirous of containing the insurrection—or independence—movement to San Domingo, but there were other factors, "some delicate considerations" in Madison's words, that had to be considered before trade with the black republic was abruptly terminated. [15]

One delicate consideration was that Britain would fill the vacuum created by the suspension of American trade. Surely, the two men reasoned, the French did not want to help their enemy at America's expense. Jefferson and Madison were concerned that some kind of indirect traffic would de-

13. Pichon to Madison, March 9, 1804, in Notes from the French Legation, NA; Pichon to Talleyrand, January 17, 1804, in AMAE, LVI, LC.

14. The British, themselves sitting on a time bomb in their slave-inhabited West Indian islands, frequently noted the impact of San Domingo news on Americans. See Thornton to Hawkesbury, August 18, 1801, May 1, June 2, August 29, 1802, in FOA 5:32, LC; Merry to Hawkesbury, March 19, 1804, in FOA 5:41, LC.

15. *National Intelligencer*, June 8, 1804, clipping enclosed in AMAE, LVII, LC: Madison to Livingston, January 31, 1804, in Diplomatic Instructions of the Department of State: All Countries, Department of State Archives, National Archives.

velop between San Domingo and the United States, and that American merchants attracted by the rich rewards the trade offered would send cargoes to nearby bases from which the goods would be forwarded to San Domingo. Vessels engaging in such transactions would become fair game for French corsairs already preying on the Americans, guaranteeing a crisis in Franco-American relations akin to the disruptions of 1796 when marauding French ships in the Caribbean were a factor in the origins of the Quasi-War.

There was another consideration. If France managed to dam the flood of foodstuffs and other goods entering San Domingo, Jefferson feared that the blacks might undertake exporting revolutions to other lands—the *National Intelligencer* story would be repeated, perhaps in America. Prudence from the President's perspective dictated a continuation of trade, making the blacks dependent on their suppliers who, in turn, might check tendencies toward rashness.[16] To placate the French, to keep the exchange going, and to curry favor with Napoleon, the President asked Congress to approve a measure curbing the activities of armed merchantmen.

Many congressmen were baffled by the so-called port clearance bill. Extreme Federalists wailed that it was a capitulation to Napoleon; blinded by prejudice, Representative Samuel Taggart of Massachusetts claimed the legislation "is as much as to say we hate to starve the black dogs, but our dear cousin Bonaparte . . . is too powerful to be affronted, therefore something must be done." Yet Nathaniel Macon thought the bill "scarcely strong enough . . . when the great profit of the trade is considered."[17] Macon was right; the act approved by Congress early in March, 1805, was weak. It was not meant to abolish or disrupt the lucrative trade with San Domingo, but to mollify the French, to prevent possible Franco-American hostilities in the Caribbean, and to aid the Florida talks. In short, a port clearance bill would demonstrate the concern of the United States for France's plight in San Domingo, suggesting to Napoleon that an equivalent act would be appreciated.[18]

16. Madison to Livingston, January 31, March 31, 1804, in Diplomatic Instructions, NA; Merry to Hawkesbury, March 19, 1804, in FOA 5:41, LC.

17. Taggart to John Taylor, December 3, 1804, in Mary Robinson Reynolds (comp.), "Letters of Samuel Taggart, Representative in Congress, 1803–1814," American Antiquarian Society *Proceedings*, n.s., XXXIII (1923), 138; Macon to John Steele, January 19, 1805, in Kemp P. Battle (ed.), *Letters of Nathaniel Macon, John Steele and William Barry Grove* (Chapel Hill, 1902), 67.

18. Passage of the port clearance bill could be viewed by France as "proof of the justice and friendly disposition of the United States." Madison to Armstrong, March 5, 1805, in Diplomatic Instructions, NA.

[II]

The Emperor and his entourage disappointed the Americans. As Armstrong had already discovered, they dismissed hints that the United States might align itself with Britain; in French eyes the militarily weak new nation could not materially affect the Anglo-French war. Furthermore, Napoleon was ready to forego America's neutral carrying capacity even though it helped France's embattled economy. Moreover, the Emperor was not deceived by the cosmetic San Domingo legislation—he was well aware that the Americans continued a large-scale trade with his insurgent black subjects and at his direction Talleyrand and Turreau continued complaining about the traffic.[19] Harboring such sentiments, the French did not intercede in the Madrid negotiations and, recognizing the futility of further discussion, the Americans withdrew, Monroe returning to London and Pinckney packing his possessions for the return trip to the United States. His successor, wealthy Massachusetts Jeffersonian James Bowdoin, did not even present his credentials in the Spanish capital, but based himself in London.

Meanwhile, another dimension was being added to America's quest for West Florida. On September 14, 1805, Armstrong was approached by an anonymous Frenchman who in the course of a conversation asserted that "the more you refer to the decisions of the Emperor, the more sure and easy will be the [Florida] settlement." The stranger then spelled out provisions providing for transfer of East and West Florida to the United States and a western boundary readjustment to the Colorado River of Texas. Spain was to receive $10,000,000 from the United States, and obligations owed American citizens for earlier spoliations were to be paid by bills drawn on Spain's New World colonies.[20]

France had sought money before from the United States. The XYZ episode, it will be remembered, had precipitated a major crisis in Franco-American diplomacy. Although that affair had occurred under the Directory, transfer payments continued to be an integral part of French diplomacy under the Consulate and Empire. Napoleon himself supposedly informed Chancellor Livingston that he would find Europe corrupt.[21] As

19. Talleyrand to Turreau, July 5, 1805, in AMAE, LVIII, LC; Talleyrand to Armstrong, August 10, 16, 1805, in *American State Papers; Class I, Foreign Relations* (6 vols.; Washington, 1832–1861), II, 726–27; Turreau to Madison, October 14, 1805, *ibid.*, 725–26; Turreau to Madison, October 22, 1805, in Notes from the French Legation, NA.

20. Armstrong to Madison, September 14, 1805, in Despatches from France, NA.

21. William Vans Murray to John Quincy Adams, April 3, 1802, in Worthington C. Ford (ed.), "Letters of William Vans Murray to John Quincy Adams, 1797–1803," American Historical Association *Annual Report, 1912* (Washington, 1914), 705; Talleyrand in-

already disclosed, Marbois and d'Hauterive had broached the question of money during Monroe's Parisian interlude. In addition, Armstrong had warned Monroe of France's lust for cash; Spain and America, he said, "will in fact be a couple of oranges in her hands which she will squeeze at pleasure, and against each other, and that which yields the most will be the best served or rather the best injured."[22] The proposal made to Armstrong on September 14, then, was in line with prevailing practices.

Jefferson was not eager to become enmeshed in questionable activities. Yet, thwarted in Madrid and aware of Spain's dependency on France, he explained to Madison that the Spaniards' "cavalier" conduct proved "that France is to settle with us for her." Besides, with the war in Europe widening, the international scene was favorable for a Spanish-American agreement in Madrid and "at Paris, through Armstrong and Monroe as negociators [*sic*], France as the mediator, the price of the Floridas as the means. We need not care who gets that; and an enlargement of the sum we had thought of may be the boit to France." Spain, the President added, might be persuaded with a permanent western boundary following the Guadalupe River, much further east than the Rio Bravo (Grande) that the United States was claiming and west of the Colorado River, the line mentioned by the anonymous Frenchman to Armstrong.[23]

In seeking a solution through France, the President opened himself to charges ranging from Francophilism to corruption. Jefferson was ready to risk outcries, however, because the reward outweighed the abuse he would have to endure. Thus he rejected Madison's fervent hope that France should not get "her hand into our pocket." It is easy to be censorious, to assert that the end did not justify the means; yet, as a writer calling himself "Timoleon" (probably Jefferson) argued in the *National Intelligencer* late in 1806, the Floridas were strategically important, they were controlled by Spain, and French influence was dominant in Madrid. In Timoleon's mind, it would be folly if the United States did not seize the opportunity circumstances created.[24] Timoleon did not say as he could have that America was

---

formed Livingston on another occasion, "You see in this country it is very difficult to do business. You need a lot of money and with that there are no difficulties that can't be ironed out." Louis Madelin, *Talleyrand* (New York, 1948), 103–107.

22. Armstrong to Madison, September 14, 1805, in Despatches from France, NA.

23. Jefferson to Madison, August 17, 1805, in Madison Papers, LC; Jefferson to Madison, October 23, Jefferson to Gallatin, October 23, 1805, in Jefferson Papers, LC. Slightly differently worded letters were sent to Robert Smith, October 24, Wilson Cary Nicholas, October 25, and Samuel Smith, November 1, 1805, all *ibid.*

24. Madison to Livingston, July 5, 1805, in Hunt, *The Writings of James Madison*, VII, 187, *n*1; Madison to Jefferson, September 30, 1805, in Jefferson Papers, LC; *National Intelligencer*, November 5, 1806. Noble E. Cunningham, Jr., The *Jeffersonian Republicans in*

following a precedent established in the Louisiana Purchase. Nor did he rationalize as he could have that Spain was hardly the most enlightened power in the world and that the Floridas would be better served being incorporated into Jefferson's "empire for liberty." Spain's tenure as a great power was ending; on the morrow her magnificent New World colonies would take flight from the motherland, the Floridas among them.

At a cabinet meeting on November 12, the President proposed that France be notified that America was making a "last effort" to reach an "amicable settlement" with Spain. America would offer Spain money for the Floridas and Spain would compensate Americans for losses suffered at Spanish hands during the hostilities sparked by the French Revolution. To guarantee fulfillment of spoliation claims, the zone between the Guadalupe and Rio Bravo rivers would serve as collateral. Shortly after the session on the twelfth, Jefferson received the proposition made to Armstrong on September 14. Happy that they were almost "equivalent to ours," Jefferson was confident that success would crown American efforts.[25]

The President outlined Spanish-American affairs to Congress on December 6, 1805. According to Jefferson's interpretation, the Louisiana Purchase had had a serious and negative impact on Spanish-American relations; before that epochal agreement Spain had willingly accepted a spoliations convention. After the Louisiana transaction, however, Spain had become intransigent: she carped at the Mobile Act and she rejected the spoliation convention. Furthermore, envoys Pinckney and Monroe had been stymied when they sought a settlement of outstanding problems in Madrid. The French, who had adopted an aloof attitude, now appeared willing to promote an accord. With France ready to lend a helping hand and with a war raging in Europe, the time seemed propitious to reach a settlement with Spain. Jefferson's message was more interesting for what it left unsaid, however. There was no mention of money being employed, although the President ended his statement with the comment "the course to be pursued will require the command of means which it belongs to Congress exclusively to yield or to deny." Paris was not named as the negotiating site. Congress was not told of the financial underworld lurking in the French capital waiting for ill-gotten gains at Spain's expense. Presumably the President felt that leaks would flesh out his sketch or that congressmen would

---

Power: Party Operations, 1801−1809 (Chapel Hill, 1963), 257, identifies Jefferson as "Timoleon" writing in the Richmond *Examiner*, June 25, 1803. For Jefferson's connection with the *National Intelligencer*, and its editor, Samuel Harrison Smith, see William E. Ames, *A History of the National Intelligencer* (Chapel Hill, 1972), 39−41.

25. Entry of November 12, 1805, in Franklin B. Sawvel (ed.), *The Complete Anas of Thomas Jefferson* (New York, 1903), 232−33; entry of November 19, *ibid.*, 233−34.

become knowing when appropriations legislation was introduced in the House.[26]

In the absence of precise information, rumors proliferated. Various congressmen—Maryland's Senator Smith and Representative Orchard Cook of Massachusetts among others—claimed to have inside knowledge of what was happening, and although there were discrepancies in accounts about the sums involved, all agreed that France, as broker, would receive money for Spain's transfer of the Floridas to the United States. In retrospect, Jefferson probably erred in not divulging his plans; airing details might have muted the self-righteous indignation of a few congressmen and stifled the rumor mongering that flourished in Washington that winter. Yet, with his followers dominating the Senate and House by overwhelming majorities, the President can hardly be blamed if he misjudged congressional reaction.

Even though he had been warned, Jefferson must have been chagrined when he found his kinsman and onetime fervent supporter John Randolph spearheading the opposition. Randolph, who had earlier piloted administration measures through the House, was infuriated at the prospect of France benefiting from a cash transaction between Spain and America. "I will never consent," he told his colleagues, "that the asses milk of the United States shall enrich the consumptive coffers of France. I will never consent to give him [Napoleon] a single cent—so help me God!" Randolph may have been sincerely vexed at the thought of Napoleon's treasury swollen by a contribution engineered by a politician he once believed moral. Yet the shrill eunuch, Randolph, had other issues in mind: he had watched Jefferson drift away from solid Republican virtues, he loathed the heir apparent Madison (saying he was for "*no more milk and water presidents*"), and he was concerned about corruption in high places—the Yazoo scandal was fresh in his memory.[27] For all of his sarcasm and oratorical flourishes, however, Randolph could not stem the tide by himself and the House eventually voted the $2,000,000 needed to fund the acquisition of the Floridas.

Federalists were generally quiet during Randolph's pyrotechnics. They were delighted to see their opponents warring among themselves; in private they applauded Randolph as an honest man (everyone was honest who op-

---

26. "Confidential Message on Spain," December 6, 1805, in Ford (ed.), *The Works of Thomas Jefferson*, X, 203–205; Secretary of the Navy Jacob Crowninshield hinted at intrigue a week after Jefferson's communication. "With Spain the only serious difficulty is the two floridas, we want them and they must be ours, but I doubt if they can be acquired except thro' France (this to yourself however)." Crowninshield to William Bentley, December 14, 1805, in Crowninshield Papers.

27. Entry of January 7, 1806, in Brown (ed.), *William Plumer's Memorandum*, 369; William Wirt to Monroe, June 10, 1806, in Monroe Papers, LC.

posed Jefferson). Their glee diminished though when Jefferson requested congressional approval of another bill restricting trade to French controlled areas of San Domingo. Again the Federalists charged that the United States was exhibiting "tameness and spanish servility" to France. They claimed San Domingo was an independent nation, that it might undertake retaliatory actions against American shipping, and that humanitarianism dictated continued provisioning of the black republic. "Sir," Timothy Pickering warned Jefferson, "the moment you sign this act (and you will sign it if it passes the House of Representatives), you seal the degradation of your country, whose honour and dignity are placed in your hands, not to be debased; but to be firmly maintained . . . against . . . any power on earth. One act of submission," he maintained, "begets further unwarrantable demands; and every subsequent compliance still further debases the nation, blunts the sense of national honour, and sinks the spirit of the people."[28] Although no record survives of Jefferson's reaction to Pickering's message, he was probably bemused at the Massachusetts senator's indignation, for few men could match Pickering's slavish devotion to Britain.

Actually Jefferson favored a new law early in 1806 for generally the same reasons he had promoted legislation in 1805. Turreau was complaining, and the President wished to still the Frenchman. The specter of race war was probably on Jefferson's mind also; certainly it figured in congressional debate of the bill.[29] Finally, Jefferson wanted West Florida and he hoped that a new San Domingo bill would favorably impress Napoleon, inducing the Emperor to bless the negotiations that would take place. Yet, as much as Jefferson desired West Florida, he was unready to abandon the lucrative exchange so profitable to his countrymen; the 1806 proposal, like its predecessor, was deliberately weak. As its chief backer, George Logan of Pennsylvania, told a fellow senator, "It was not his intention to prohibit the trade—but only pass a bill that would please the French . . . and not injure our traders."[30] The Federalists and more zealous Republicans never did

28. Pickering to Jefferson, February 24, 1806, in Jefferson Papers, LC; and Plumer to Jedediah Morse, February 24, 1806, in Plumer Papers, LC. Donald R. Hickey, "The Federalist View of the Slave Revolt in Haiti: A Letter from Timothy Pickering to Thomas Jefferson in 1806" (unpublished paper), places Pickering's letter in perspective.

29. *Annals of Congress*, 9th Congress, 1st Session, 27–42, 510–16 (December 20, 1805, February 25, 1806).

30. Entry of January 15, 1806, in Adams (ed.), *Memoirs of John Quincy Adams*, I, 382; figures prove Logan right. Exports to the French West Indies increased from $3.6 million in 1804 to $7.4 million in 1805. Thereafter exports dropped to $6.7 million in 1806 and $5.8 million in 1807 and, because of the embargo, to $1.5 million in 1808. John H. Coatsworth, "American Trade with European Colonies in the Caribbean and South America, 1790–1812," *William and Mary Quarterly*, Series 3, XXIV (1967), 262.

fathom such reasoning; they adhered tenaciously to the view that Jefferson obeyed Napoleonic injunctions. Thus when Turreau objected to certain parts of the 1806 act, Senator James Hillhouse suggested that the French envoy draft his own measure.[31]

Having aroused Randolph and his disciples as well as the Federalists with his requests for negotiating money and seemingly stricter regulation of the San Domingo trade, Jefferson stirred up Congress further when he asked the Senate's approval of John Armstrong and James Bowdoin to negotiate jointly in Paris. The President hoped to placate New Englanders wary of southern expansion and to recognize what in fact already existed, since Bowdoin had joined Armstrong in Paris of his own volition. It was not Bowdoin who prompted the Senate's subsequent convulsions, but Armstrong; for although he had been in France less than eighteen months, the New Yorker had made many enemies. Samuel Smith still resented the loss of the ministerial post to Armstrong; the influential Marylander was more certain than ever that Armstrong was an incompetent. "Armstrong is again honored, at a time when all America believes he is recalled," Smith complained after Armstrong's nomination. "I speak a truth when I say, that there is not a man in either house or of the cabinet (the P[resident] and M[adison] excepted) that approves his appointment."[32] Randolph, meanwhile, was portraying the New Yorker as part of a ring of "renegades" and "harpies of the French bureau" accumulating money from claims cases initiated by Americans against the French government.

Illustrating Randolph's charge and a primary reason for the Senate's hesitation in approving Armstrong for the Spanish negotiations was the *New Jersey* case. Returning to America from a voyage to China in 1798, the *New Jersey* had been captured by French privateers—the Quasi-War was then in process—and adjudged a lawful prize by the Council of Prizes. The insurers, who put up a $203,000 deposit for the release of the cargo and ship, naturally appealed the decision. Years later, in September, 1804, their claim was upheld. At this point Armstrong recommended disallowance of the claim chiefly because the owners, Philip Nicklin and Robert Griffith, were said to be British citizens. When the rumor proved untrue, Armstrong argued that claims could only be settled in proportion to the limited amount of money provided by the Louisiana treaty. Despite the

---

31. Turreau was seen as a prime reason for enactment of the bill. "The insulting menace of a brute of a fellow, miscalled a French Ambassador," Samuel Taggart wrote with his usual exaggeration, "back'd with the threat of Talleyrand to the same purpose . . . convinced many legislators that the trade is wrong." Taggart to John Taylor, February 24, 1806, in Reynolds (comp.), "Letters of Samuel Taggart," 180–81.

32. Smith to Wilson Cary Nicholas, March 11, 1806, in Carter-Smith Family Papers.

intervention of Jefferson's friend Samuel Du Pont de Nemours as agent for Nicklin and Griffith, Marbois, with Armstrong's concurrence, awarded less than a third of the amount originally allowed.[33]

Jefferson's willingness to forgive Armstrong for a "monetary error as to the rights of insurors" was not shared by the Senate.[34] Despite intense lobbying for a favorable vote, the upper house deadlocked fifteen to fifteen on Armstrong; Kentuckian John Adair fled the Senate chamber to avoid voting for his fellow Republican and it was only through the intervention of Vice President George Clinton (who knew Armstrong) that approval came sixteen to fifteen. Jefferson decided to assuage senatorial anger and give complete sectional balance to the negotiating team by asking his Virginia friend and former senator, Wilson Cary Nicholas, to join Armstrong and Bowdoin. Although he shared the President's passion for West Florida, Nicholas, begging responsibility for his flock of a dozen children, declined Jefferson's offer.[35] The Senate remained unappeased.

The House was also in an uproar. Federalists were baffled by the $2,000,000 appropriation; they wondered why money was needed for West Florida if that territory had been included in the Louisiana Purchase as the administration maintained. Soon they convinced themselves that the warship *Hornet* was conveying cash to France for the enrichment of Napoleon and Talleyrand. A quarter century later, so dogged was the Federalist mind, the tale was repeated that $2,000,000 "was actually sent to France . . . for no other reason than that *France wanted money and must have it.*" Randolph, meanwhile, continued his verbal assaults on Jeffersonian corruption. "The nation is stigmatized—it has received a blot which all your India rubber cannot efface," he told his former Republican cohorts.[36]

Jefferson remained unshaken by Randolph's onslaught, but others were not so sturdy. For example, Fulwar Skipwith, commercial agent in Paris, had returned to America late in 1805 hoping for a government position in

33. Ambrose Saricks, *Pierre Samuel Du Pont de Nemours* (Lawrence, 1965), 323–24; *American State Papers, Foreign Relations*, II, 774–75.

34. Jefferson to Samuel Latham Mitchill, March 1, 1806, in Jefferson Papers, LC. The previous August the President called Armstrong's error "a very palpable and unfortunate one." Jefferson to Madison, August 17, 1805, *ibid.*

35. Jefferson to Nicholas, March 26, 1806, Nicholas to Jefferson, April 2, 1806, *ibid.* Nicholas, informed of the situation by Samuel Smith (see note 32), may have wished to avoid involvement in the political battle.

36. William Sullivan, *Familiar Letters on Public Characters, and Public Events: From the Peace of 1783 to the Peace of 1815* (Boston, 1834), 291; *Annals of Congress*, 9th Congress, 1st Session, 959–60 (April 7, 1806); for the evolution of a New Hampshire Federalist's thoughts on Louisiana and the Floridas, see Samuel Tenney to Josiah Bartlett, February 18, 1803, February 15, 1800 [1804], April 3, 13, 1806, in Josiah Bartlett Papers.

Louisiana. Failing that, he was recruited to accompany important dispatches to Armstrong and Bowdoin in February, 1806.[37] "I was an eyewitness . . . of many things while at Washington," he confessed later. "I wish my Country as well as myself had been utter strangers to such things."[38] What bothered Skipwith's conscience is not clear, but evidence indicates that he knew he was carrying authorization for the negotiators to utilize the recently appropriated Florida money. Unlike Jefferson who worried about the impact of Randolph's rhetoric abroad, Skipwith was uneasy about his homeland demeaning itself by indulging in shady bargaining.

Monetary reward, the San Domingo legislation, the European scene, and self-interest all dictated France's cooperation, and by the summer of 1806 the President's dream of a Spanish settlement had revived. Thus Jefferson told his close friend William Short in July, "From Paris we may expect now daily to hear something . . . notwithstanding the efforts made here to render that negotiation abortive."[39] Even as the President wrote these words, however, events were occurring in Paris that permanently dashed hopes for a French-aided settlement of the Florida question.

The primary reason was Napoleon's European ambitions: "The affairs of France are today in Europe," Talleyrand lectured the French ambassador in Madrid, "those of America are of secondary order." In Europe Spain was uppermost in the Emperor's mind. Theoretically in bondage to France, Spain and its sovereign Charles IV were proving most recalcitrant vassals. Manuel Godoy, chief minister of the nation for most of the 1792–1808 period, had been extremely critical of France's disregard of her ally. Napoleon, meanwhile, doubted that Charles IV's regime could repulse English landings in the Iberian Peninsula and he was skeptical about Spain's adherence to the unfolding Continental System. Thus he concocted a plan for the dismemberment of Portugal that would permit large numbers of

37. Skipwith to St. George Tucker, February 14, 1806, in Tucker-Coleman Papers; Armstrong and Bowdoin were authorized to draw up to $2,000,000 in accord with the act passed February 13, 1806. Gallatin to Bowdoin and Armstrong, March 18, 1806, in *Bowdoin and Temple Papers*, Massachusetts Historical Society *Collections*, Series 7, VI (Boston, 1907), 306; Skipwith sailed on the *Hornet* from New York on March 29 "the Bearer of Remittances to the Amount of Two Millions of Dollars to pay for the Purchase of Florida should that Negotiation succeed." Merry to Mulgrave, April 6, 1806, in FOA 5:48, LC.

38. Skipwith to St. George Tucker, August 10, 1806, in Tucker-Coleman Papers. Mayor DeWitt Clinton was overheard by Armstrong's brother-in-law denouncing the grant of "authority to the President to expense $2,000,000 in the purchase of East Florida. That the Country was not worth a Cent. That it was a measure disgraceful to the Administration." Morgan Lewis to John Smith, March 23, 1806, in John Smith of Mastic Papers, New-York Historical Society. Lewis added, "If you experience as much Intrigue in the general government as we do in that of the State [New York], I pity Mr. Jefferson from my soul."

39. Jefferson to Short, July 9, 1806, in William Short Papers, Library of Congress.

French troops to transit Spain; once in the Bourbon realm they would pressure Charles to follow Napoleon's orders. Eventually Charles was deposed and Joseph Bonaparte occupied the Spanish throne. Then on May 2, 1808, the Spanish nation rose up against its French oppressors. The May 2 uprising inaugurated a bloody six-year struggle that, besides sapping French strength, led to British intervention and the opening of Spain and her colonies to British merchandise, precisely what Napoleon did not want. In mid-1806, however, Napoleon was bent on humoring Spain. Consequently he urged the Spaniards to strengthen their defenses in the Floridas and he refused aid to Armstrong and Bowdoin in their negotiations. Indeed, Turreau was instructed to caution the Americans about precipitous action against Spanish possessions.[40]

The absence of French cooperation had a direct bearing on the feud that flared between Armstrong and Bowdoin, a subsidiary factor in the destruction of Jefferson's Florida dream. Bowdoin had been in Paris but a short time when he became uneasy about the situation. *"Things . . . don't look so prosperous here as I expected,"* he observed.[41] Bowdoin recognized that little could be accomplished while the French waged the Austerlitz campaign, and he waited impatiently for the return of Napoleon. Unfortunately Bowdoin used his spare hours—there were many—to evaluate Armstrong. He found the New Yorker deficient in all respects. After the joint commission arrived, Armstrong insisted on negotiating with the French by himself because he claimed that he alone was commissioned minister to France. Bowdoin never recovered from this snub. He noted that Armstrong had limited contacts with Frenchmen; Marbois monopolized most of the New Yorker's time. The Americans Armstrong did know were a curious lot. Since many were active in financial and commercial circles, it was easy for Bowdoin to imagine Armstrong's complicity in a ring of what Bowdoin called stock-jobbers or money lenders.[42]

As Bowdoin repeated the tale, Pierre Cesar Labouchère, Amsterdam agent of the House of Hope, had visited him "that I might give credence to his substitute, Mr. Daniel Parker." It was "Parker's intrigues with

40. Talleyrand to Eugene de Beauharnais, November 9, 1806, in Cox, *The West Florida Controversy*, 267; Talleyrand to Turreau, July 31, 1806, in AMAE, LIX, LC; Napoleon to Talleyrand, June 23, 1806, in *Correspondance de Napoléon*, XII, 484–85.

41. Bowdoin to Erving, November 3, 1805, in *Bowdoin and Temple Papers*, 255–56.

42. See Bowdoin to Erving, February 3, March [?], April 13, June 12, September 16, 1806, and Bowdoin to Madison, March 9, 1806, all *ibid.*, 288, 305, 307–308, 312–13, 332, 296–97; Bowdoin to Armstrong, May 3, 1806, in Despatches from France, NA; Bowdoin to Jefferson, October 20, 1806, in Jefferson Papers, LC; Bowdoin to Monroe, January 20, 1806, in Monroe Papers, LC; Bowdoin to Monroe, February 26, 1806, in Monroe Papers, New York Public Library.

Armstrong which has [*sic*] done all the mischief; he is daily closeted with him," Bowdoin stressed. A ring including Parker and Labouchère claimed to have Manuel Godoy's blessing to convey the Floridas to America for a stipulated sum. These insiders would obtain three to six million acres of land from Spain for a nominal price; their claim would be protected in the territorial transfer; and, if the past was a precedent, their investment would appreciate handsomely as settlers flocked to the new lands.[43]

Bowdoin's suspicions about Armstrong's corruption were bolstered by his fellow Americans, James Sullivan and Skipwith. Sullivan, Bowdoin's private secretary, had been warned either by Pichon or another foreign office functionary, Jean Baptiste Petry, that the French government was determined to profit from the Florida question. Worse, Armstrong was in "collusion with Speculators." Complaining that Armstrong "blasts all the blooming honors of Mr. Jefferson's administration," Sullivan concluded "in no instance of the general['']s conduct shall we find the fairness of a man of honor or the frankness and candor of a man of truth." Skipwith, the recipient of a visit by an insider named Dautremont, insisting he had never known "a man more destitute of any worthy motives" than Armstrong, called him a liar and "his conduct, if possible, more reproachable than" Livingston's. Pointing out that Armstrong associated with men of dubious reputation including Parker and another international speculator, James Swan, Skipwith professed his allegiance to Jefferson "but I fear it will be found that he had been the dupe of his Minister."[44]

Armstrong, who knew of some of these charges, was not the kind of man to remain silent when his integrity was questioned. For Bowdoin's edification, Armstrong interpreted his instructions: he was to await Spanish overtures and to utilize France's good offices in making a settlement about which the French were to be informed. Furthermore, until he was told otherwise, Armstrong felt completely justified conferring "*exclusively*" with Talleyrand. To Jefferson and Madison, Armstrong traced Bowdoin's unhappiness to his indignation over British insults to America. Arriving in Paris "red-hot" about British crimes against America, Bowdoin desired to enlist

43. Bowdoin to Jefferson, May 20, 1806, in Jefferson Papers, LC. Labouchère had married a daughter of Sir Francis Baring, whose firm had helped finance the Louisiana Purchase; Bowdoin to Erving, September 9, December 31, 1806, in *Bowdoin and Temple Papers*, 326, 357; Bowdoin to Jefferson, March 1, 1806, in Jefferson Papers, LC (mistakenly filed in 1807). For information on the House of Hope and brief mention of Parker, see Marten G. Buist, *At Spes Non Fracta: Hope & Co., 1770–1815* (The Hague, 1974).

44. Sullivan to Erving, May 5, 1806, in Monroe Papers, New York Public Library; Sullivan to Monroe, May 5, 1806, *ibid.*; Skipwith to Monroe, May 3, 31, 1806, *ibid.*; Skipwith to George Logan, July 13, 1806, George Logan Papers, Historical Society of Pennsylvania.

French support in the quest for West Florida because as soon as this territory was in American hands, the United States could take appropriate measures to curb the English. When Armstrong pointed out that Bowdoin's expectations for an immediate response from France was unrealistic, the Massachusetts Republican threatened to appeal directly to Napoleon, then campaigning in Central Europe. Bowdoin was only dissuaded from headlong flight to the Emperor's headquarters by Daniel Parker.[45]

Parker was inextricably linked with American expansion into Louisiana and the Floridas, yet his name was and is largely unknown. A native of Watertown, Massachusetts, Parker headed Daniel Parker & Company, a firm engaged in supplying provisions to the Continental army. Washington, who had contact with Parker, described him as "a Gentleman of amiable manners and dispositions, and as a Man of great integrity and capacity in business."[46] After the Revolution, Parker established a financial house with William Duer and a former French agent in America, John Holker, and dabbled in various commercial ventures including the financing of the *Empress of China*, the first American ship to sail to China.

Parker was not in New York when the *Empress of China* returned in 1786, for late in 1784 he fled to Europe when irregularities were uncovered in his accounts. "I can with all solemnity and truth declare, that however unfortunate and Distress[ed] I may be, that the rectitude of my Intentions has always been supported by the fullest testimony of my feelings and Conscience," he wrote from London on New Year's Day, 1785. For several years Parker maintained that he would return to America and clear his name, reimbursing Holker for the losses he had suffered.[47] Europe proved irresistible, however, and Parker steadily increased his fortune speculating in American securities and commerce during the French Revolution. In 1803 he acquired Draveil, a great estate on the Seine River about fifteen miles outside Paris where, as a gentleman farmer, he raised high grade Merino sheep and practiced scientific farming. At Draveil Parker entertained members of the trans-Atlantic community including Lafayette; Sir Benjamin Thompson, the American Loyalist known to the scientific world as Count

45. Armstrong to Bowdoin, September 16, 1805, in *Bowdoin and Temple Papers*, 371; Armstrong to Bowdoin, May 4, 1806, in Bowdoin and Temple Papers, Massachusetts Historical Society; Armstrong to Jefferson, February 17, 1806, in Jefferson Papers, LC; Armstrong to Madison, May 4, 1806, in Despatches from France, NA.

46. Washington to Superintendent of Finances, March 12, 1783, in Fitzpatrick (ed.), *Writings of Washington*, XXVI, 212.

47. Parker to Andrew Craigie, January 1, 1785, in Andrew Craigie Papers, American Antiquarian Society, Worcester, Mass.; the Holker Papers at the Library of Congress contain much correspondence relating to Holker's unsuccessful attempts to collect compensation for Parker's activities.

Rumford; Massachusetts merchant Thomas Handasayd Perkins; and William Short. Parker knew or was known by all the American envoys to France from Jefferson to Albert Gallatin. While Jefferson apparently had little contact with Parker, others like Gouverneur Morris, Monroe, Livingston, Armstrong, Jonathan Russell, and Joel Barlow were well acquainted with their fellow countryman. Barlow, for example, had met Parker in 1788 and during his brief tenure as minister he saw Parker frequently; indeed he even entrusted one of his diplomatic ciphers with the wealthy American. No wonder Barlow's successor, William H. Crawford, reported that Parker "has been in fact the minister for the last ten years." [48]

Parker's interest in the Floridas went back to the summer of 1802. In June of that year, Thomas Sumter later wrote, he had seen Livingston and Parker poring over a map of the Floridas. Parker seemed quite knowledgeable about the remote Spanish possession, placing a value of $20,000,000 on what he estimated to be the 30,000,000 acres of land included in the region. Parker claimed that Sir Francis Baring was ready to finance any bargain that could be struck and that a land transfer would be "of great consequence to the United States—it might be accomplished and a man might make his own fortune too." Finishing his account of what had transpired, Sumter not unexpectedly concluded, "I always had an impression too that Mr. P[arker] tho' apparently and perhaps really a true friend to the United States might nevertheless be disposed to allow individuals to serve their own fortunes at the public expense." [49] There is no proof, however, that Parker realized any profit from the Louisiana transaction.

Parker may not have benefited but his interest in the Floridas continued undiminished. Through his friendship with Talleyrand, Sir Francis Baring, Théophile Cazenove, and a Spanish intermediary, Eugenio Izquierdo de Ribera y Lazaun, Parker planned on securing a huge grant of land in the Floridas just before a territorial transfer. "Nothing forbad[e] me from buying from the King of Spain what certainly belonged to him and what of course he had a right to sell," the financier protested later; "a Deed given one hour before the transfer of the Country would have been as good as if dated half a Century back." [50] Despite his best efforts and with all of his

48. See Joel Barlow to Peter Stadnitski, April 23, 1789, Peter Stadnitski Papers, Gemeente-Archief, Amsterdam. My former colleague James C. Riley called this letter to my attention. Barlow to Ruth Barlow, November 12, 1812, in Barlow Papers, Houghton Library, Harvard University; entries of July 28, 30, 1813, in Knowlton (ed.), *The Journal of William H. Crawford*, 30–31.

49. "Mr. Sumter's remarks respecting [the] Floridas" [October 1, 1803], in Monroe Papers, LC.

50. Parker to Armstrong, May 25, 1810, in Despatches from France, NA; Parker was not the only American interested in securing Florida lands. Juan Ventura Morales, Inten-

connections, not even Parker could get the negotiations for the Floridas moving. Nonetheless his interest in the area remained strong and during the flurry over the Floridas in 1810–1811 he was again involved in acquisition efforts.

With such shifty figures inhabiting Paris, Bowdoin's suspicions were never allayed. Throughout the winter of 1806–1807 he continued fuming. "A minister," he complained, "is neither a source of pleasure or profit; it will not afford the first because deception and deceit characterize those with whom you must associate" and profit was impossible because a minister's salary was grossly inadequate. Unable to exercise the equal rights that Jefferson said he shared with Armstrong, Bowdoin, having experienced one indignity heaped on another, left Paris late in 1807 with a final blast at Armstrong. "French and Americans here have but one opinion in regard to him, which is that he is as unfit as unworthy of the place he holds."[51] With the *Chesapeake-Leopard* affair clouding Anglo-American relations, the negotiations in Paris were no longer pressed. Bowdoin returned unnoticed to America where he died in 1811; his abortive mission is largely overlooked in American historiography.

Jefferson was certainly dismayed with the outcome in Paris. With more hindsight than accuracy, he protested that he had "yielded (with a reluctance well remembered by all)" to the nominations of Bowdoin and Armstrong. The fact was that the President was bent on securing West Florida and would have asked Senate confirmation of anyone except perhaps Aaron Burr to speed negotiations. When Armstrong and Bowdoin clashed, the President was so apprised, but, hoping the unpleasantness would disappear, he characteristically contented himself with writing soothing messages to his envoys, remaining aloof from the squabble.[52] It may well have been that Jefferson overlooked the pettiness of his subordinates because of a serene confidence that sooner or later East and West Florida would be American.

If so, Jefferson was right, for eighteen months after he left office American settlers in the area east of Baton Rouge, Louisiana, staged a successful revolt delivering a section of the Floridas to the United States. There is

---

dant of West Florida, made large land grants in his fiefdom to Edward Livingston and Daniel Clark, among others. Thomas Perkins Abernethy, *The South in the New Nation, 1789–1819* (Baton Rouge, 1961), 332–33.

51. Bowdoin to Erving, October 27, 1806, in *Bowdoin and Temple Papers*, 346; Bowdoin to Erving, October 11, 1807, *ibid.*, 434.

52. Jefferson to Monroe, April 11, 1808, in Monroe Papers, LC; Bowdoin never formally accused Armstrong of being involved in land speculation. Madison to Armstrong, October 29, 1810, "Private," in Rokeby Collection.

much evidence suggesting the complicity of the Madison administration in the uprising. In July, 1810, for example, Joel Barlow mentioned the presence of William Charles Coles Claiborne, governor of the Louisiana territory, in Washington. "It seems that the Floridas will come to us and if properly managed it may be a good thing," the usually reliable Barlow reported.[53] Furthermore, the first and only leader of the West Florida Republic was Fulwar Skipwith, the same Skipwith who had been so alarmed at what he had observed in Washington during the winter of 1805–1806.[54] Another chunk of the Floridas was obtained during the War of 1812. The Spanish surrendered the territory remaining in their possession in the Adams-Onís Treaty of 1819. Far away on his mountaintop near Charlottesville Jefferson must have felt satisfaction.

Napoleon's thoughts, if any, on the Adams-Onis Treaty of 1819 are unknown. Choked with the details of conquering and ruling Europe, he had never known much about the Floridas except that they, like much else that he knew, were something to be dangled or manipulated as the case should demand to further France's interests. Thus after the suspension of the American quest for the Floridas in mid-1807, the Emperor attempted to utilize the Floridas to galvanize the Americans against Britain in 1808. As desirous as he was for the region, Jefferson did not rise to the bait.

Napoleon had spurned a chance to bring France and the United States closer together. The Floridas were lost anyway; the hardheaded Emperor knew that. Instead of letting the Americans have the territory with French cooperation, the Corsican pursued his illusory Spanish dreams, losing American good will on the one hand and, ultimately, Spain on the other. A grateful United States, its domain including the Floridas and convinced of French friendship, might have protested English violations of American neutrality more vigorously. An Anglo-American war might have come before 1812, benefiting France and the United States equally. Ever the prisoner of expediency, Napoleon missed his opportunity.

53. Barlow to Henry Dearborn, July 10, 1810, in J. S. H. Fogg Collection, Maine Historical Society, Portland.

54. Skipwith settled near Baton Rouge because of economic opportunity, and in time he became one of the most prominent planters in the area. He was pleased that West Florida was incorporated into Orleans Territory "altho under circumstances which I cannot at this moment reconcile with my ideas of honor, justice, and sound policy on the part of the government under whose orders you act." Skipwith to W. C. C. Claiborne, December 10, 1810, in Monroe Papers, New York Public Library. Skipwith's friends were disconcerted by his activities in the remote region; as Joseph Cabell pointed out, "we regret exceedingly that you had any connection with the business as your enemies will always make a handle of it to your annoyance and detriment." Cabell to Skipwith, June 12, 1812, in Fulwar Skipwith Papers, Causten-Pickett Collection, Library of Congress.

FOUR

Economic Coercion

October 20 and 21, 1805, were ordinary days in the United States but in Europe events of far-reaching consequence were taking place. Most important was the great naval engagement off Cape Trafalgar on October 21 which resulted in a complete victory for Great Britain. The previous day France won the Battle of Ulm and her armies were only six weeks away from Austerlitz, the scene of Napoleon's greatest triumph.

Trafalgar Day also witnessed the appearance of *War in Disguise; or the Frauds of the Neutral Flags*, a lengthy pamphlet authored by a stern-minded Englishman named James Stephen. Among other points, Stephen focused on the maritime growth of the United States, and he charged that the Americans were benefiting from Britain's war with France by exploiting the erosion of the so-called Rule of 1756. This measure specified that no trade could exist in war that had not existed in peace: for example, the United States could not participate in France's colonial trade in wartime when the French monopolized it in peacetime. The Rule of 1756 had fallen into disuse as Britain's war against France waned at the turn of the century. The English could afford to be generous then, but in Stephen's view the time for charity had passed and the Rule of 1756 needed to be enforced.

Actually the *Essex* decision the previous spring anticipated Stephen's call. Bound for Cuba from Spain, the *Essex* had paid nominal duties on her cargo in the United States before sailing for the Caribbean. En route from America she was taken into British custody and condemned. The English maintained that His Majesty could not allow American participation in Spain's colonial trade in war when the Spanish excluded the United States from that traffic in peace. The *Essex* case, the appearance of *War in Disguise*, the balance produced by Britain's hegemony on the high seas and Napoleon's control of the European landmass, all these events boded ill for the mushrooming commerce of the neutral United States.

[I]

Early in the Anglo-French war Stephen Cathalan, Jr., the veteran American consul in Marseilles, observed that the conflict "must become very advantageous to the Commerce of the United States."[1] Cathalan's forecast proved accurate as American foreign trade made impressive gains throughout 1804, 1805, and 1806. Along the Atlantic coast, ports throbbed with prosperity; the old Federalist stronghold of Newburyport, Massachusetts, was typical of coastal towns flourishing from wartime commerce. Newburyport apparently had matured by the late eighteenth century with a stable population and settled economic order. The wars of the French Revolution stimulated fresh growth, however, and further expansion came with the Napoleonic Wars. The impact of the cycle of European conflicts was evident from population and economic statistics: by 1807 Newburyport's population stood at 7,500, 50 percent greater than in 1792. Even more impressive, between 1792 and 1807 the average wealth of adult males tripled to more than $5,000, while the median value of the population's holdings almost quadrupled from $440 to $1,600. By 1807 over 100 Newburyport residents were worth at least $10,000, a fair sum by contemporary standards.[2]

Newburyport's growth was stimulated by the enormous surge of foreign commerce, especially the re-export segment of that trade.[3] Merchants from the picturesque town on the Merrimack River might invest $5,000 in a cargo of fish products; the $5,000 shipment would be exchanged in the

1. Cathalan to Madison, July 13, August 18, 1803, in Despatches from Marseilles, NA.

2. Newburyport's population in 1980 was estimated at 15,910; details about Newburyport are drawn from Benjamin W. Labaree's *Patriots and Partisans: The Merchants of Newburyport, 1764–1815* (Cambridge, 1962), 132–33.

3. Burton Spivak, *Jefferson's English Crisis: Commerce, Embargo, and the Republican Revolution* (Charlottesville, 1979), and "Republican Dreams and National Interest: The Jeffersonians and American Foreign Policy," Society for Historians of American Foreign Relations *Newsletter*, XII (1981), 1–20, distinguishes between exports of American origin and the re-export trade. According to Spivak, Jefferson never really believed in the re-export trade, but domestic politics and the ballooning of the "carrying trade" led him its defense with the disastrous end results of embargo and war. As interesting as this interpretation is, I am not convinced that Jefferson reasoned or acted as Spivak would have his audience believe.

Caribbean for sugar and molasses worth $8,000 or more. To satisfy the belligerents, the shipment would be Americanized via a nominal customs payment (as in the *Essex* case), then it would be sent to Europe where the value might double to $16,000. By 1807 Newburyport's re-exports were worth $1,500,000; knowledge of this figure makes the town's prosperity and growth understandable. Of course, unsettling problems accompanied this growth in international trade that was so beneficial economically to Newburyport and the nation. The trade was artificial and when peace was restored, the economy would have to undergo painful readjustment. Conversion difficulties lay in the future; in 1805, 1806, and 1807 the dual problems of impressment and tighter restrictions on neutral carriers were on men's minds.

Impressment had long plagued Anglo-American diplomacy. The rapidly expanding United States merchant marine needed manpower, and Britain's fleets contained thousands of sailors willing to work under the American flag where they were treated better and were paid substantially higher wages than in the Royal Navy. Some of these men became American citizens, but His Majesty's government refused to recognize the transfer of allegiance to another nation. These naturalized Americans as well as American-born citizens fell victim to English search parties combing the crews of United States vessels on the high seas.[4] Americans have always focused on this affront to national dignity, ignoring the fact that His Majesty's Navy spared no one. If Americans were impressed, so too were other nationals.

The British had various defenses besides indefeasible allegiance for their actions. The Royal Navy had been practicing impressment for a century. Indeed, during the colonial era, press gangs, as the parties seizing men were called, had sometimes depopulated towns of their male inhabitants. In a notorious case in 1757, more than a quarter of New York's adult males were forced into duty on British ships. Perhaps half were returned following strenuous objections, but several hundred remained in the Royal Navy's control. Impressment had also accompanied the outbreak of the Anglo-French war in 1793, and the British largely ignored the protests made by the United States.[5] Having successfully utilized manstealing in the 1790s,

4. Even before Anglo-American diplomatic relations were firmly established, the English impressed Americans. In October, 1803, Daniel Mulford reported a sailor who left New York in 1789 "in an India-bound Ship—was sold by his Capt[ai]n in India to a British Man of War, where he remain'd till about a year ago." Entry of October 30, 1803, in Daniel Mulford Diary, Library of Congress. For another instance of impressment in 1790 see "The Impressment of Hugh Purdie and Others" in Boyd (ed.), *The Papers of Thomas Jefferson*, XVIII, 310—42.

5. Jesse Lemisch, "Jack Tar in the Streets: Merchant Seamen in the Politics of Revolu-

the English assumed they could continue it with impunity in the 1800s.

Thus the resumption of war in May, 1803, brought new cases of impressment. English warships even kidnapped men from vessels in American waters. Unlike his predecessors, Jefferson did not ignore the situation and a steady stream of complaints was directed to annoyed English envoys. When H.M.S. *Boston* pressed two Americans, Secretary of State Madison quickly lodged a complaint with Edward Thornton, England's representative in Washington; Thornton was disturbed by Madison's protest and he indignantly informed his superior, "I was sorry to see a bitterness of tone and of insinuation, partaking too much of the character of the public papers as well as the assertion of doctrines, which if allowed to utmost extent would be in contradiction to all the hitherto received opinions of general law, and destructive of the well-being of every civilized state."[6] Like other Englishmen, Thornton assumed that impressment was essential to the United Kingdom's survival. Consequently American protests fell on deaf ears and Britain adhered to the practice.

France also offended the United States through its erratic treatment of American sailors marooned in French ports. Some of these men joined French or Spanish privateers operating out of Bayonne or Bordeaux. Others journeyed to England seeking transportation home. Most stranded crewmen looked to American consuls in ports such as L'Orient, Marseilles, Le Havre, or Bordeaux or they appealed to the minister in Paris for help. In April, 1809, Consul Isaac Cox Barnet in Le Havre reported that seventy seamen seeking assistance had written since December. Barnet had already secured the release of four "and shall probably be instrumental in getting them all liberated." He claimed that Armstrong could effect the release of "every American in France" if he would lift his pen. This was an important revelation. American seamen in France were subjected to varying treatment—some never encountering any difficulty whatever while others were humiliated, even confined—but there can be no valid comparison of French and British actions because France simply did not impress United States citizens. James Coleman's New York *Evening Post* exaggerated when it described seamen "marched without shoes to their feet or clothing to their backs in the most inclement weather some hundreds of miles into the interior of France; lashed along the highway like slaves, treated with every

---

tionary America," *William and Mary Quarterly*, Series 3, XXV (1968), 383; the number of Americans impressed in the 1790s and 1800s is unknown. That many were is beyond dispute; doubtful persons need only examine manuscripts of contemporary American diplomats. The standard account of impressment, sorely in need of replacement, is James F. Zimmerman, *Impressment of American Seamen* (New York, 1925).

6. Thornton to Hawkesbury, August 26, 1803, in FOA 5:38, LC.

possible indignity and then immured in the infernal dungeons of Arras or Verdun."[7] As the United States marched down the road to war in 1811–1812, impressment was notably missing from the catalog of American grievances against France.

American diplomats in London worked diligently to outlaw impressment. Finding the English unalterably opposed to abandoning this policy, James Monroe and his conegotiator William Pinkney, a Federalist lawyer from Maryland, accepted a compromise, the so-called Monroe-Pinkney treaty of December 31, 1806; the two envoys bartered a curb on impressment for preferential treatment of re-exports.[8] Unwilling to sanction impressment in any manner, and disturbed because the English reserved the right to retaliate against France in the steadily expanding economic war, Jefferson refused to submit the Monroe-Pinkney treaty to the Senate.[9]

Meanwhile, the United States had joined the commercial struggle in mid-April, 1806, when Congress approved a diluted version of a bill first introduced by Representative Andrew Gregg of Pennsylvania. Gregg, a revolutionary war soldier and veteran congressman, was tired of repeated British insults—even then English warships were operating just off the coast, screening vessels entering American ports—and he was convinced that Jefferson and his government "cannot long expect the support of the people" with a policy of passiveness.[10] Gregg therefore proposed banning all English imports, but his fellow Republicans shied away from such strong medicine. The result was that Gregg's bill was changed to ban English goods of peripheral importance such as beer and flax cloth. Weakening the bill further, the Congress stipulated that the measure would not become effective until November, 1806; in fact, the law was not applied against Britain until December 14, 1807.

Gregg's bill upset the English and Jefferson alike. Anthony Merry, a

7. Barnet to Skipwith, April 17, 1809, in Skipwith Papers; New York *Evening Post*, July 12, 1809. There is no work on Americans in Napoleonic France; Michael Lewis, *Napoleon and His British Captives* (London, 1967), details the experiences of Englishmen in France and notes that their treatment ranged from good to monstrous.

8. If the United States surrendered to Britain on impressment and neutral rights in general, warned Vice Consul John Mitchell at Le Havre, "we shall be accused of want of firmness and of sacrificing our rights and those of other neutrals, altho' they from not opposing the principle have tacitly ceded it." Mitchell to Livingston, September [?], 1806, in Robert R. Livingston Papers, New-York Historical Society.

9. Spivak, *Jefferson's English Crisis*, 66, argues that Jefferson rejected the proposed treaty because he realized that "saving American victims from royal press gangs and ensuring their future safety through treaty stipulation would ravage the nation's foreign commerce."

10. Gregg to William Jones, April 17, 1806; fellow Pennsylvanian John Smilie concurred with Gregg, telling Secretary Gallatin, "If the government does not do 'something' it

zealous defender of British commercial hegemony, was not the only Briton to interpret Gregg's measure as being "beneficial to France in the present War." Jefferson, who foresaw just such an English reaction to Gregg's legislation, had favored milder resolutions or no action at all until a more friendly English government had been given sufficient time to alter British policy.[11] House and Senate Republicans were not as patient as their chief, however, and they felt that even a mild measure might prod Great Britain into respecting American rights. Gregg's revised legislation marked the beginning of America's employment of commercial warfare as an instrument of foreign policy in the troubled years prior to 1812.

[II]

Speculation was rife in Washington during the winter of 1806–1807 about Pinkney's and Monroe's negotiations—John Randolph claimed that Napoleon would never permit Jefferson to accept a reasonable treaty. Speculation was widespread also about the nature and meaning of the newly proclaimed Berlin decree whereby France announced the blockade of the British Isles. There were some Republicans, including Nathaniel Ames (brother of staunch Federalist Representative Fisher Ames) and Thomas Paine, who applauded the proclamation as part of a great man's plan for ending England's oceanic tyranny. Other Republicans were more reserved about the new Napoleonic measure. Probably relying on John Armstrong's favorable assurances, Henry Clay blandly billed the decree as a "new measure . . . of a most gigantic nature" but one that should leave American commerce unscathed. Armstrong's explanation also reached the ears of William Eaton, a virulent anti-Jeffersonian who reported Washington asleep following receipt of Armstrong's message. The cautious Senator Plumer attempted to verify Armstrong's interpretation with Turreau, but the Frenchman said that he had not received an official explanation from his government.[12]

---

will lose the confidence of the people." Smilie to Gallatin, March 9, 1806, both cited in Sapio, *Pennsylvania and the War of 1812*, 83. See also George Washington Campbell to John Overton, March 7, 1806, in John Overton Papers, Tennessee Historical Society.

11. Merry to Mulgrave, March 19, 1806, in FOA 5:48, LC; Jefferson's friend Barlow, recently returned from Europe, thought that the British could be induced into more desirable conduct but not through coercive legislation. Barlow to Jefferson, January 31, 1806, in Jefferson Papers, LC.

12. Clay to William Prentiss, February 13, 1807, in James F. Hopkins (ed.), *The Papers of Henry Clay* (5 vols. to date; Lexington, 1959—), I, 280; Eaton to Edward Preble, February 20, 1807, in Dudley W. Knox (ed.), *Naval Documents Related to the United States War with the Barbary Powers* (6 vols.; Washington, 1939–1944), VI, 507; entries of February 13, 19, 1807, in Brown (ed.), *William Plumer's Memorandum*, 608–10, 613–14.

In mid-1807 Armstrong's assessment seemed accurate. The Berlin decree was not enforced against the United States; indeed, large numbers of American ships were reaching European ports although troublesome problems remained. The Berlin edict and the subsequent British order in council of January 7, 1807, disrupted normal traffic in northern European waters. In the Mediterranean, the English and Russians interrupted commerce, the English by enforcing the new order, the Russians by blockading Turkish lands. The French also were administering annoying pinpricks: tariffs were variable; some American vessels lacking proper certification were denied entry into French ports while others or their cargoes were confiscated in a whimsical manner with appeals delayed by the ponderous port bureaucracies. "How unwisely the French act with their embargo and exorbitant duties," Jacob Crowninshield fumed on one occasion. "They will never learn what is best for their interest and the worst of it is they injure us without benefitting themselves."[13] If impressment had not clouded Anglo-American relations, a survey probably would have revealed that many citizens were more irked with French actions than English provocations at this time.

Impressment did exist, though, and its ugly face appeared again in the infamous *Chesapeake-Leopard* affair in the summer of 1807. The Royal Navy believed that the American warship *Chesapeake* was "being used as a kind of fly-paper for picking up deserters and other wandering British seamen." On June 22 H.M.S. *Leopard* hailed Commodore James Barron's heavily laden and totally unprepared vessel, which had just departed from Norfolk for the Mediterranean. When Barron discovered the *Leopard's* intent, he refused the English permission to examine the *Chesapeake's* crew. The *Leopard* proceeded to fire on the American warship for ten minutes, killing three men and wounding twenty more, twelve seriously.[14] With no alternative but utter destruction, Barron struck his colors and was forced to watch the removal of four of his crewmen. A few days later, even as news about the *Chesapeake's* ordeal spread through the United States, an American cutter bearing Vice President George Clinton and his daughters was fired upon by an English warship off the Capes of Virginia.[15]

13. Crowninshield to Silsbee, January 13, 1805, in Crowninshield Family Papers.

14. Anthony Steel, "More Light on the *Chesapeake*," *Mariner's Mirror*, XXXIX (1953), 265. See also *"Occurrences and remarks, on board the United States Frigate "Chesapeake" of 40 Guns*, James Barron Esq. Commander, on Teusday [*sic*] the 23 [*sic*] *day* of June *year* 1807," in Edward H. Tatum, Jr., and Marion Tinling (eds.), "Letters of William Henry Allen, 1800–1813," *Huntington Library Quarterly*, I (1938), 209–12; and Jay D. Smith, "Commodore James Barron: Guilty as Charged"? United States Naval Institute *Proceedings*, XCIII (1967), 79–85.

15. Edwin M. Gaines, "The Chesapeake Affair: Virginians Mobilize to Defend Na-

The *Chesapeake-Leopard* incident created a near unanimity of opinion in the United States. From Maine to Georgia, from the counting houses of Philadelphia to the ramshackle dwellings of Ohio frontiersmen, national anger swelled into a great roar demanding apologies or war. As Jacob Crowninshield explained to Jonathan Williams, "when our sovereignty is attacked, our independence threatened and attempts made to heap disgrace upon us . . . it becomes us to rally round the standard of our country" and support the President with no dissent and "with one mind to resolve to chastise the insidious invaders of our rights."[16]

There were good reasons for going to war. Great Britain had been wantonly violating neutral rights for years; she was, of course, also guilty of practicing impressment. In the *Chesapeake* episode she had added invasion of another nation's sovereignty to the list of offenses. National unity was present and national unity was absolutely indispensable to waging war successfully. It was true that the United States was poorly prepared for an armed struggle in mid-1807, but the situation was not significantly different in 1812 when war was finally declared. In addition, British Canada was completely vulnerable to an American thrust in 1807, and under American control it was widely believed that Canada would guarantee England's good conduct.[17] In summary, the United States had justification for declaring war against Britain, and public opinion was ready to accept a presidential call for action.

Thomas Jefferson did not ask for war. In retrospect, this decision, not his maneuvering for West Florida, not the embargo, not his assault on the judiciary, may have been his greatest error as president.[18] Jefferson's refusal to request a declaration of war led to reliance on economic coercion: the

---

tional Honor," *Virginia Magazine of History and Biography*, LXIV (1956), 139; for another aspect of the episode, see Edwin M. Gaines, "George Cranfield Berkeley and the *Chesapeake-Leopard* Affair of 1807," in John Boles (ed.), *America: The Middle Period* (Charlottesville, 1973), 83–96.

16. Crowninshield to Williams, August 4, 1807, in United States Military Philosophical Society Papers, New-York Historical Society; Boston merchant Thomas H. Perkins was one of the few dissenters. He wrote that war "will be owing to the Madness of our Rulers, or their Masters, the Sovereign People." Cited in Carl Seaburg and Stanley Paterson, *Merchant Prince of Boston: Colonel T. H. Perkins, 1764–1854* (Cambridge, 1971), 185.

17. "I [have] no doubt that the first blow that will be struck will be directed against Canada." Isaac A. Coles to Joseph C. Cabell, July 17, 1807, in Cabell Papers. Coles was Jefferson's private secretary. See also Jonathan Russell to Samuel Smith, January 10, 1809, in Russell Papers, Brown University.

18. For amplification of this point, see Clifford L. Egan, "Thomas Jefferson's Greatest Mistake: The Decision for Peace, 1807," in David H. White and John W. Gordon (eds.), *Proceedings* of The Citadel Conference on War and Diplomacy, 1977 (Charleston, S.C., 1979), 94–97.

embargo, non-intercourse, and Macon's Bill #2, measures the American people supported less enthusiastically than they would have war in the summer of 1807. Surrendering to desires for immediate answers can be dangerous, of course, but the crisis provoked by the *Chesapeake* incident came after years of maritime restrictions and many impressment cases. By not pressing for war, Jefferson did not take advantage of Britain's continued preoccupation with the Napoleonic Wars. Certainly the President could not know that the Anglo-French conflict would last another seven years; on the other hand, Madison apparently gambled that the great struggle would continue when he sought war in 1812.

If Jefferson's decision not to ask for war was an error, it was also an understandable one. Initially the Virginian rejected a call to arms because Congress was not in session and because he wanted to allow time for ships and sailors to return home. Much more important, the British would be given the opportunity to apologize and to return the men abducted from the decks of the *Chesapeake*, as Madison told Monroe in diplomatic instructions dated July 6. Privately Jefferson explained that "if nations go to war for every degree of injury there would never be peace on earth."[19]

Louis Turreau was a firsthand observer of the *Chesapeake-Leopard* crisis. To the French minister, the President's only choice was war. As Turreau said, "Blood, blood alone can wash out that stain." When Jefferson did not summon Congress into special session, the bewildered general complained to Talleyrand about a "people not comprehending the concept of glory, grandeur and justice." Indicting Americans for their materialism, Turreau fumed that citizens of the young nation were "disposed to suffer every kind of humiliation" as long as their "sordid greed" was satisfied.[20]

Turreau's assessment was wrong. The vast majority of Americans paid no attention whatsoever to the balance sheet in the immediate aftermath of the *Leopard*'s offense. Nor was Jefferson calculating profit versus loss when he recoiled from war with Britain. A reasonable man himself, he expected the British to be reasonable and to make amends for what had happened. Nor was it the President's fault that, while he vainly waited for apologies, the French stupidly deflected some of the public's anger by enforcing the

19. Jefferson to Madame de Staël, July 16, 1807, in Marie G. Kimball, "Unpublished Correspondence of Mme. de Staël with Thomas Jefferson," *North American Review*, CCVIII (1918), 65. Spivak, *Jefferson's English Crisis*, 72, 75, argues that Jefferson preferred war between June and October and prepared the United States for hostilities.

20. An Inchiquin Letter quoted in Turreau, *Aperçu des États-Unis*, 66–67; Turreau to Talleyrand, September 4, 1807, in AMAE, LX, LC. Napoleon contented himself with declaring the *Chesapeake* episode "most abominable," and he expected an Anglo-American war. Armstrong to Madison, August 15, 1807, in Despatches from France, NA; Napoleon to Savary, October 30, 1807, in *Correspondance de Napoléon*, XVI, 126.

Berlin decree in the case of the American ship *Horizon*. Operating out of Charleston, the *Horizon* was shipwrecked within French territorial waters late in May, 1807, and her cargo condemned.[21] News of the *Horizon* decision coupled with the *Chesapeake* insult and rumors of another order in council convinced Jefferson that extraordinary times demanded extraordinary remedies.

The embargo was the result. Although it appeared to be merely a hasty expedient, commercial restrictions actually had always been in Jefferson's mind. On the eve of the American Revolution the Virginian had promoted economic warfare in the form of the non-importation agreement. Two decades later Secretary of State Jefferson wrote that "free commerce and navigation are not to be given in exchange for restrictions and vexations." He was certain four years later that "*our commerce*" was the proper "instrument for obliging the interested nations of Europe to treat us with justice."[22] Furthermore, the United States had already employed trade restrictions in the form of embargoes against Britain during the crisis preceding the Jay Treaty and against France at the height of the Quasi-War in mid-1798.

Besides witnessing commercial warfare in action during the nation's formative years, Jefferson had men close to him urging him to employ this weapon. From France John Armstrong suggested a withdrawal from the international commercial arena "till the present storm passes by." In 1806 Elbridge Gerry deemed an embargo on shipping wiser than allowing unrestricted sailings in the face of certain depredations, and Joel Barlow described an embargo as something to be used in the "last interval of peace."[23] James Madison, who as a young congressman had helped push through the adoption of the embargo of 1794, also supported such a measure. Others added their voices to those of these men and assured Jefferson that he was not alone in favoring commercial restrictions.

Meanwhile, although war fever had diminished, there was still a considerable contingent of citizens agreeing that Britain should be punished. "I am ready to do anything to vindicate our honor," Massachusetts Republican Jacob Crowninshield wrote six weeks after the *Chesapeake* outrage; six

21. *National Intelligencer*, December 28, 1807; "Decision du Conseil Imperial des Prises dans l'affaire du navire naufragé l'Horison," in AMAE, LX, LC.

22. "Report on the Privileges and Restrictions on the Commerce of the United States in Foreign Countries" [December 16, 1793], in Ford (ed.), *Works of Thomas Jefferson*, VI, 480; Jefferson to Thomas Pinckney, May 29, 1797, *ibid.*, VII, 129. Shortly after becoming president, Jefferson reaffirmed his belief in the power of commercial curtailment, in this case against Britain. Pichon to Talleyrand, March 25, 1801, in AMAE, LIII, LC.

23. Armstrong to Madison, September 24, 1807, in Despatches from France, NA; [Joel Barlow] "Remarks on Neutrality," January 29, 1806, in George Logan Papers, Historical Society of Pennsylvania.

months after the incident Crowninshield's feelings were unchanged and the New Englander supported the embargo. George Poindexter, Mississippi delegate in Congress, was infuriated by what he deemed excessive caution by the administration. "Peace is the darling object of the Government," he grumbled. Other politicians including Madison's brother-in-law, James Jackson, Joseph B. Varnum, and John Quincy Adams were exasperated with what Adams called "procrastination" and desired some kind of action. Having waited nearly half a year, however, Jefferson would not be stampeded; Poindexter, Jackson, and other congressmen did not represent everyone's thinking.[24] Besides, significant and favorable news from Britain was expected aboard the schooner *Revenge*.

The anticipated dispatches arrived in late November and dashed all hopes for an amicable solution to the *Chesapeake* affair. To Jefferson, the United States now had three options: continuation of the status quo, a stance which the President equated with submission; application of an embargo; or resort to war. Submission was not considered; in Jefferson's mind, English insolence had been tolerated long enough. For a fortnight the President fluctuated between urging war or embargo, but the embargo won out for several compelling reasons. Most important, an embargo might be sufficient to bring the British to their senses. America supplied Britain with a sizable percentage of her imports; coupled with the curtailments of British imports embodied in Gregg's resolution that had finally been implemented, England would certainly recognize America's significance to the British economy and remove the thorns afflicting Anglo-American relations.[25] The embargo also postponed war yet punished Britain. There re-

24. Crowninshield to Caesar A. Rodney, August 3, 1807, in Jefferson Papers, LC; John H. Reinoehl, "Post-Embargo Trade and Merchant Prosperity: Experience of the Crowninshield Family, 1809–1812," *Mississippi Valley Historical Review*, XLII (1955), 230–31; Poindexter to Cowles Mead, October 27, 1807, in J. F. H. Claiborne Collection, Mississippi Department of Archives and History; Jackson to Madison, November 8, 1807, in Madison Papers, University of Virginia; Varnum to Plumer, December 6, 1807, in Plumer Papers, LC; entry of November 25, 1807, in Adams (ed.), *Memoirs of John Quincy Adams*, I, 480–81; Isaac A. Coles to William Cabell [late 1807], in Cabell Papers. Uninformed Federalist congressmen either ridiculed Jefferson or saw the French dictating American policy in late 1807. Samuel Dana to Oliver Wolcott, November 23, December 18, 1807, in Oliver Wolcott Papers, Connecticut Historical Society; John Davenport to John Cotton Smith, December 15, 1807, in John Cotton Smith Papers, Library of Congress.

25. Crouzet, *L'economie britannique et le blocus continental*, points out the significance of the American market to Britain. An observer residing in British Canada claimed "America [has] got such a hold of England, that she can almost regulate the pulse of the nation by her movements." "Uniacke's Memorial to Windham, 18 February, 1806," cited in Brian Craig Uniacke Cuthbertson, "The Old Attorney General: Richard John Uniacke, 1753–1830" (M.A. thesis, University of New Brunswick, 1970), copy in Public Archives of Nova Scotia.

mained the chance that dramatic developments in Europe might alter the situation: Napoleon could be victorious, his armies could be defeated, or the Emperor could be assassinated. Whatever the case, peace had to come someday and the reasons for the embargo would be eliminated. Jefferson also knew that the war spirit, so strong in the summer of 1807, had dwindled. In sum, the embargo made sense, and with only Secretary of the Treasury Albert Gallatin dissenting, the cabinet concurred with the President's wishes. On December 18 Jefferson recommended to the Congress "an inhibition of the departure of our vessels from the ports of the United States." The proposal quickly cleared the Senate and House and was signed into law mid-afternoon on December 22.[26]

[III]

The embargo was favorably received. In the vanguard of its champions was the *National Intelligencer*, which editorialized that "the ocean presents a field only where no harvest is to be reaped but that of danger, of spoliation and of disgrace." Other newspapers echoed the *Intelligencer*, including the Federalist Newburyport *Herald* which admitted that "all things considered the existing state of things undoubtedly requires it." Scores of people added their approval of the measure. Nathaniel Macon noted that British and French arrogance proved the necessity for such a step while John Binns, a Pennsylvania newspaperman, thought the embargo "asserts our rights and preserves the peace." Freshman Representative Daniel Durrell of New Hampshire believed that economic coercion was just the tool to prod the belligerents into respecting neutral rights.[27] Whatever the rationale, general support existed for the embargo, and that support cut across both party and sectional lines.

There was opposition to the embargo, of course. Some Federalists charged that a French hand was discernible in the Jeffersonian scheme because the embargo would have a more severe impact on Britain than France.[28] Then they contradicted themselves by claiming that George III's

26. Gallatin to Jefferson, December 18, 1807, in Henry Adams (ed.), *The Writings of Albert Gallatin* (3 vols.; Philadelphia, 1879), I, 368; "To the Senate and House of Representatives of the United States," December 18, 1807, in James D. Richardson (comp.), *A Compilation of the Messages and Papers of the Presidents* (10 vols.; Washington, 1912), I, 42; Jefferson to Thomas Mann Randolph, December 22, 1807, in Jefferson Papers, LC.

27. *National Intelligencer*, December 23, 1807; Newburyport *Herald*, December 29, 1807, cited in Labaree, *Patriots and Partisans*, 152; John Binns to Jonathan Roberts, January 11, 1808, cited in Sapio, *Pennsylvania and the War of 1812*, 93–94; Daniel M. Durrell to Plumer, February 14, 1808, in William Plumer Papers, New Hampshire State Library.

28. Perkins, *Prologue to War*, 150, echoes this belief: "That the Embargo aimed chiefly at England was, however, understood in Washington, London, and Paris."

Portrait of Thomas Jefferson, by Gilbert
Stuart (1805)
Fogg Art Museum, Harvard University

James Madison, by Thomas Sully
In the Collection of the Corcoran Gallery of Art,
gift of Frederick E. Church
Washington, D.C.

James Monroe, by James Sharples
Independence National Historical Park
Collection, Philadelphia

John Armstrong, by John Vanderlyn
Courtesy of Mrs. W. Vincent Astor

James Bowdoin III, by Gilbert Stuart
Bowdoin College Museum of Art, Brunswick,
Maine

Jonathan Russell
Courtesy of the John Hay Library, Brown
University

Joel Barlow, by John Vanderlyn (1796)
Musée de Blérancourt

William Lee
Courtesy of Mrs. J. H. N. Potter,
Jamestown, R.I.

David Bailie Warden
From W. T. Latimer, "David Bailie Warden,
Patriot, 1798," *Ulster Journal of Archaeology*, XIII
(1907), 29.

realm would benefit economically from the embargo and would favor its continuance. The embargo was also described as a sectional weapon with the allegation made that "southern men" supported it as a means to extinguish commerce. "We are directed by . . . a Vilanous [*sic*] Administration," one angry young Federalist complained as he contemplated the spectacle of scores of ships tied up indefinitely.[29] These Federalists did not share the sense of outrage harbored by so many of their countrymen. They were willing to continue the status quo, amassing profits and chancing the growing hazards faced by neutrals in Atlantic and European waters.

Such thinking undermined the embargo from the beginning. Even before the embargo was law someone, presumably a Federalist, divulged news about the act to British envoy David Erskine. Erskine was among the first informed, but messages about the probability of an embargo swept up and down the coast in amazingly short time. Boston merchants had reports by Christmas Day while British authorities in Halifax, Nova Scotia, received unconfirmed stories on January 3.[30] The intelligence was acted upon immediately: in Boston, New York, Baltimore, and lesser ports there were wild melees to load and clear vessels before official word of the embargo reached local authorities. Thus one of the embargo's purposes, that of keeping American shipping out of circulation, was partially nullified at the start.

There were other problems also. Authorities had to await receipt of official copies of the embargo law, but copies were transmitted so slowly that as late as January 28, 1808, the collector of customs in New Orleans had not received formal notification. The port was emptied of cotton and flour in the interim between December 22 and January 28. Far more serious, however, were loopholes leaving overland trade unhampered and the coasting trade unregulated. These openings were speedily exploited and although Congress moved three times (January 9, March 12, and April 25) to remedy these oversights, illicit trade continued.

New England was most guilty in this respect. In Vermont, trade over the Canadian boundary continued throughout 1808; with approximately 100 men to screen the border, customs officials, even if they were inclined, were overwhelmed by the flow of goods. Where there were attempts at

29. William Ely to Plumer, January 24, 1808, in Plumer Papers, New Hampshire State Library; Nathaniel Saltonstall, Jr., to Nathaniel Saltonstall, Sr., December 22, 23, 1807, in Saltonstall Family Papers.

30. Erskine to Canning, December 21, 1807, in FOA 5:52, LC. B. Davis to Gideon White, December 25, 1807, in Gideon White Papers, Public Archives of Nova Scotia; J. Shortland to J. Wentworth, December 28, 1807, in Letters to the Secretary of State, Vol. 214, *ibid.*; J. Wentworth to Castlereagh, January 3, 1808, in Letters of the Secretary of State, Vol. 58, *ibid.*

enforcement, Vermonters devised ingenious methods to circumvent the law: ships were blown off course on Lake Champlain and consequently reached Canada; people transported items overland to the boundary and carried them over when opportunity arose; and some inspired souls built huts on the border with the front door opening on the American side, the back door on the Canadian—with goods passing from American to Canadian hands. Of course, bribery also facilitated the movement of trade northwards.[31] An observer in Quebec who witnessed the willful evasions gloated that "notwithstanding all the supplements & attempts to enforce the embargo . . . immense quantitys of products come in by every fair wind from Lake Champlain, & the inhabitants of Vermont publickly declare they will not allow it to be stopped."[32] One estimate is that the flow of goods northwards increased by 31 percent in 1808. Whatever the volume, the embargo suffered.

British authorities in Canada initially fretted that the embargo would halt the importation of food and materials from the United States, hurting Canada and other British possessions. "From all the information I have had it in my power to obtain," Sir George Prevost wrote, "I cannot discover any thing like a sufficiency of Flour or Lumber in British America to answer the present demands of our Plantations." Prevost therefore liberalized regulations governing the entry of neutral shipping into Nova Scotia producing, he gleefully recounted, "numerous attempts and uncommon exertions on the part of the residents of the Sea Coast of the adjacent States to evade and violate the non-importation Law." Prevost was not exaggerating. American ships continued to enter Halifax, Shelburne, Liverpool, and Digby, Nova Scotia, and British Canada; and Britain's plantations survived the embargo with little trouble.[33]

31. Embargo violations continued even after Secretary of War Henry Dearborn authorized the use of the militia to uphold the law. Henry Dearborn to Israel Smith, April 19, 1808, in War of 1812 Collection, William L. Clements Library, University of Michigan. See also H. N. Muller, "Smuggling into Canada: How the Champlain Valley Defied Jefferson's Embargo," *Vermont History*, XXXVIII (1970), 5–21.

32. William Armstrong to Lieutenant-Governor Gore, May 26, 1808, in H. A. Innis and A. R. M. Lower (eds.), *Select Documents on Canadian Economic History, 1783–1885* (Toronto, 1933), 228–29.

33. Prevost to Castlereagh, May 28, 1808, in Letters of the Secretary of State, Vol. 58, Public Archives of Nova Scotia; Prevost to E. Cooke, July 30, 1808, *ibid.* See also the entry of November 24, 1808, in "Journal and Proceedings of the House of Assembly, of the Province of Nova Scotia," 4, copy *ibid*; not even the War of 1812 dampened New England's trade with Nova Scotia. "Throughout the war the naval and military contractors at Halifax purchased large quantities of goods from Americans who, in return, bought British manufactures imported by Halifax merchants." Walter Ronald Copp, "Nova Scotian Trade During the War of 1812," *Canadian Historical Review*, XVII (1937), 141.

Embargo violations in New York State also contributed to British Canada's well being. Part of the problem in the Empire State arose from the necessary navigation of Lake Ontario; salt was carried via the lake from the Onondaga salt springs to northwestern Pennsylvania, eastern Ohio, and Michigan territory. Curtailing this commerce might halt violations of the embargo, but serious damage would be inflicted on many isolated frontier settlements. The traffic continued, and an illicit trade with British Canada developed. Vessels also reached Canada when masters paid a fee to one enterprising New Yorker who captured ships on Lake Champlain and disposed of them in Canadian waters. Tariff collectors in the Champlain district as well as at small posts such as Oswego and Sacketts Harbor were either fearful or unwilling to enforce economic coercion. As was the case in Vermont, along the New York frontier a greater volume of merchandise reached Canada in 1808 than in 1807.[34]

The South joined in violating the embargo too. Along the Georgia-Florida boundary, illegal trade flourished at Amelia and St. Mary's Island. "I am sorry to say," one anguished Georgian said in April, 1808, "that a large Portion of our Leading Citizens will not be restrained by Patriotism if there be any possibility of making money, by a violation of the embargo act." Twice Secretary Gallatin authorized the use of additional force to curb illicit exportation. Yet in January, 1809, vessels were reported scarce in Savannah "and there has been a great demand for them for the trade from Amelia to England."[35] A thousand miles away, in the trans-Mississippi West, an overland trade between Louisiana and Spanish Texas arose. Still infractions in the South hardly compared to the large-scale evasions in the North.

Administration bungling also damaged the embargo. For instance, hundreds of ships were cleared for the recovery of merchandise that was supposedly American-controlled before the embargo became law; it is debatable just how much of this property belonged to American citizens before December 22, 1807. Furthermore, the government was lax in enforcing the embargo, Federalists' cries to the contrary notwithstanding. State governors (James Sullivan of Massachusetts was the most flagrant example)

34. Peter Porter to Henry Dearborn, May 6, 1808, in Letters Received by the Secretary of War, April, 1808–December, 1809, National Archives; Israel Rubin, "New York State and the Long Embargo" (Ph.D. dissertation, New York University, 1961), 138; Richard P. Casey, "North Country Nemesis: The Potash Rebellion and the Embargo of 1807–1809," *New-York Historical Society Quarterly*, LXIV (1980), 30–49.

35. Hugh McCall to George M. Troup, April 23, 1808, in Letters Received by the Secretary of War, NA; Samuel Charles Howard to King, January 8, 1809, in William King Papers, Maine Historical Society.

were allowed too much discretion in granting clearance permits; customs officers were often in league with violators or inadequate in number for the task confronting them. "Our government deserves censure for the inefficiency of their measures to effect submission to the laws," complained an American in New Brunswick, "instead of sixty men [to guard the Maine–New Brunswick border], five hundred ought to have been sent—commanded by none but the most active and the most trustworthy officers."[36]

There were other gaps. Hundreds of American registered vessels never returned to home ports from belligerent waters because their owners preferred profits available in Europe to losses certain under the embargo; these ships augmented the supply of carriers serving the continent and thus undermined one of Jefferson's goals, depriving the belligerents of American bottoms. In addition, many craft continued at sea by engaging in the coasting trade along the Atlantic seaboard, some winding up in Halifax when fortuitous and unexpectedly powerful winds blew them hundreds of miles off course. The *Clarissa* out of New York cunningly evaded the embargo by feigning distress while she passed her cargo of cotton "without loosing [*sic*] a bale" to a conveniently available English vessel. Unscrupulous federal officers were among the embargo violators: the always avaricious General James Wilkinson took over three months to sail from Washington to New Orleans. "He left with a ship full of flour and apples," one historian has recorded, "and visited first Havana and then Pensacola, where, while plotting with Spanish officials, he apparently picked up some pocket money."[37]

The most serious trouble was not the smuggling, bribing, or indirect violations, but the instances where mobs or individuals challenged national authority. Nowhere was the defiance as great as it was in Federalist Massachusetts where by the end of 1808 vessels openly loaded at Beverly, Manchester, and Cape Ann with the avowed intention of clearing for non-American ports. In Salem, a ship arriving from Guadaloupe, having been taken by a revenue cutter, was seized by a crowd that "cut away her masts to prevent her being carried to the navy yard in Charleston." Massachusetts

36. Leonard Jarvis to Jonathan Russell, January 1, 1809, in Russell Papers, Brown University.

37. Jarvis to Russell, January 15, 1809, *ibid.* An English historian claims that "embargo breakers" in vessels "blown off the coast" and mainly "from New York and New Jersey" helped manufacturers overcome shortages. S. G. Checkland, "American versus West Indian Traders in Liverpool, 1793–1815," *Journal of Economic History*, XVIII (1958), 155. David F. Long, *Nothing Too Daring: A Biography of Commodore David Porter, 1780–1843* (Annapolis, 1970), 47–48.

Federalists were among the staunchest supporters of law and authority; in 1808 they willfully violated a statute enjoying national support.[38]

Manifestations of the public attitude was readily available: "If it was not for the embargo, we should have a Bloody War," one orator told a band of Republicans in Williamsburg, Virginia; the embargo demanded sacrifice, he admitted, but it was not "cutting off the existence" of fellow Americans. Other commentators lauded the increasing economic self-reliance the embargo promoted in the United States. "We shall . . . substitute domestic culture, domestic manufactures, domestic commerce, domestic consumption through the territories of the Union," one nationalist wrote Jefferson. Dreams of an economically independent country had been widespread in the perilous days of the Confederation; they were still harbored during Jefferson's presidency, and toward that end the embargo promoted domestic investment and domestic enterprises. Another theme of embargo supporters was the insistence that the treatment accorded America would improve as the French and British economies felt the embargo's impact. Probably the greatest number of those supporting economic coercion concurred simply that something had to be done and that the embargo represented a positive step in the right direction. "The Embargo I only consider as taking time for consideration—not as a final measure," Representative Orchard Cook explained to a constituent.[39]

It has been argued that Jefferson wearily fled Washington and his "Frankenstein" in March, 1809, following months of confusion and drift. Certainly President Jefferson was overjoyed casting off the burdens of office and moving to Monticello permanently; he was tired and ill that winter. He did

38. Joseph White, Jr., to Story, December 11, 1808, in Story Papers. See also White to Story, December 25, 1808, *ibid*; Discussing the "discontent in the eastern Yankee country," Robert Vaux of Philadelphia admonished, "If they are oppressed as they doubtless are let them appeal to *reason but not to arms*." Vaux to Samuel Robbins, January 16, 1809, in Vaux Papers, Historical Society of Pennsylvania. About the support for economic coercion English minister Erskine, who frequently ridiculed the embargo and laughed at the crude results of American manufacturing enterprises, candidly admitted "that it [the embargo] will certainly continue to be approved of by a large Majority of the People." Complaints emanated "from a comparatively small Number [of?] the Mass of the People" and were exaggerated "from the free Manner in which Sentiments upon public Measures are given in New[s] Papers and other Publications." Erskine to Canning, May 2, 1808, FOA 5:52, LC.

39. "Speech by a Dr. Roberts," September 5, 1808, in Tucker-Coleman Papers; Marshall Smelser, *The Democratic Republic, 1801–1815* (New York, 1968), 174; William Tatham to Jefferson, May 6, 1808, in Jefferson Papers, LC; Ramsay to John Coakley Lettsom, October 29, 1808, in Robert L. Brunhouse (ed.), *David Ramsay, 1749–1815: Selections from His Writings*, American Philosophical Society *Transactions*, n.s., LV (1965), 163; Cook to William King, February 8, 1808, in King Papers; and Cook to Representatives of the Lincoln District, November 20, 1808, *ibid*.

not flee a monster, however; rather the Congress, as it had with Gregg's resolution, asserted its legislative prerogative and replaced the embargo with non-intercourse. In taking this action the people's representatives were impatient for favorable results and fearful for the life of the Union. "I am satisfied that N. England will not bear the Embargo," Massachusetts Republican Ezekiel Bacon announced in opposing its continuation.[40]

Disunionist sentiments were uttered with increasing frequency in New England. "There appears a spirit hostile to the existence of *our* [new?] government," William Plumer testified. Although prominent New Englanders including Joseph B. Varnum tried to counter the impression that the region was ripe for revolt, many Americans remained unconvinced. Faced with choosing between the embargo and the federal Union, the populace through their solons chose the nation. A chagrined Varnum pointed an accusing finger at the press for fostering an image of New England united against the embargo.[41] Actually the press was but one segment of the antiembargo battle; the other part was a well orchestrated letter writing and petition campaign directed at the president. One bellicose letter writer, Bostonian John Lane Jones, asked Jefferson, "How much longer are you going to keep this damned Embargo on to starve us poor people[?]," adding "one of my children has already starved to death of which I [am] ashamed and declared that it died of apoplexy." Jefferson tired of answering letters and petitions demanding repeal, and he asked Samuel Harrison Smith of the *National Intelligencer* to draft form replies. Significantly (aside from personally answering such mail), the President requested only 150 copies from Smith and he specifically commented about being "overwhelmed with petitions from Massachusetts."[42] Jefferson was unaware of it, but he was being

40. Perkins, *Prologue to War*, 140–83; Ezekiel Bacon to Joseph Story, January 22, 1809, in Story Papers.

41. Plumer to Nicholas Gilman, January 24, 1809, in Plumer Papers, New Hampshire State Library; "When the political pot boils, the *scum* will rise," Plumer told Jefferson, July 22, 1808, in Jefferson Papers, LC; Varnum to William Eustis, December 5, 1808, in William Eustis Papers, Library of Congress; compare Wilson C. Nicholas to Joseph C. Cabell, January 23, 1809, in Cabell Papers; and Littleton Waller Tazewell to Monroe, January 26, 1809, in Monroe Papers, New York Public Library.

42. John Lane Jones to Jefferson, August 8, 1808, in Worthington C. Ford (ed.), *Thomas Jefferson Correspondence Printed from the Originals in the Collections of William K. Bixby* (Boston, 1916), 166–67. The Jones letter was one of many abusive communications Jefferson received. He told Madison, "You will receive thousands [as President] . . . they are almost universally the productions of the most ill-tempered and rascally part of our country, often evidently written from tavern scenes of drunkeness. They never merit one moment's attention." Jefferson to Madison, August 5, 1808, in Madison Papers, LC. A decade earlier John Adams received remarkably similar letters, one of which—aside from threatening assassination—was signed *"a ruined merchant, alas! with ten children!! made beggars by the*

subjected to one of the nation's earliest organized pressure group campaigns. A determined and vocal minority convinced their fellow Americans that disunion or revolution or both were imminent unless the embargo was terminated.

Impatience played a significant and perhaps decisive role in the embargo's demise. Simply stated, too many Americans expected Jefferson's economic weapon to work miracles overnight. They forgot that a month elapsed before the embargo became effective; they did not remember that even if the measure hurt Britain or France, the governments of those nations would never acknowledge the havoc wrought, and they were unprepared to live with a policy that needed to be strictly adhered to for at least eighteen to twenty-four months. Thus even before the embargo began to be felt there were complaints of economic hardship and shipyard personnel were reputedly fleeing to Nova Scotia. The outcries increased steadily in 1808; unwillingness to bear the pain caused by the law forces melancholy agreement with a Jefferson biographer that the embargo's "fate leads one to wonder if human beings are really willing to pay the high price of peace."[43]

The apparent negative economic impact of the embargo has inspired much comment. According to a recent historian of Massachusetts Federalism, "within a few months, American trade was at a standstill, the national economy had collapsed, ships stood idle—and New England Federalism was up in arms."[44] Indeed, virtually every history of the early republic is replete with details of the economic distress along the coast, rotting ships, idled seamen, and soup lines. In reality, what may have been true in a few ports has been generalized into fact for the nation.

Actually, the embargo had far from the deleterious effect usually ascribed to it. This is not to argue that the nation remained undamaged during 1808; it is beyond dispute that the price of staple crops plummeted in the South, that certain industries were hurt, and that some shipowners suffered severe losses. In New York State, to cite a few examples, the value of securities and real estate plunged and the farm product index declined

---

French," in De Conde, *The Quasi-War*, 182. Jefferson to Samuel Harrison Smith, September 9, 1808, in Jonathan Bayard Smith Family Papers, Library of Congress.

43. Burwell Bassett to St. George Tucker, December 11, 1808, in Tucker-Coleman Papers; George Poindexter to Cowles Mead, December 26, 1808, in J. F. H. Claiborne Collection; John Rhea to his constituents, February 13, 1809, in Rhea Family Papers, Tennessee Historical Society; Rubin, "New York State and the Long Embargo," 150–51, quotes a report of workers leaving New York on January 9, 1808, scarcely a fortnight after Jefferson signed the embargo law; Dumas Malone, "Presidential Leadership and National Unity: The Jefferson Example," *Journal of Southern History*, XXXV (1969), 11.

44. Banner, *To the Hartford Convention*, 294.

approximately 16 percent. In New York City one observer complained that "the streets are almost crowded with beggars and our almshouse have frequently issued 5,000 rations a day—most of which have been to able bodied people who if they could only get employment would easily earn more than [what is] sufficient for their maintenance." Under the leadership of Mayor Marinus Willett, the municipality coped with unemployment through public works projects as well as relief. On the other hand, during 1808 and 1809 the New York legislature granted eleven manufacturing charters compared to four from 1795 to 1807. Again during 1808 and 1809, sixty-seven turnpike and road companies received charters compared to seventy-three during the span from 1791 to 1807. The embargo, then, had a dual effect on New York State, perhaps increasing unemployment in the short run, but laying the foundation for significant business expansion over the long haul.[45]

Other states benefited from the embargo. Federalist Delaware's industrialization was spurred, especially in the Wilmington area. Neighboring Pennsylvania and its chief city, Philadelphia, underwent a boom in 1808 and 1809 as capital formerly used in commerce was shifted into manufacturing units. Individuals not absorbed in the new enterprises, which enjoyed strong demand generated by westward expansion, found ready employment in the mushrooming construction field. In western Pennsylvania the embargo encouraged manufacturing, and area agriculture was undisturbed. Even Massachusetts benefited to the degree that investment capital was forced into non-maritime activities. Furthermore, contrary to popular belief, Massachusetts seaborne activities did not grind to a halt nor were mercantile houses as devastated as some of their spokesmen claimed. Boston shippers shifted their vessels into the coastal trade and the port "had its busiest though perhaps not most profitable year during Jefferson's Embargo of the entire period 1783–1815." Merchants found that cargoes arriving in Europe early in 1808 were selling "at capital prices" and that the embargo was helping keep prices high. They used profits to scale down debt, they reduced inventories, and they firmed prices.[46] In sum, the em-

45. Peter De Witt to John De Witt, March 8, 1808, in War of 1812 Collection, William L. Clements Library, University of Michigan; Rubin, "New York State and the Long Embargo," 151–56, 169, 174, 176–78; Raymond A. Mohl, *Poverty in New York, 1783–1825* (New York, 1971), 111–12, argues that unemployment and poverty were widespread and getting worse before the embargo.

46. "Thus do we advance to real independence," Wilmington *American Watchman and Delaware Republican*, January 10, 1810, quoted in John A. Munroe, *Federalist Delaware, 1775–1815* (New Brunswick, 1954), 223; Louis M. Sears, "Philadelphia and the Embargo, 1808," American Historical Association *Annual Report, 1920* (Washington, 1925), 253–63, and "Philadelphia and the Embargo of 1808," *Quarterly Journal of Economics,*

bargo sparked the growth of manufactures which, in turn, minimized economic hardships and promoted self-sufficiency. Jefferson was hardly aware of the far-reaching ramifications of the embargo, but he sensed that the measure was making the United States less dependent on Europe, a cardinal aim of the Virginian in the 1780s and still a goal in the 1800s. No wonder Jefferson as an elder statesman expressed satisfaction with economic warfare.

[IV]

Uncertainty gripped the Congress during the winter of 1808–1809 because most of the assembled wisdom of the country was unsure about what course the nation should follow. While there were abundant testimonials supporting economic coercion from Americans everywhere, and strong backing for the embargo from organized bands of Republicans as well, there were calls also for action. Do not "agree to a *perpetual embargo*" one correspondent implored Joseph Story. "By God we had better be destroyed in honorable war than thus succomb [*sic*] and pine away in self denial and apathy."[47] In the end, enough congressmen concurred that another solution

XXXV (1921), 354–59; Martin Kaufman, "War Sentiment in Western Pennsylvania: 1812," *Pennsylvania History*, XXI (1964), 446; William E. Lingelbach noted the relationship between economic warfare and American industrialization in "Historical Investigation and the Commercial History of the Napoleonic Era," *American Historical Review*, XIX (1914), 257–81; Robin Higham, "The Port of Boston and the Embargo of 1807–1809," *American Neptune*, XVI (1956), 189–213, effectively demolishes the myth of rotting ships and unemployed sailors. See also John D. Forbes, "European Wars and Boston Trade, 1783–1815," *New England Quarterly*, XI (1938), 729–30; L. Lenox and Company to King, January 31, June 21, 1808, in King Papers; Seaburg and Paterson, *Merchant Prince of Boston,* 198.

47. Plumer to Clement Storer, April 19, 1808, in Plumer Papers, New Hampshire State Library; John Haywood to Steele, May 25, 1808, in H. M. Wagstaff (ed.), *The Papers of John Steele* (2 vols.; Raleigh, N.C., 1924), II, 551; Macon to Nicholson, June 22, 1808, in Nicholson Papers; James Winchester to John R. Eaton, July 11, 1808, in J. G. de Roulhac Hamilton (ed.), "Letters of John Rust Eaton," *The James Sprunt Historical Publications* (Raleigh, N.C., 1910), IX, 50; H. Taylor [Clark County, Kentucky] to Madison, December 10, 1808, in Madison Papers, LC; "Address of Frederick County, Md., Residents, February 18, 1809, Signed by twelve hundred and four," in Jefferson Papers, LC. Congressman Bacon found that strong pro-embargo sentiment existed in western Massachusetts early in 1809. Bacon to Story, March 23, 1809, in Story Papers. One westerner wrote that the "word Embargo issued from the mouth of almost every Woman and Boy I have met since I entered the settlements and was often used by men who did not know whether it related to Vessels, Horses or Cornfields." George Hoffman to Bates, October 25, 1808, in Thomas M. Marshall (ed.), *The Life and Papers of Frederick Bates* (2 vols.; St. Louis, 1926), II, 37. Nathaniel Williams to Joseph Story, December 21, 1808, in Story Papers.

to America's predicament must be found, and the embargo was replaced by non-intercourse.

How Congress would have acted if either France or Britain had indicated even mild respect for neutral rights is unknown. The two belligerents had been apprised that a modification of their practices might sway the United States into the camp of one against the other; in David Erskine's words, America "will remove the Embargo towards Great Britain *or* France should either of those Powers withdraw their Restrictions upon Neutral Commerce." The British ignored the proposal, however, and the French not only ignored the American proposition, but they continued their contradictory policy of agitating for an Anglo-American war while raining new blows on the United States with the Milan and Bayonne decrees. The measure bearing the name of the northern Italian city ostensibly strengthened the Berlin edict and replied to Britain's orders in council. It provided that every vessel visiting Britain, allowing itself to be screened by the Royal Navy, or paying a fee to the English government was "denationalized" and considered to be English property. Ships contaminated by the English entering French ports or the ports of certain French controlled states or intercepted on the high seas by French privateers were declared "good prize." In the catalog of economic restrictions the Milan decree was not as significant as the Berlin statement issued thirteen months previously. Its purpose was clearly to force neutrals to make Britain respect their flags. Thus it was announced that the Milan decree would not be enforced against those "nations who will have the firmness to compel the English Government to respect their flag."[48]

The Bayonne decree of April 17, 1808, was based on the clever logic that the embargo had halted all American commerce. Therefore vessels arriving in French and European ports were not American but British; rebuking General Andoche Junot in Portugal for allowing colonial products to enter that country, Napoleon reminded him that everyone knew such goods came via England. Armstrong, who had fruitlessly sent twenty protest notes about the Berlin and Milan decrees, was reduced to muttering, "it is very ingenious" when he disclosed the Emperor's latest stroke.[49]

48. Erskine to Canning, April 26, 1808, in FOA 5:57, LC; "Both Gov." seem to be equally ignorant of our character or rather of human nature," Madison complained, and "each is seeking the means of embroiling us with the other." Madison to Robert R. Livingston, July 18, 1808, in Naval History Collection, New-York Historical Society; "Decret," Milan, December 17, 1807, in *Correspondance de Napoléon*, XVI, 192–93.

49. Napoleon to Murat, April 19, May 10, 1808, in *Correspondance de Napoléon*, XVII, 25, 86; see also Napoleon to Gaudin, March 28, April 17, 1808, *ibid.*, XVII, 60, 205, 329, 364; Armstrong to Madison, April 23, 1808, in Despatches from France, NA. Armstrong

The Bayonne decree may have seemed an ingenious move to Napoleon and Armstrong, but, coupled with earlier acts, it thwarted any possibility of an Anglo-American war, the goal uppermost in the Emperor's mind. Ironically he was keenly aware of American sensibilities from Armstrong's regular complaints and from Turreau who, for all of his wishful thinking and irritation with the United States, advised his master that French policies diverted American anger from Britain. In addition to these channels, Armstrong used Talleyrand to put the same message across to the Emperor, while Decrès, still the chief of the navy ministry, reminded Napoleon of the advantages accruing to France from continued American trade. The Emperor not only ignored or dismissed the counsel of those around him, but he paid no attention to the fact that the embargo was hurting Britain far more severely than France because England depended on her maritime industry to a much greater extent than the First Empire. To Napoleon the embargo was a step in the right direction, but it was not enough; he believed that the Americans should do more to safeguard their rights.[50] A despairing Armstrong, convinced that the embargo had outlived its usefulness, cried out to Madison, "For God's sake let your measure be such as will correct this erroneous estimate."[51]

Armstrong's letter (dated August 30) unintentionally helped undermine the embargo when its contents became common knowledge early in November. "Armstrong as usual with him is very brief & pungent in his remark[s]," Massachusetts congressman Bacon wrote his good friend Joseph Story. "Those measures of our Govt. which are founded on any

---

did not relay official notice of the Bayonne decree at this time, and as late as July, 1808, Madison still complained about the lack of official notification.

50. Turreau to [Champagny], May 20, 1808, in AMAE, LXI, LC; Armstrong to Talleyrand, August 26, 1808, in Despatches from France, NA; "États-Unis d'Amérique," September, 1808, in AMAE, LXI, LC, which reflected Armstrong's view; and Decrès to Napoleon, September 15, 1808, in Frank E. Melvin, *Napoleon's Navigation System: A Study in Trade Control During the Continental Blockade* (New York, 1919), 74–75; Crouzet, *L'economie britannique et le blocus continental*, I, 319–20, 387; Turreau to Champagny, June [28?], 1808, in AMAE, LXI, LC; Robert L. Livingston, who had an audience with Napoleon on July 6, said Napoleon applauded the embargo as a "wise measure" and that he "did not desire" an American declaration of war on Britain. The Emperor promised "to give every facility to your commerce in my Ports, *but I repeat that I never will consent that any nation shall pay tribute to the English to carry on a neutral trade* [author's emphasis], Robert L. Livingston to Jefferson, September 22, 1808, in Jefferson Papers, LC.

51. Armstrong to Madison, August 30, 1808, in Madison Papers, LC; Two months previously, however, Fulwar Skipwith assured Madison that the embargo was felt equally by both belligerents. Skipwith to Madison, June 20, 1808, in Despatches from United States Consuls in Paris, Department of State Archives, National Archives.

supposed justice or good faith in other Nations towards us do no good for us but make mischief—that they think in Bonaparte's Court that *Words* in some shape or other are the only means which we possess of vindicating ourselves & that if we have other means that we won't use them." Bacon then described Napoleon's rejection of milder treatment for the United States and his feeling that as he had "taken his ground he hopes that we shall take ours." Finally, Bacon divulged Armstrong's opinion that America had "overestimated our ability to coerce the belligerents and that in France, it [the embargo] was not felt." Bacon was already doubtful of the embargo's effect on the belligerents and he was also keenly aware of the bitterness Jefferson's brand of economic coercion inspired among many of his fellow New Englanders. Thus Armstrong's revelations drained the small reservoir of enthusiasm that Bacon still held for the embargo and by mid-January he was openly opposing the measure. He was joined by Story and together the two men led the drift away from the embargo. Jefferson never forgave Story and Bacon for their heresy; however, the embargo was scrapped not because of the actions of two congressmen, but because of impatience for results, fears of disunion, and the intractability of the two great warring powers. The President's private secretary, Isaac Coles, recognized these factors a month before Congress met in November, 1808, and privately Jefferson must have admitted their force.[52]

Annoyed as Jefferson was by the defection of Story and Bacon, he still abstained from congressional deliberations. His aloofness has prompted charges that he was counting the days before the expiration of his term. Knowing that his power was waning ("Mr. Jefferson's influence is I conceive on the decline and will continue so, he is the setting sun and all Idolaters and Sycophants worship the rising," Nathaniel Macon philosophized) and bereft of any alternatives to the embargo, Jefferson was president in name only. There is no evidence, however, to substantiate the charge that he retreated into a shell and allowed events to take their course.[53] Instead, in line with his conception of government, in his last months in office the Virginian continued to give Congress the opportunity to initiate legislation. If Congress hesitated, Jefferson cannot be blamed for

52. Bacon to Story, November 4, 1808, in Story Papers; Coles shared Jefferson's viewpoint that America had three alternatives: embargo, submission, or "war with Britain, or with France, or with both of them—Yes Damn them, with both." Coles to Joseph C. Cabell, October 10, 1808, in Cabell Papers.

53. Macon to Joseph Nicholson, March 28, 1808, Nicholson Papers; for a different view, see Richard Mannix, "Gallatin, Jefferson, and the Embargo of 1808," *Diplomatic History*, III (1979), 170.

the vacillation of the legislative branch. The President's alternative to the embargo was war and he admitted occasionally that hostilities might be preferable to continued economic coercion, but he was not interested in saddling the administration of his friend Madison with an inherited conflict.

Considerable war sentiment existed in the Congress simply because the alternatives, submission or more of the embargo, were utterly unacceptable.[54] Outside of Federalist circles there was unanimous concurrence that the United States should never meekly submit to the belligerents. "If peace cannot be preserved without a sacrifice of the honor, rights and independence of the United States," Tennessee representative John Rhea announced, "that sacrifice will never be made: that sacrifice would reduce the United States below the level of colonial degradation. Ten millions free sovereign people will never bend the knee of servility to any foreign power." War proponents confronted at least two major hurdles, however. First, the majority of the group were southerners and westerners. If war were to be declared, they faced the impossible task of winning adherents from the New England and Middle Atlantic states. Second, identification of the most guilty belligerent was a genuine dilemma. "It [is] an idle Enquiry to ask whether France or England first assailed us," fumed an exasperated Joseph Nicholson. "God knows we have Cause of quarrel enough with both, and if we stop to enable by metaphysical Discussions and logical deductions, whose Conduct we are first to resent; they will both continue to laugh at our Mediations." The idea of a triangular war featuring the United States against Britain and France developed, but cooler heads and majority opinion prevailed and the prospect of any type of war diminished early in 1809.[55]

With hostilities ruled out and submission unthinkable, non-intercourse

54. See Reginald C. Stuart, "James Madison and the Militants: Republican Disunity and Replacing the Embargo," *Diplomatic History*, VI (1982), 145–67.

55. Rhea to Constituents, February 13, 1809, in Rhea Family Papers; see also Wilson Cary Nicholas to [?], December 3, 1808, in Carter-Smith Family Papers; Joseph B. Varnum to William Eustis, November 7, 1808, in Eustis Papers; Joseph H. Nicholson to Monroe, November 30, 1808, in Monroe Papers, LC; Caesar A. Rodney to Madison, January 16, 1809, in Madison Papers, LC; Nicholson to Monroe, November 30, 1808, in Monroe Papers, LC; the Olivers of Baltimore wrote that "it is generally believed that we shall soon be at War with France." A fortnight later they were reporting, "It is said by the friends of the administration that a war with England is nearly certain." The Olivers to P. Escheverria, November 12, 1808, to W. Pinkney, November 29, 1808, in Stuart Bruchey, *Robert Oliver, Merchant of Baltimore, 1783–1819* (Baltimore, 1956), 344. For letters and arguments in support of France, see Arthur Campbell to Madison, December 29, 1808, in Madison Pa-

had its day. This type of economic warfare was neither more effective than the embargo nor less costly than war. Rather all involved viewed non-intercourse as an interim measure. Advocates of action viewed it as another expression of American discontent; they reasoned that half a loaf was better than none. Embargo opponents considered non-intercourse to be less restrictive because trade would be permitted with non-belligerent areas. Even the British liked non-intercourse if one accepts David Erskine's view that the Royal Navy's maritime superiority and the certain flouting of the new law by greedy Yankees assured His Majesty's realm receipt of needed commodities. As Jefferson's term expired in early March, non-intercourse applicable to public British and French shipping became the law of the land "until the end of the next session of Congress." Beginning May 20 private British and French ships and goods were barred from entering the United States.[56] Although it was not understood at the time, non-intercourse was another step on the road to war. Impatience had helped kill the embargo in fifteen months; non-intercourse would survive scarcely a year. By 1810 the frustrations of another year would further swell the ranks of the war party. In mid-1812, after two more years of experimentation with economic warfare, the executive and legislative branches of government would agree that war was America's only recourse.

Meanwhile, the embargo was not forgotten. "You all know why and how it failed," Wilson Nicholas addressed his constituents, "and will not be surprised that the men whose opposition very materially contributed to its failure, should, deduce an argument to prove its original incompetency." Singling out Massachusetts, Nicholas was disturbed that one state could force alteration of national policy. All the hardships and sacrifices of 1808 seemed to have been made in vain. "Posterity will scarcely credit, when recorded by history, that the agricultural interest of the nation is contending & actually making the greatest sacrifices to maintain our pretensions to the just rights of commerce, & that a great portion of the com-

pers, New York Public Library; Caesar A. Rodney to Jefferson, December 6, 1808 (mistakenly filed in 1806), in Jefferson Papers, *ibid.* Turreau to Champagny, January 15, 1809, in AMAE, LXII, LC, claimed that France was not seriously considered as a foe in case of hostilities.

56. Erskine to Canning, February 10, 1809, in FOA 5:62, LC; non-intercourse, Erskine assured Canning on February 13, was designed "to leave open as many places for their Commerce as they can consistently with keeping up an appearance of resistance to the Belligerent Restrictions, but it is thoroughly understood that the whole Measure is a mere Subterfuge to extricate themselves from the Embarrassments of the Embargo System, and is never intended to be enforced." FOA 5:62, LC; *Public Statutes at Large of the United States of America* (79 vols. to date; Boston and Washington, 1845–), II, 530–31.

mercial interest of the Nation are using their utmost endeavors to oppose these measures," one distraught citizen wrote. An exasperated William A. Burwell proclaimed, "United we stand, divided we fall." Nathaniel Macon saw events from another perspective: "The Lord, the mighty Lord must come to our assistance, or I fear we are undone as a nation."[57]

57. "An Address from Wilson C. Nicholas, a Representative in Congress from Virginia to his Constituents" (Richmond, 1809), 7–8, copy in Carter-Smith Family Papers. A young Massachusetts resident, attributing repeal to "the firmness of New England," lauded Federalists, for "to their courage and exertion we may owe the safety of our Country; for if our country remains safe under the present administration, it be from their fear [of division], not their principles." Saltonstall to Nathaniel Saltonstall, March 11, 1809, in Saltonstall Family Papers; MacCreery to McHenry, February 10, 1809, in James McHenry Papers, Library of Congress; Burwell to Madison, February 10, 1809, in Madison Papers, LC; Macon to Nicholson, February 28, 1809, in Nicholson Papers.

FIVE

*From the Coles Mission to
the Cadore Letter*

"James the first of America will take
possession of the throne the fourth of March," Samuel Taggart wrote sar-
castically early in 1809. "I think Friend James will have rather a troublesome reign."[1] The Massachusetts Federalist's forecast proved to be accurate,
for only the last two years of James Madison's two presidential terms were
tranquil. Madison's first three years in power were marked by sincere attempts to avoid war, but these efforts failed. When the War of 1812 commenced, ill-preparedness, military incompetence, and sedition jeopardized
the young republic. In short, Madison deserved the serenity of 1815 and
1816.

[I]

If experience is a criterion for the presidency, Madison should have been a
great leader. "Father of the Constitution," co-founder of the Republican
movement, then leader of House Republicans, Madison finished his prepa-
ration for the nation's highest elective office by serving as secretary of state
for eight years. This period was marked by such a close working relationship with Thomas Jefferson it is difficult to determine which one of the
Virginians formulated policy and which one executed it. Ironically, his
credentials did not impress Madison's contemporaries at home or from
abroad. In 1806, for example, Senator William Plumer asserted that Madison was too timid for presidential consideration. A French diplomat

1. Taggart to John Taylor, February 12, 1809, in Reynolds (comp.), "Letters of Samuel
Taggart," 331–32.

claimed indecisiveness was another shortcoming; the new president was a "bright but irresolute man," incapable of mustering the audacity necessary to follow a specific course. English observers cited more deficiencies: Madison was merely a philosopher dominated by Jefferson.[2]

Credentials have not deterred Madison's detractors among historians either. The fourth president's overall reputation might best be described as weak; he has usually been portrayed as a puny man overwhelmed by events and other men. Thus Madison did not lead the nation from economic coercion to war. Rather he was overpowered by a band of men who once were called War Hawks, but who are now seen as nationalistic Republicans. Similarly, historical interpreters suggest Madison yielded to political pressures and accepted Robert Smith of Maryland (brother of Senator Samuel Smith) as secretary of state even though he preferred Albert Gallatin for the post.[3]

Madison was acutely aware of the problems he faced the day he took the oath of office. "The present situation of the world," he told his audience in a scarcely audible voice, "is largely without a parallel." Proposing a continuation of Jefferson's program of "sincere neutrality," Madison tried to preserve American neutrality by preparing mutually acceptable arrangements with the two great belligerents.[4] When peaceful strategies finally proved impossible, he sanctioned hostilities and gradually moved the country toward war from the summer of 1811 to 1812. All the while Madison, not the retired Jefferson, navigated the ship of state.

2. "Bulletin," Beaujour to Champagny, January 25, 1809, in AMAE, LXII, LC; Minister Jackson passed along Benjamin Stoddert's assessment of Madison as "merely a Metaphysician, often the dupe of his own School-boy Sophistry, ignorant of Men, and easily imposed on by Curring." Though Stoddert had not been active in the cabinet since John Adams' administration, Jackson described him as one "who to a very Strong and correct understanding adds a perfect knowledge of the interior of this Government." Stoddert to [?], December 6, 1809, enclosed with Jackson to Canning, December 13, 1809, in FOA 5:64, LC. The next year chargé d'affaires John Morier asserted that Jefferson and Joel Barlow were "the secret Advisers of the President." Morier to Wellesley, October 26, 1810, in FOA 5:70, LC. After the start of the War of 1812, an Englishman wrote: "It is yet an enigma whether he [Madison] is a traitor to his country, or the dupe of French politics." William Playfair, *Political Portraits in the New Era* (2 vols.; London, 1814), II, 181.

3. Theodore Clarke Smith, "War Guilt in 1812," 345. See the brief discussion of Madison in recent American historiography in my "The Origins of the War of 1812: Three Decades of Historical Writing," *Military Affairs*, XXXVIII (1974), 73–74; the Smith affair is examined in the next chapter.

4. "First Inaugural Address," March 4, 1809, in Richardson (comp.), *Messages and Papers of the Presidents*, I, 451. Among those present was Turreau, a "body of gold," Nathaniel Saltonstall described him to Leverett Saltonstall, March 6, 1809, in Saltonstall Family Papers.

Fortune initially seemed on Madison's side when David Erskine signed an accord promising that the English orders in council affecting America would be withdrawn no later than June 10, 1809. The United States would suspend non-intercourse against Britain in return. As an Anglo-American reconciliation appeared underway, Franco-American relations seemed deadlocked and considerable opinion existed to punish France through restrictive trade measures.

All of this suited Erskine immensely. The Englishman realized that Madison desired a rapprochement with Britain; he was intelligent enough also to recognize that Britain needed to sacrifice very little to gain many advantages, not the least of which would be to isolate France. "As things are at present," Erskine exulted on May 4, "either France will be compelled to withdraw her Decrees, or the United States will inevitably make War upon her, and in mean time all Intercourse with her and her dependencies is prohibited." For the moment Erskine enjoyed the limelight and favorable publicity; for Turreau, who departed abruptly for Baltimore, he had pity.[5]

Americans were also happy with the new arrangement, although Britain had placed "us with regard to France just where She wished us." Feverish activity gripped seaports as merchants took advantage of the legalization of Anglo-American commerce (they had, of course, as the English and French foresaw, been violating non-intercourse) to dispatch hundreds of ships to English ports.[6] While few thought of it, the export surge sparked by the Erskine accord negated all the hardships and sacrifices endured during the embargo, and the British war economy was bolstered with badly needed transfusions of yankee goods.

The bubble of excitement created by the Erskine agreement burst on July 21 when information reached Washington that Foreign Minister George Canning had rejected the Erskine accord. While Canning was technically correct in asserting that Erskine had violated his instructions, his action reflected English contempt for America and a monumental ignorance of the United States. As an English trader admitted, "there is a dreadfully low, degrading, malignant and envious spirit in this country towards the rising greatness of America."[7]

News of Canning's disavowal of Erskine's handiwork rocked the land

5. Erskine to Canning, May 4, March 17, 1809, in FOA 5:63, LC.

6. James Kent to Moss Kent, April 28, 1809, in James Kent Papers, Library of Congress; Turreau to Champagny, April 15, 1809, in AMAE, LXII, LC.

7. William Rathbone IV to Dugald Bannatyne, August 27, 1808, in Checkland, "American versus West Indian Traders in Liverpool, 1793–1815," 156; see also the perceptive comments of William Tudor, Jr., to Madison, May 18, 1808, in Miscellaneous Letters of the Department of State, NA.

and diverted American public attention from France's posture. "I cannot express my detestation of it," John Rodman wrote. "I consider it infinitely more base and treacherous than anything that has been done by France toward us." A correspondent of Madison's asserted that "the attack on the *Chesapeake* did not produce half so violent a sensation." Former president Jefferson, who had rejected Monroe's and Pinkney's treaty less than three years before, railed at Britain for its "total want of morality." The English constitution was a "stupendous fabric of human wisdom" riddled with the "most corrupted & corrupting mass of rotteness whichever usurped the name of government." Public fury was rekindled in late 1809 when Erskine was replaced by Francis James Jackson, a caustic, acid-tongued diplomat who did not conceal his disgust for the crude, bumptuous inhabitants of the United States. "At bottom," he generalized, "they are all alike except that some few are less knaves than others."[8] Jackson proceeded to subsidize pro-English journalists, ridicule Madison, hobnob with Federalists (notwith-standing his gibe that "they are all alike") and infuriate the populace at large. Between Canning's handling of the Erskine accord and Jackson's tactless diplomacy, Napoleon had two major assists in promoting the Anglo-American war he so ardently wished.

Having been aided by the British, Napoleon spurned a chance to promote an Anglo-American war by nonaction during the little-known mission of Isaac Coles in the spring of 1809. Coles, who had been Jefferson's private secretary,[9] conveyed a proposal to Paris suggesting that should France revoke or modify her decrees as they affected the United States: "It is the opinion of the Executive that Congress will, at the ensuing special session authorize acts of hostility [against Britain]." The same offer (with France the object of American action) was extended to Great Britain, but His Majesty's government gave it less consideration than Erskine's agree-

---

8. Rodman to Harmanus Bleecker, December 15, 1809, in Harmanus Bleecker Papers, New York State Library, Albany; Richard Forrest to Madison, July 25, 1809, in Madison Papers, New York Public Library; Jefferson to William Lambert, September 10, 1809, in Jefferson Papers, LC. "I am sincerely one of those, and would rather be in dependence on Great Britain, properly limited than on any nation upon earth, or than on no nation," Jefferson wrote in 1775. "But I am one of those too who rather than submit to the right of legislating for us . . . would lend my hand to sink the whole island in the ocean." Jefferson to John Randolph, August 15, 1775, in Boyd (ed.), *The Papers of Thomas Jefferson*, I, 242; Jackson to George Jackson, October 20, 1809, in Lady Jackson (ed.), *The Bath Archives*, 29.

9. Although situated near the center of power, Coles remains an obscure figure. Lyon Gardiner Tyler (ed.), *Encyclopedia of Virginia Biography* (5 vols.; New York, 1915), for example, contains nothing on Coles. Dumas Malone, *Jefferson the President: Second Term, 1805–1809* (Boston, 1974), 140, 529, mentions Coles's resemblance to Jefferson.

ment.[10] The bid carried by Coles anticipated by more than a year the measure called Macon's Bill #2.

Coles's departure for Europe had been held up for a month because of the uncertainties and turmoil in the Tenth Congress. Consequently it was mid-March before the youthful Virginian left America, and April 20 when he landed at L'Orient. Rushing to Paris, Coles was chagrined to discover that Napoleon had marched against Austria and that Champagny was leaving also.[11] It was the old and recurring story of American hopes and expectations being thwarted by France's preoccupation with European affairs.

Meanwhile Armstrong, who knew that the Emperor was unhappy with the bill, addressed notes to Champagny carefully explaining the reasons for the adoption of non-intercourse. It had been "forced upon" America "by the extraordinary circumstances of the times" and was meant to protect American "property and rights." Having tried to smooth ruffled French feelings, the diplomat then explained the offer carried by Coles. He was careful to point out that "a mere modification of his Majesty's decrees relating to Neutral Commerce, will immediately put an end to" non-intercourse. Armstrong anticipated the major objection that a change in French policy might be misinterpreted as a craven surrender to a minor power: "Knowing how difficult it is for the head of a great Empire to tread back the steps he shall have taken, the United States do not demand a revocation of these decrees, nor do they ask as a preliminary, that any property shall be stored . . . in a word—they will be satisfied with such interpretation of it as shall *hereafter* exempt American ships from vexation and capture."[12]

For a time the Emperor may have entertained thoughts of placating Armstrong and the Americans. He knew that the British had modified their

10. Smith to Armstrong, March 15, 1809, in Diplomatic Instructions of the Department of State, NA; for two remarkably different interpretations of the offers made to Britain and France, see Perkins, *Prologue to War*, 233–34; and Brant, "Madison and the War of 1812," 51–67.

11. Turreau to [Champagny], March 19, 1809, in AMAE, LXII, LC; Erskine to Canning, February 13, March 16, 1809, in FOA 5:63, LC; Coles to Cabell, February 25, 1809, in Cabell Papers; Coles to Jefferson, March 13, 1809, in Jefferson Papers, LC. "Advices from Washington say, that these private dispatches are written by Mr. Jefferson, without even the privity of Mr. Madison . . . it certainly has a queer appearance," *The Nova-Scotia Royal Gazette* (Halifax), February 28, 1809; Coles to Cabell, July 28, 1809, in Cabell Papers, gives April 24 as his arrival date in Paris; Coles to Jefferson, July 26, 1809, in Jefferson Papers, LC, supports April 23.

12. Armstrong to Champagny, April 29, 1809, enclosed with Armstrong to Smith, May 26, 1809, in Despatches from France, NA; Armstrong to Champagny, May 2, 1809, in AMAE, LXII, LC, emphasis in the original.

orders in council permitting American trade in the Baltic and had moved to curtail discrimination against American trade. Meanwhile, the Austrian war was not going well; after early victories, the French barely escaped disaster at the Battle of Aspern-Essling (May 21 and 22). Finally, while Armstrong held the carrot of conciliation, he also investigated returning home for several months, and rumors that the diplomat was about to leave circulated in French circles.[13] Given his precarious situation, prudence dictated that Napoleon show at least some interest in accommodation.

Therefore the Corsican approved Champagny's suggestion that d'Hauterive, the foreign minister's Paris-based understudy, conduct conversations with Armstrong. Significantly, despite the pressure of events, the French position hardly changed: Champagny, echoing Napoleon, spoke of France favorably interpreting her decrees provided that the United States shunned "tribute" to Britain. The Emperor's major concession consisted simply of contemplating a restoration of Franco-American relations to the footing that prevailed before the Milan decree.[14] While rolling back the Milan edict and presumably voiding the Bayonne decree, such a move would scarcely have been a major surrender. American vessels still would be fair game under the Berlin decree; it will be recalled that France began enforcing the Berlin edict in the *Horizon* case months before the Milan decree.

Nonetheless, a restrained optimism developed in America. Coles brought some hope when he landed in New York late in July. He reported that Armstrong was leaving nothing "undone" seeking an arrangement with the French; indeed, he suggested that something might have been accomplished "but the peculiar circumstances around which the Emperor has been placed has delayed it so long." Coles explained that while the Austrian campaign continued "every one was prohibited to speak to him [Napoleon] of Politics—for once he has found in the duties of a General alone enough to occupy him." After reporting the gossip that the French ruler was tiring of his version of commercial war, Coles, who knew of fresh seizures of American ships in Holland, Spain, and Italy, wisely added that "on the subject of our affairs I have not been able to learn any one fact which ought to be relied on as indicating the disposition or feelings of the French Government."[15]

13. Champagny to d'Hauterive, May 13, 1809, and Champagny to Napoleon, May 26, 1809, in AMAE, LXII, LC. See too François Cottier to Dominique André, July 20, 1809, in Hémardinquer, "Une correspondance de banquiers parisiens (1808–1815): aspects socio-politiques," 517.

14. Note "dictée a Schoenbrunn," May 18, 1809, and Napoleon to Champagny, June 10, 1809, both in *Correspondance de Napoléon*, XIX, 21–22, 95.

15. Coles to Cabell, July 28, 1809, in Cabell Papers; Coles sent Jefferson a similar letter

Madison's spirits were already high because of the Erskine agreement, and he was confident that the French would alter their policy because of the new situation. In occasional letters to Jefferson from May to July, Madison emphasized positive reports from Turreau and Armstrong (he admitted seizures continued but noted that they were taking place under the "municipal operation of the Berlin Decree," accepting a differentiation that contributed much mischief to Anglo-American relations). Madison's cheerfulness was relayed to others besides Jefferson. Joel Barlow, for example, in frequent contact with the president, passed word that "Our chiefs are in confident expectations that Armstrong will soon send them a new commercial convention with France."[16]

Armstrong's conversations with d'Hauterive were conducted in a cordial fashion. The Frenchman may have known Armstrong from his days of American exile and, as mentioned earlier, he had a certain ambivalent sympathy for the United States. In the harmonious atmosphere recounted by d'Hauterive, Armstrong may have become too expansive, unfairly ridiculing William Pinkney in London as an Anglophile, concurring that the various Napoleonic decrees were necessitated by the scope of the struggle against Britain, and, finally, discussing a plan whereby the United States would declare war against Britain and France; Franco-American hostilities would terminate immediately, however, and the two nations would then join in a common struggle against Britain.[17]

Armstrong's version of what transpired differed somewhat from d'Hauterive's. The French diplomat stressed finding a common ground satisfactory to America and France. "Having neither colonies nor commerce," he assured Armstrong, "it will be much both within our power and disposition to form with you a connexion of the most liberal character" if the United States preserved its rights against British encroachments. Armstrong re-

---

dated July 26, in Jefferson Papers, LC. An individual acquainted with Cabell or his brother, William, reported that "Bonaparte has been much more candid with us, though not less dishonorable—He says in answer to the proposals of this country 'I am too much engaged as a general to attend to the trifling politicks of America [.] my Decrees in councils [*sic*] are given and must be enforced.'" Arthur Sinclair to John H. Cocke, August 2, 1809, in Cabell Papers.

16. Madison to Jefferson, June 27, 1809, in Madison Papers, LC; Joel Barlow to Stephen Barlow, August 19, 1809, in Barlow Papers, Harvard University; Barlow to Henry Dearborn, August 16, 1809, in Fogg Collection. Erskine, who may have been misled by Secretary of State Smith, thought that there would be no Franco-American accord. Erskine to Canning, July 3, 6 ("Separate"), in FOA 5:53, LC; by September, however, Erskine disclosed that Armstrong and d'Hauterive hoped for a speedy and amicable agreement. Erskine to Canning, September 13, 1809, *ibid.*

17. Artaud de Montor, *Histoire de la vie et des travaux politiques du comte d'Hauterive*, 232–34, 261–62.

minded d'Hauterive of the continuing seizures of American shipping and he alluded specifically to the cargoes sent to Europe through Holland. "Translated into plain English," Armstrong concluded late in July, d'Hauterive's comments meant that "unless you resist the British doctrine of *search* and *blockade*, you need expect, no relaxation on the part of the Emperor." In this environment Armstrong recommended an immediate declaration of war on France and Britain, then immediate peace with France. A "political gulph wide as the ocean" separated Britain and America, Armstrong explained in transmitting a proposal which he admitted had, somewhat "the air of paradox."[18]

Possibly frustration motivated Armstrong's suggestion; perhaps it was Anglophobia, or maybe both. The American recognized that Napoleon no longer felt compelled to humor the United States. On June 5 news appeared in the *Gazette de France* that the English government would not honor Erskine's work. Then the Austrian war ended on a victorious note for France with the Battle of Wagram (July 6). In short, there were no overriding reasons to placate the Americans and in August the d'Hauterive-Armstrong talks petered out. Champagny (elevated to duc de Cadore) continued restating familiar points: neutral vessels allowing themselves to be visited by the Royal Navy were denationalized while Britain's patently illegal blockade forced French retaliation. Thus the hopes stirred by the Erskine agreement and the summer conversations in Paris evaporated. A disappointed and angry Armstrong queried Samuel Smith, "How long shall we submit to this system of indignity and injustice? Some measures of stronger character than any you have yet taken, must be adopted, or we shall become a proverb of weakness and irresolution."[19] In America, where denunciation of Britain filled the air, hardly anyone except Federalists noticed the termination of negotiations.[20]

18. Armstrong to Smith, June 30, 1809, in Despatches from France, NA; Armstrong to Smith, July 24, 1809, *ibid*; Armstrong to Madison, September 18, 1809, in Madison Papers, LC; for a different reading of this letter, see Skeen, *John Armstrong, Jr.*, 100–103; see also Armstrong to Jefferson, September 19, 1809, in Jefferson Papers, LC.

19. Jackson to Bathurst, February 16, 1810, in FOA 5:69, LC, agreed that Wagram had "induced" Napoleon "to delay the signature" to an Armstrong-d'Hauterive accord; Cadore to Armstrong, August 23, 1809, in AMAE, LXII, LC; the foreign minister followed Napoleon's instructions of August 21, 1809, in *Correspondance de Napoléon*, XIX, 374–75; Armstrong to Smith, September 16, 1809, in Dreer Collection, Historical Society of Pennsylvania. Contrary to what some of Armstrong's contemporaries believed, the envoy did not consider leaving France because of the lapse in talks. Armstrong to Warden, August 13, 1809, in David Bailie Warden Papers, Maryland Historical Society.

20. The Federalists concentrated on two aspects of Franco-American relations in mid-1809. First, there was the Coles mission, about which some Federalists had accurate information. Rufus King, for example, passed along Daniel Parker's assessment (dated July

[II]

Surveying the wretched state of American commerce in Holland, longtime consul Sylvanus Bourne wondered wearily, "How long are we to suffer these cruel indignities? Will the forebearance [*sic*] of our Country never be exhausted? Will it never take a manly position or evince a correct sense of national honor"[?]. The same question was on the lips of a good many men beside Bourne late in 1809. For years it seemed that the belligerents had been humiliating the United States, yet neither of the *"tormentors"* (as Ezekiel Bacon styled them) showed the least intention of modifying its position.[21] The abortive Erskine agreement and the stillborn Armstrong-d'Hauterive conversations were but the latest proofs of this.

Clearly sentiment was building for action to break the deadlock in foreign policy, to wrench one or both the great powers off America's back. Unfortunately for the new nation, no one quite knew how to accomplish this feat during the fall and early winter of 1809. The President, still smarting from the Erskine shock, not to mention the dashed hopes of a Franco-American settlement, freely admitted to a visitor that there was "no hope of accommodation with either France or England." Beyond this, he said little. The Congress was a vacuum. "Not a single member of Congress . . . ap-

1, 1809) that Franco-American differences were about to be settled. King to Christopher Gore, August 6, 1809, in Charles R. King (ed.), *The Life and Correspondence of Rufus King* (6 vols.; New York, 1894–1900), V, 167–68; Timothy Pickering had a more conventional Federalist viewpoint: Coles was bringing back Napoleon's assent to the repeal of the embargo, the alternative being the destruction of French influence in America, but the Emperor "may in a passion expose the fatal secret" should Jefferson act prematurely. Pickering to S. P. Gardiner, n.d., in Henry Adams (ed.), *Documents Relating to New England Federalism, 1800–1815* (Boston, 1905), 379–80. Four years later Armstrong alleged that "there was no doubt of the influence of France upon Jefferson and Madison," citing the Coles mission— Coles carried a letter from Gallatin to d'Hauterive (they were friends) and one from Jefferson to Napoleon providing for Armstrong's recall if the Emperor found him disagreeable. King, *The Life and Correspondence of Rufus King*, V, 370–71. It was in 1813 also that the Federalists dredged up a letter sent by Turreau to Smith early in June, 1809. The French envoy, despairing of American even-handedness ("I have never doubted that England's ascendancy over the United States would end in triumph in spite of our efforts," Turreau to [Champagny], April 20, 1809, in AMAE, LXII, LC) and unhappy with the non-intercourse bill, addressed a sharp albeit unofficial note to Smith which the secretary of state rejected. Ignoring this, the Georgetown *Federal Republican and Commercial Gazette*, August 25, 1813, puffed that "no American can read it without a blush of shame and indignation; that a depraved Chevalier d'Industrie, the tool of a reptile, which has crawled into a throne, should use such language with impunity and without reproof." Copy in Madison Papers, LC.

21. Bourne to Armstrong, September 6, 1809, enclosed with Armstrong to Smith, September 18, 1809, in Despatches from France, NA; Bacon to Story, November 27, 1809, in Story Papers.

pears to have formed a definite opinion as to the course to be pursued,"
Senator Andrew Gregg reported glumly. The Pennsylvania Republican did
not exaggerate: whether from the North or the South, Republicans and
most Federalists, elected officialdom shrugged its collective shoulders and
pondered how to proceed. According to New York Republican Ebenezer
Sage, congressmen "now see the mischief & folly of letting go of the
embargo." [22]

While the Congress wandered through the winter, two facts became
evident. First, war would be considered as a last resort only, years of rebuffs
and antineutral acts notwithstanding. "They don't want war," Sage wrote
of his colleagues, "but to continue some scheme, to beat and discomfort all
the belligerents without any fighting." Second, bitterness and vexation
increasingly filled congressmen, breeding self-criticism and condemnation
of Madison. "To expect from the efforts of a heterogenous mass composed of
two hundred wire heads & blockheads, in pursuit of popularity, a correct
well digested political course of proceeding toward the great powers at war,
is to my mind irrational," Nicholas Gilman of New Hampshire commented. Only one person, the president, "must devise and recommend
measures, as the Constitution unequivocally recquires." [23]

Madison was a careful man, however. Like his predecessor Jefferson, he
wished to avoid hostilities, and he could not quite bring himself to believe
that the warring states would not recognize the wisdom of placating the
United States. Thus Madison speedily accepted Erskine's offer and thus he
made similar proposals to Britain and France in mid-March, 1809. These
prospects having foundered, Madison was in temporary distress. Ultimately he would work with the Congress in utilizing Macon's Bill #2, but
he would not lead in the sense Gilman asked. Such executive initiative was

22. Christopher Fitzsimons to Wade Hampton, November 28, 1809, in Charles E.
Cauthen (ed.), *Family Letters of the Three Wade Hamptons, 1782–1901* (Columbia, 1953), 7;
Gregg to A. J. Dallas, December 4, 1809, cited in Sapio, *Pennsylvania and the War of 1812*,
110; Sage to Henry P. Dering, December 12, 1809, in Dering Family Papers, William L.
Clements Library, University of Michigan. See also Poindexter to Cowles Mead, April 20,
1810, in J. F. H. Claiborne Collection; Varnum to Campbell, March 15, 1810, in George
Washington Campbell Papers; Jonathan Robinson to Plumer, January 4, 1810, in Plumer
Papers, LC.

23. Sage to Dering, January 16, 1810, in Dering Family Papers. See also John Rhea to
John Overton, April 14, 1810, in Overton Papers; Jenkin Whiteside to Overton, February
1, 1810, *ibid.*; Wilson C. Nicholas to Jefferson, December 22, 1809, in Carter-Smith
Family Papers; Gilman to Plumer, December 30, 1809, in Plumer Papers, LC; see also
Gilman to Josiah Bartlett, March 18, 1810, in Bartlett Papers. Shortly after leaving office,
Jefferson scored "the wonderful credulity of the members of Congress in the floating lies of
the day. And in this no experience seems to correct them." Jefferson to Madison, March 17,
1809, in Madison Papers, LC.

decades or even a century away. The Father of the Constitution would fulfill the role he had envisioned for the president; later leaders would interpret what they thought Madison meant in 1787.

While Madison interpreted executive leadership, Armstrong began campaigning anew for more favorable treatment of American shipping. The New Yorker would have been ineffective by himself, but he was joined by an assortment of interested Americans, thoughtful Frenchmen, and concerned Napoleonic subordinates who were motivated by a common desire to awaken the Emperor to economic reality. Anticipating the crisis which scarred the Imperial economy during 1811–1812, they concurred that France needed trade and they agreed that it was senseless to alienate the United States, the most important neutral carrier. Jean Baptiste Bachasson, comte de Montalivet, readily admitted that "France must admit your commerce. Our merchants need it. Our manufactures will perish without it, and our national industry be lost."[24]

There had been other occasions when Napoleon's ministers had tried to modify the Continental System. Some had disagreed with or did not understand the need for the Berlin and Milan decrees in 1806 and 1807. In mid-1807 Secretary of the Treasury Gallatin had received a letter, probably from d'Hauterive, hinting that a cadre of the French ruler's underlings favored "a relaxation of the commercial policy of the Emperor" and that the Corsican was "disposed to listen" to other viewpoints provided that any hint of a humiliating retreat was avoided. Furthermore, late in 1808, Navy Minister Decrès pleaded against singling out the Americans for harsh treatment; he reminded the mercantilist emperor that American merchants paid for French goods in specie.[25] Napoleonic policy remained firm.

Now stronger pressure was brought to bear on the Emperor. Joseph Fouché, duc de Otranto and minister of police, carried Lafayette's reminder that France was foolishly skipping opportunities to conciliate the United States, and the famous French officer urged more lenient treatment of the Americans. Montalivet, Decrès, and d'Hauterive also spoke up so that the Emperor was enlightened about America's importance.

Armstrong believed that reason would finally influence Napoleon. "I have but one moment to say that appearances are favorable," he reported on New Year's Day, 1810. "By the 10 of Jan[uar]y the present system will be irretrievably fixed, or entirely altered. Of the two events, the latter is the most probable." On the sixth the American diplomat was more restrained

24. Quoted in Lee to Mrs. Susan Palfrey Lee, January 16, 1810, in Mann, *A Yankee Jeffersonian*, 109.

25. Madison to Jefferson, July 7, 1807, in Madison Papers, LC; Decrès to Napoleon, September 15, 1808, cited in Melvin, *Napoleon's Navigation System*, 74–75.

as he relayed rumors of a crackdown on Holland. "The Emperor sees things in a way almost peculiar to himself." If Napoleon dethroned his brother from the kingship of Holland, Armstrong wondered, "what will avail our appeals to law, to justice, and to moderation?" On the tenth (the time by which Napoleon was supposed to have acted), Armstrong was still repeating that "of our business here, it is very difficult to speak with any degree of certainty almost every day giving appearances peculiar to itself." He still maintained that any decision made with the First Empire in mind "cannot be unfriendly to us."[26]

Armstrong was not alone in his optimism. William Lee, consul in Bordeaux temporarily assisting Armstrong, boasted in mid-December that he was producing "short and pithy" *mémoires* for Napoleon's perusal. A fortnight later he proclaimed exultantly that "hourly you may expect to see a decree in favor of American commerce." By mid-January, a more restrained Lee noted that Napoleon did not "appear friendly." Echoing Armstrong, he commented on the Emperor's unpredictability; the French ruler had just ordered action taken against American shipping in Naples, Bilbao, Santander, and San Sebastian.[27]

At least two historians have claimed that Armstrong was responsible for Napoleon's quixotic actions in the winter of 1809–1810: the Emperor, they explain, was under heavy ministerial pressure to treat the Americans more generously. In fact, he was on the verge of agreeing to a treaty exempting American ships from seizure on the high seas and allowing the free entry of United States flag vessels into French and French-controlled ports when Armstrong delivered strongly worded protests about French confiscations. Infuriated at the American's impertinence, Napoleon promptly rejected conciliatory gestures.[28]

Armstrong was an awkward figure in diplomatic circles, and his prose and his manners could be excessively formal. His deficiencies had little if anything to do with Napoleon's behavior, however. The Emperor's order concerning American vessels in Spanish ports was dated December 19, well before his supposed displeasure with Armstrong. In any case, Armstrong had delivered vigorous protests on numerous occasions during his years in France. It seems likely therefore that the Corsican turned on the American

26. Armstrong to Smith, January 1, 1810, in Despatches from France, NA; Armstrong to Smith, January 6, 1810, *ibid*; Armstrong to Russell, January 10, 1810, in Russell Papers, Brown University.

27. Lee to Mrs. Susan Palfrey Lee, December 15, 1809, January 2, 13, 16, 1810, in Mann, *A Yankee Jeffersonian*, 94–95, 103, 107, 108–109.

28. Melvin, *Napoleon's Navigation System*, 154–58; Phoebe Anne Heath, *Napoleon I and the Origins of the Anglo-American War of 1812* (Toulouse, 1929), 124.

envoy to mask his decision to continue his usual short-sighted and contemptuous treatment of the United States. In a business-as-usual note to Cadore on January 10 the French leader reiterated a familiar position: he welcomed American commerce provided that the United States prohibited the levying of dues on its trade to the Continent and rejected England's paper blockades. Until America took these steps, Napoleon considered the Berlin pronouncement justifiable retribution against Britain. Armstrong realized that the First Empire would continue treating the United States in the disdainful fashion it always had. Outraged, he demanded of Senator Smith, "Why should you fear a war with this country?"[29]

Napoleon acted on other fronts also. He launched an anti-Armstrong drive that stretched from Washington to St. Petersburg. He struck at American commerce in Dutch and Italian ports, and he pressured the Swedes to exclude American vessels from their homeland. Finally, on March 23, 1810, he signed what became known as the Rambouillet decree (not officially published until May 14), approving past and current seizures of American shipping throughout the Empire. "I cannot see with indifference," Armstrong was informed after the customary professions of friendship, "measures which expressly favor the trade of my enemy. Such is the non-intercourse law."[30] Having struck at Armstrong, having moved to fill Imperial coffers, and having strengthened the Continental System, the Emperor busied himself with plans for his forthcoming wedding to Marie-Louise of Austria.

[III]

Gloom enveloped the American people and their representatives during the late winter and spring of 1809–1810. The Erskine fiasco still lingered in many memories and non-intercourse was regarded as an unsuccessful experiment. The country again seemed to have the alternatives of submission to the belligerents, war, or another variation of economic coercion. Submis-

---

29. See Chapter I herein and Lee to Mrs. Susan Palfrey Lee, February 5, 1810, in Mann, *A Yankee Jeffersonian*, 114; Napoleon to Berthier, Prince de Neuchatel, December 19, 1809, in *Correspondance de Napoléon*, XX, 78; Napoleon to Cadore, January 10, "Projet de note au Ministre d'Amérique," January 25, and "Note pour le général Armstrong," January 25, 1810, all *ibid.*, XX, 110–11, 141–43; Armstrong to Samuel Smith, January 17, 1810, in Dreer Collection.

30. For some of Napoleon's comments (labeling Armstrong an "imbecile" and "morose") and directives concerning the American representative, see Napoleon to Cadore, January 19, 1810, in *Correspondance de Napoléon*, XX, 132; Napoleon to Cadore, January 24, March 11, 1810, in Léon Lecestre (ed.), *Lettres inédites de Napoléon Ier* (2 vols.; Paris, 1897), II, 6, 55; Armstrong to Madison, May 25, 1810, in Madison Papers, LC.

sion was unthinkable, and only a minority of congressmen favored hostilities. "All is still & torpid," one observer despaired in Washington, "the patriotism & honor of the Country is gone." So an appeal was made to Nathaniel Macon for yet another version of commercial warfare. The North Carolinian had opposed termination of the embargo rather bitterly, and he tartly suggested "that those who brought the nation into the present strange situation ought to be here, and try to get us out of it."[31] Nonetheless, with Albert Gallatin's assistance, he brought forth a document that became known as Macon's Bill #1, permitting American ships to venture anywhere, but prohibiting French and English vessels from entering American ports. Should one or both belligerents relax restrictions directed against the United States, President Madison could lift entry curtailments affecting one or both. With little enthusiasm the House approved Macon's Bill #1.

There was tepid support at best for Macon's Bill #1 in the Senate. Seeing Gallatin's hand, Samuel Smith called the measure a "disgrace." "The House," Smith explained, "tries to hide the disgrace under a cloak, the Senate pulled off the cloak." Smith argued that Macon's bill was pusillanimous to the point that it would invite retaliation. After what seemed an interminable time, the Senate approved a modified version of Macon's Bill #1. The measure was then returned to the House where further modifications sponsored by South Carolina Representative John Taylor were accepted. Even then the two chambers clashed about the content of the new law. House debate raged until one exasperated congressman muttered, "If God in his mercy does not restrain this perpetual tornado of wind and words, the Government will be puffed out of existence in five years," and it was not until May 1, 1810, that the by now misnamed Macon's Bill #2 became effective.[32]

The new legislation barred armed French and British vessels from American waters and it provided for the imposition of non-intercourse against one great power should the other revoke or modify its measures as they applied to the United States before March 3, 1811. Allegations have been made that Macon's Bill #2 marked the end of a positive American foreign policy. Certainly there were those who felt that way in 1810 and it is

---

31. "A return to the embargo could alone save us," Jefferson to Madison, June 27, 1810, in Madison Papers, LC; Elisha Tracy to Samuel Huntington, February 25, 1810, in *Letters from the Samuel Huntington Correspondence, 1800–1812* (Cleveland, 1915), 141; Macon to Joseph H. Nicholson, November 30, 1809, in Nicholson Papers.

32. Samuel Smith to Wilson Cary Nicholas, March 17, 1810, in Carter-Smith Family Papers; see also the assessment of Turreau to Champagny, March 15, 1810, in AMAE, LXIII, LC; Sage to Dering, March 15, 1810, in Dering Family Papers.

equally true that there was nationwide despair when Macon's Bill #2 became law. Far from being an abject surrender of neutral rights, however, Macon's bill represented one final attempt to secure relief from foreign interference with American trade. It was risky, but after years of buffeting gambling was in order. Finally, Macon's Bill #2 was not a bold new concept; it had been preceded by the proposals extended to Britain and France in March, 1809, and by a roughly similar suggestion during the embargo. These earlier overtures are largely forgotten.

Macon's Bill #2 seemed destined for oblivion too. Congressman Macon himself, still favoring an embargo, had no confidence in the vehicle bearing his name. "When we shall adjourn or what we shall do before we adjourn God only knows," he wailed; in his judgment maritime war appeared most likely. While President Madison acknowledged the shortcomings of the legislation, he hoped that the misnamed measure might produce the positive results previous propositions had not. To British minister Francis Jackson, Macon's bill was the product of a demented mob, and about the best that could be expected from the Congress of the United States. "They have covered themselves with ridicule and disgrace," Jackson jeered. What started in "blood and thunder" had "ended in a drunken frolic."[33]

Jackson's offensive conduct, meanwhile, prompted the administration to demand his recall.[34] His diplomatic mission had gone awry from the beginning; he loathed Madison and democracy, and the English gentleman expressed his contempt openly. To Jackson the United States was an impotent nation under French influence, a country that unfairly protested British actions while demonstrating a remarkable forbearance under Napoleonic insults. Firmness was the only way to deal with such impertinence, and with Federalists counseling him he advised his government to avoid immediate negotiations, to maintain the orders in council, to cultivate other trading outlets, and to leave the position of minister plenipotentiary to the United States vacant. Jackson was convinced that such a program would make even the Americans come to their senses. Having made his recommendations, the Englishman foolishly journeyed to Massachusetts at the invitation of Federalist governor Christopher Gore. Though he became the

33. Macon to Joseph H. Nicholson, April 27, 1810, in Nicholson Papers; see also Macon to Nicholson, April 3, 10, 1810, *ibid.*; Jackson to George Jackson, May 7, 1810, in Lady Jackson (ed.), *The Bath Archives*, 116–17.

34. "I have little Doubt that a Demand to this Effect [Napoleon ordering Madison not to receive Jackson] was made by Bonaparte as soon as my Appointment was known, and that it would have been willingly acquiesced in by Mr. Madison, if he had not conceived the Step to have been too decisive and ostensible a Proof of his Devotion to French Interests." Jackson to Bathurst, December 30, 1809, in FOA 5:64, LC; FOA 5:69 is filled with Jackson's angry comments on the United States.

toast of hardshell Federalists, Jackson's antics had a serious impact on Anglo-American relations.[35] John Philip Morier and Augustus John Foster, England's chargé and minister respectively in 1810, 1811, and 1812 were unable to undo the resulting damage.

The United States experienced other pains for being a leading neutral in 1810. The English used forged papers to gain entry into European ports, leading to French retaliation against authentic American-owned vessels. It was in 1810 also that the license trade between Britain and France zoomed. Begun in 1796, this commerce remained a relatively minor operation until 1808 when the French government issued approximately 5,000 licenses, almost double the number granted in 1807, and more than had been allowed during the whole 1803–1806 period. In 1809 more than 15,000 licenses were approved while in 1810 the number climbed to over 18,300.[36] While these figures may seem high—not all licenses signed were delivered and not all those delivered were used—the license trade between the belligerents was flourishing while neutral America's trade was being victimized by Britain and France.

The license trade seemed like a calculated insult aimed at the United States. Jefferson's friend William Short reported on a voyage he made from

---

35. Andrew Jackson raged that "no act of insult, degradation or contumely offered to our government will arouse them from their present lethargy and temporising conduct until my name sake sets fire to some of our seaport Towns and puts his foot aboard a British man of war." Jackson to Jenkin Whiteside, February 10, 1810, in John Spencer Bassett (ed.), *Correspondence of Andrew Jackson* (7 vols.; Washington, 1926–1935), I, 200.

36. Sir William Scott admitted in 1810 that "it is a matter perfectly notorious that we are carrying on the whole trade of the world under simulated and disguised papers." Quoted in Roland G. Ruppenthal, "Denmark and the Continental System," *Journal of Modern History*, XV (1943), 16; the figures are from Adam Seybert, *Statistical Annals . . . of the United States of America* (Philadelphia, 1818), 70; John Quincy Adams reported rumors that the British and French were about to sign a commercial treaty in the midst of the war. Adams to Robert Smith, May 19, 1810, in Ford (ed.), *Writings of John Quincy Adams*, III, 440. Though the number of licences was at a record high in 1810, Anglo-French trade peaked in 1813.

French trade with Great Britain: (in francs)

Year	Imports	Exports
1802	6,738,725	15,560,315
1803	2,163,996	17,199,426
1810	46,117,900	38,918,100
1811	32,428,700	29,987,300
1812	26,437,200	96,973,000
1813	44,552,700	114,632,250

A. Chabert, *Essai sur les mouvements des revenus et de l'activité économique en France de 1798 à 1820*, 325–26.

Dieppe to Liverpool early in June, 1810: "The owner of the ship in which I came was on board & very much amused at this state of things as to commerce & admired the Emperor's talents & *savoir faire* in making it penal in other countries to furnish England with any thing in order that his own subjects might have the exclusive benefit of it." When Short objected to the peculiar commerce between belligerents, the ship owner blandly replied that neutrals could trade with each other. Napoleon contended that Anglo-French wartime trade was a matter of convenience and design: France wanted to export surplus wheat from Brittany and the British needed foodstuffs. The Emperor therefore approved wheat exports for specie imports, hoping in the process to cripple the English economy.[37] Although French wheat helped Britain through a difficult year, what the specie did for France is questionable. The license trade meanwhile confirmed the convictions of many Americans that the belligerents were scheming against neutral trade. The license system seemed but the tip of an economic iceberg, the bulk of which consisted of a maze of French decrees, announced and unannounced, enforced and unenforced, all of which together spelled uncertainty and confusion about the status of American shipping in Continental ports.

An apparently endless number of cases testified to the absurdities and inconsistencies of the various French restrictions. The experience of the ship *America* was typical. According to Jonathan Russell, the *America* violated a code specifying that a vessel *"forced into a French port* by a French privateer had been condemned *for arriving* there."* Following heated protests the *America* was spared condemnation, losing valuable travel time in the process. The Crowninshields, a politically prominent merchant family of Massachusetts, also encountered trials and tribulations at French hands. Their ship *Belisarius* was wrecked off the coast of Tunis in February, 1810; her cargo was saved only to be seized by a French privateer because the ship was allegedly heading for British-controlled Lisbon. Another Crowninshield vessel, the *Hind*, carried tobacco, whale and fish oil, and cotton to a north German port close to Hamburg. The tobacco and fish oil were admitted without penalty; a six percent duty was applied to the cotton before transportation to Hamburg. In Hamburg the French claimed two-thirds the cotton in additional duties.[38]

37. Short to Jefferson, June 19, 1810, in *The Jefferson Papers*, Massachusetts Historical Society *Collections* (Boston, 1900), 138–40; Melvin, *Napoleon's Navigation System*, 89, cites "the irresistible trend of events and . . . the choice of the only expedient offered for the pressing need of the moment," in the development of the license trade.

38. Russell to Armstrong, July 15, 1810, and Merrit Bates to Russell, August 11,

France itself ultimately was the chief victim of these Napoleonic controls. A generous policy toward the United States would have spurred Franco-American trade. A greater commercial exchange coupled with curtailment of the activities of French seaborne raiders would have promoted Franco-American harmony in sharp contrast to the Anglo-American disharmony caused by British impressment policy and the oppressive orders in council. Finally, a more judicious treatment of the United States might have meant more tranquil Franco-Russian relations because the Americans would not have been driven to the Russian market. Seeking less risky and more financially rewarding markets, however, American merchants did turn their attention to Russia in 1810 and 1811; whereas no Russian-American trade existed in 1803 and 1804, by 1810 almost $4,000,000 in American exports and in 1811 more than $6,000,000 worth of exports reached Russia. The Continental System was breached; imported items from the United States appeared in Western Europe.[39] To close the break Napoleon launched his Russian adventure and precipitated the collapse of his empire. History is often the story of missed opportunities; nowhere is this more true than with Napoleonic France and its relations with Jeffersonian America.

[IV]

"Our vessels are every where seized, not by the municipal authority or conformably to the usual forms of judicial proceedings; but by the strong arm of military power; not in detail, but in mass," editorialized Washington's *National Intelligencer* about the French in June, 1810. The bleak picture would remain unchanged, the *Intelligencer* forecast, for Napoleon acted solely in defense of French interests, not in consideration of American wishes.[40]

The summer of 1810 bore out the *Intelligencer's* prediction, for the Emperor made structural changes in his commercial policies. He adjusted tariff

1810, in Russell Papers; Reinoehl, "Post-Embargo Trade and Merchant Prosperity: Experience of the Crowninshield Family, 1809–1812," 235–37.

39. E. V. Tarlé, "Kontinental'naia Blokada," *Soch.*, III, 33, quoted in N. N. Bolkhovitinov and S. I. Divil'kouskii, "Russian Diplomacy and the Anglo-American War of 1812–1814," *Soviet Studies in History*, I (1962), 21. "In the interests of the Russian landowners and merchants, the Tsarist government encouraged expansion of Russo-American trade and was not deterred even when it came to direct violation of the Continental Blockade."

40. *National Intelligencer*, May 28, 1810; see also the issues of June 15, 23, 1810.

rates upwards and he stipulated that exports must equal imports; he even specified what products should leave France. To Napoleon's dismay, the Continental System was not strangling Great Britain's war economy; indeed, England continued to subsidize her European allies. Thus at a June meeting of the *Conseil du Commerce et des Manufactures* (including Napoleon, Montalivet, Cadore, Decrès, and Gaudin, minister of finance) the Emperor discussed further revision of trade regulations. The *Conseil*, which dealt with the interrelated issues of smuggling, trade with the United States, and the state of the Imperial economy, had members who were very familiar with the economic mischief caused by the various overlapping restrictions that had evolved.[41] These men were nonetheless unable to change the Napoleonic system. The Emperor simply would not tolerate any dramatic alteration of his complex economic instrument.[42]

Instead, early in July, 1810, the license system became the law of the empire with Napoleon proposing to sign every authorization personally. French subjects alone were eligible for what were called "normal licenses." In the St. Cloud decree of July 5, however, Napoleon allowed American participation in the license trade; American vessels from Charleston and New York certified by French consuls could enter Bordeaux, Nantes, or Marseilles carrying cotton, logwood, indigo, and pot-ashes. Thirty "permits" (licenses) were granted initially with thirty to fifty more possible.[43] In accord with earlier rules, exports (furniture, brandy, wines, and silks) had to equal imports.

Then in late July, as rumors circulated in Paris that the American Congress would meet in special session perhaps to declare war on France, the Emperor decided that the Berlin and Milan decrees would no longer be applied against the United States. On August 2 the French leader forwarded an outline to Cadore to be used in constructing a note for Armstrong ("the simpler . . . the better," His Majesty stipulated condescendingly). After some remarks approving the embargo and condemning nonintercourse, Napoleon stated that France would reciprocate the reopening of American ports under Macon's bill by ending the Berlin and Milan de-

41. There were many Frenchmen favoring trade restrictions. See the pamphlet "A sa Majeste l'Empereur et Roi sur la question de l'admission des navires americains dans les ports de l'empire" by Guerault, de Fontaine-Guerard of the Départment de l'Eure, copy in AMAE, LXIV, LC.

42. "Notes pour le Ministre de l'Intérieur, dictées en Conseil d'Administration de Commerce," June 25, 1810, in *Correspondance de Napoléon*, XX, 431–32.

43. Armstrong to Smith, July 15, 1810, in Despatches from France, NA; Lefebvre, *Napoleon: From Tilsit to Waterloo*, 125–26.

crees effective November 1 with the proviso that England withdraw her orders in council and her blockade or, alternately, that the United States force "the English to respect their rights."[44] Armstrong received this message on August 5. He did not seek clarification of the conditional wording in the communication.

The Cadore letter, as the French note became known, was "so unexpected" according to a Lexington, Kentucky, newspaper that "universal astonishment appeared to prevail in town." Yet the Cadore letter was bereft of new ideas: the French had made their displeasure with non-intercourse known before; and they had been offered the opportunity to promote an Anglo-American war at the start of Madison's presidency. Repeatedly the relish with which the Emperor had insisted that cannon alone could vindicate American rights had been reported to Madison and Smith.[45] Furthermore, limitations on Napoleonic generosity were evident by mid-September; the Berlin and Milan decrees would be enforced against violators until November 1. In addition, fresh restrictions were imposed on traders in the Trianon tariff of August 5 and in the Fontainebleau decree of October 18. The Trianon tariff featured still higher duties on imports and provided for the disposition of sequestered merchandise and detained ships while the Fontainebleau decree was designed to halt smuggling and the introduction of unwanted goods. Finally, to make the Continental System more effective, France took control of the coastal zones of the Baltic, Mediterranean, and the Adriatic.[46]

Despite this catalog of inconsistency, President Madison favorably interpreted the Cadore letter and chose to employ it against Britain. Madison's decision was not made because of ignorance, fear, timidity, or wishful thinking. The President clearly understood that the Cadore letter was con-

44. Napoleon to Cadore, July 31, 1810, in *Correspondance de Napoléon*, XX, 554–55; Napoleon to Cadore, August 2, 1810, *ibid.*, XXI, 1–2; Cadore to Armstrong, August 5, 1810, in AMAE, LXIV, LC.

45. *Kentucky Gazette* (Lexington), October 9, 1810; when a young Philadelphian told Napoleon he did not know what the British would do about their orders, the Emperor reputedly said, "I have set them the example and they ought to follow it and if they do not, the cannon of the Republic should make them. They alone command the respect of nations." Armstrong to Madison, late August, 1810 [?], quoted in Heath, *Napoleon I and the Origins of the Anglo-American War of 1812*, 144–45.

46. Cadore to Armstrong, September 7, 1810, in AMAE, LXIV, LC; Armstrong to Smith, September 10, 1810, in Despatches from France, NA; for guides to the maze of decrees and decisions during the summer of 1810, see Melvin, *Napoleon's Navigation System*, 166–230; Lefebvre, *Napoleon: From Tilsit to Waterloo*, 124–27; Bonnel, *La France, les États-Unis et la guerre de course*, 267–70, 461.

ditional. He was equally familiar with Britain's adamant opposition to partial repeal and he knew that the British would reject the Cadore letter and that an Anglo-American war would result.[47] Madison desperately wanted to avoid hostilities, but accumulated grievances forced him to recognize that war was on the horizon. Another year and a half of frustration caused by blockades, impressment, and English arrogance would bring the chief executive and Congress together on the war question. On November 2, 1810, Madison took yet another step on the road to war; he proclaimed French compliance with Macon's Bill #2, giving Great Britain three months to satisfy American expectations.

Madison's acceptance of the Cadore letter has made Napoleon seem a more clever statesman than he was. It is true that Macon's Bill #2 was published in Paris on June 24 and the opportunities it offered readily appreciated.[48] It is also true that many historians have linked Macon's bill with the birth of the Cadore letter. Still, the French had long known that modification of their restrictions would satisfy the United States. Secretary of State Smith had even informed David Erskine in September, 1809, that America would not object if France barred English goods through municipal regulations. Every "nation had a Right either entirely to exclude from their Ports any Articles or Commodities, or to determine the Conditions upon which they should be received," Smith explained.[49] Napoleon, the self-proclaimed protector of neutrals, could live with such a doctrine; the

47. "It [the Cadore letter] promises us at least an extrication from the dilemma of a mortifying peace, or a war with both the great belligerents. The precise course which G. B. will take remains to be seen. *Whatever the immediate one may be, it is probable that we shall ultimately be at issue with her or her fictitious blockades*" [author's emphasis], Madison to Caesar A. Rodney, September 30, 1810, in Rodney Family Papers, Library of Congress. See also Madison to Armstrong, October 29, 1810, in Rokeby Collection, Barrytown-on-Hudson, New York.

48. Turreau's replacement as minister, Louis-Barbé-Charles, comte Sérurier, pictures Napoleon eagerly snatching the opportunity offered by Macon's Bill #2. Sérurier Papers, Centre de Microfilm des Archives de Seine et Oise, France, copy in Kent State University Library, Kent, Ohio, Reel #1, 18–19. Although cited as the Sérurier Papers, this collection is made up of a short manuscript (written probably in 1846) describing events leading to the War of 1812; the bulk of the papers is made up of official communications available in AMAE, LC.

49. For a sampling of opinion on Madison's decision, see Perkins, *Prologue to War*, 250–52; Patrick C. T. White, *A Nation on Trial: America and the War of 1812* (New York, 1965), 73, 79, 84; Irving Brant, *James Madison: The President, 1809–1812* (Indianapolis and New York, 1956), 214; Bonnel, *La France, les États-Unis et la guerre de course*, 273; Robert Lacour-Gayet, "Napoléon et les États-Unis," *Revue d'histoire diplomatique*, LXXXIII (1969), 301; Erskine to Canning, September 13, 1809, in FOA 5:63, LC.

British could not. They insisted that municipal rules were half measures; repeal had to be unconditional. In the summer of 1810, with the First Empire at its zenith, the time appeared propitious to test the British and the Americans. Macon's Bill #2 was a convenient instrument and Napoleon used it. His interest was in an Anglo-American confrontation; if a unilateral proclamation conditionally repealing the Berlin and Milan decrees would promote discord, Napoleon would have issued one regardless of the actions of the American Congress.

SIX

Interregnum

Late in 1810 John Armstrong re-
turned home enjoying high standing with the public and the administration alike. Among the general population the prevailing opinion was that
Armstrong had steadfastly defended America's interests. Resident "at the
court of the most despotic and mighty monarch the world has ever seen,"
one newspaper proclaimed, he had "acted with the firmness of a soldier and
spoke[n] with all the firmness and simplicity of a republican." His behavior
was in striking contrast to William Pinkney in London, who "like a spaniel
has fawned upon those who have kicked him." President James Madison
was pleased with Armstrong because the Cadore letter seemed to be a diplomatic wedge the United States might employ against Britain. The success
which seemed to crown Armstrong's mission was particularly gratifying
because it came when he had despaired of accomplishment. "We shall be all
packed off together," the minister had prophesied pessimistically in June,
1810. Weary and frustrated, the New Yorker had asked Madison to provide
transportation home for his wife and children the previous September; in
May, 1810, Robert Smith authorized the departure.[1] The Cadore message,
coming on the eve of Armstrong's long anticipated leavetaking, seemed like
a gift from heaven.

Even Armstrong's enemies appeared routed. Pinkney, whom he imagined conspiring against him in Britain, was stymied in his attempts to

1. *Kentucky Gazette*, September 25, 1810. Napoleon had called Pinkney a "haberdasher
of nouns & pronouns." Russell to Armstrong, June 27, 1811, in Russell Papers; Armstrong
to Russell, June 10, 1810, *ibid*; Armstrong to Madison, September 18, 1809, in Madison
Papers, LC; Smith to Armstrong, May 22, 1810, in Diplomatic Instructions of the Department of State, NA.

achieve a settlement. Skipwith, agent for prize cases in Paris, had been removed in 1808 and was living in the wilds near Baton Rouge in the newly acquired West Florida district. Armstrong had also fired Skipwith's successor, David Bailie Warden, an Irish-born family friend, for "calumny and ingratitude." Warden returned home to attack Armstrong and to seek another government position in France. He was, however, overshadowed by his erstwhile benefactor who was basking in the acclaim of his countrymen and being boomed for secretary of state, the presidency, and governor of Pennsylvania (where he planned to live).[2] Equating popularity with political influence, Armstrong began testing his standing by suggesting that Jonathan Russell be named the next United States minister to France.

[I]

Jonathan Russell was a thirty-nine-year-old native of Providence, Rhode Island. A graduate of Rhode Island College (Brown University), Russell became a merchant with global business connections, traveling to such exotic places as Buenos Aires and Calcutta. Although a successful businessman, Russell's real fascination was politics. In 1800 he threw himself into the political wars, writing a pro-Jeffersonian pamphlet that ran through twenty editions in a decade and earned him consideration for the editorship of a Republican newspaper in New York. Russell's zeal did not go unnoticed; he became acquainted with such luminaries as Levi Lincoln, Jefferson's first attorney general, and the redoubtable Aaron Burr.

Russell yearned for public office, and he expected to receive a diplomatic post in Britain or France. As positions in those countries were reserved for Republican notables, Russell was offered a less prestigious consulship in Tunis. He declined the marginal position. A less ambitious man would have acknowledged political reality and turned his attention to other matters, but Russell was cut from different cloth; personal satisfaction would come only through service in Paris or London. Thus he set about cultivating

---

2. "The most palpable and infamous lies are told of you here and have made some unfavorable impressions," a London source told Armstrong as he awaited transportation home. Armstrong to Russell, September 30, 1810, in Russell Papers, Brown University, entry of September 14, 1810, *ibid.* Armstrong to Warden, September 10, 1810, in Warden Papers. "Warden—poor wretch—came to me after your departure to explain and apologize for his conduct towards me—I wished he had kept away—he could say nothing about me that would give me half the pain I suffered at witnessing the mean & snivelling manner in which he cried [illegible]." Russell to Armstrong, September 23, 1810, in Russell Papers, Brown University; Lee to Mrs. Susan Palfrey Lee, December 12, 1810, in Mann, *A Yankee Jeffersonian*, 134; Morier to Wellesley, November 21, 1810, February 22, 1811, in FOA 5:70, 74, LC; Armstrong to Short, November 21, 1810, in Dreer Collection.

more powerful men, Armstrong and Samuel Smith being among the more noteworthy. In 1808, using the *nom de plume* Hancock, he authored a thirty-eight-page pamphlet entitled *The Whole Truth* attacking the Federalists and appealing for Madison's election. Shortly after Madison became president, presumably expecting a reward for his service, Russell solicited an appointment through Secretary of War William Eustis. For the second time he was frustrated: he was advised that it was an inauspicious moment to fill positions in France, Spain, or Portugal. While on business in the old Hanse city of Hamburg in 1810, Russell received the appointment he so ardently sought. Conveniently forgetting his heretofore unsuccessful officeseeking, Russell assured Armstrong that "I am ready to do whatever you desire and to set off for Paris three days after I receive your answer to this letter—but the acceptance of the trust which you repose in me is dictated by duty and not by ambition." Thus Russell became chargé d'affaires for the United States. Having told Armstrong that duty dictated his acceptance of the Paris post, Russell moved heaven and earth to become the next American minister to France. He assumed that Armstrong's popularity would be an asset in securing this plum in the American diplomatic establishment, and Armstrong promised to lend his support.[3]

Sad to say for Russell, he had little chance for an appointment. Madison was determined to dispatch the ablest talent to France to cement a permanent settlement with Napoleon, thereby freeing the United States to take whatever action necessary against Britain. While Russell's vigorous defense of American interests caused the Emperor to complain about the tone of his notes, he was by no stretch of anyone's imagination the best choice for the ministerial opening. As an American in Paris observed, "It is of the utmost consequence that we have in this country a minister of the first rate talents—he should be a man of information, shrewdness, address & no little intrigue, and speak the french language with [ease?]—this last is absolutely essential for English is as little known in Paris as Arabic." Russell fell short of these qualifications; he was too much a personal intriguer, too conniving and too obsequious, and his French was too limited. Armstrong's support killed whatever chances Russell had, however, for the former diplomat became a thorn in Madison's political hide during the winter of

3. Russell to Armstrong, July 15, 1810, in Russell Papers. No Russell biography exists; the sketch I have written draws mostly on the large collection of Russell Papers at Brown University; "Permit me to express my felicitation on your appointment made by Gen[era]l Armstrong which I am confident will be confirmed by the President," Samuel Smith wrote Russell on July 25, 1810, *ibid.*, ten days after Russell had accepted Armstrong's offer while in Hamburg. "I am a great favorite with both parties," Armstrong announced. "This cannot from its own nature be of much duration." Armstrong to Russell, November 18, 1810, *ibid.*

1810–1811. Unhappy with the Smiths who were also in Russell's camp and fearful of the Clinton faction in New York State, the President rightfully connected Armstrong with these wayward Republicans. Besides this, Madison's ears were ringing with public toasts to Armstrong's future as governor of Pennsylvania and president of the United States. A coolness soon separated the President from his former servant in France. Thus Armstrong told Russell that he had no chance of getting the French mission, claiming that the Rhode Islander had "no friends in the administration"; more to the point, Armstrong also admitted that his support had damaged Russell's candidacy.[4]

While Russell was learning the bitter truth from Armstrong, Joel Barlow made ready to leave his attractive home, Kalorama ("beautiful view"), to return to France. There was a good deal of irony in Barlow's being named Armstrong's replacement, not the least of which was Barlow's pronouncement in 1804 that he would never again set "foot in the land of the Corsican. I have disposed of the property I had there and have quitted with great joy a nation that had long become insupportable to me from the follies of the many and the rogueries of the few."[5] That was in 1804, though, and now, seven years later, Barlow's friend Madison had requested his services. Besides, Washington was a small and backward community compared to the majestic city of Paris where Joel and Ruth Barlow had lived many happy years.

Barlow was the most able American diplomat in France between Thomas Jefferson and Albert Gallatin. He knew the people and the land exceedingly well because he had lived in France most of the years from 1788 to 1804. He was fluent in the language, unlike his predecessor Armstrong or his successor, William H. Crawford. He was familiar with many of the ruling elite including Napoleon, whom he had met when the Corsican was a young artilleryman, and Hugues-Bernard Maret, duc de Bassano, Cadore's successor at the Foreign Ministry. Similarly he had been a fixture in the Franco-American community, and he was well known to many of its members including Lafayette and Daniel Parker. The Emperor had called Armstrong an "imbecile" and claimed that the envoy had erected a wall around himself, precluding adequate representation of America. He could not and he did not make similar assertions about Barlow.

---

4. John Rodman to Harmanus Bleecker, October 3, 1810, in Bleecker Papers; "General Armstrong is considered as a Man on whom no Dependence can be placed, and whom People are more afraid than desirous to be connected with, from his Character for Duplicity." Foster to Wellesley, July 18, 1811, in FOA 5:76, LC; Armstrong to Russell, "Private," March 5, 1811, in Russell Papers, Brown University.

5. Barlow to Abraham Baldwin, November 2, 1804, in Barlow Papers, Harvard.

Joel Barlow was a native of Redding, Connecticut. Graduating from Yale College in 1778, he spent a short time teaching school and then returned to Yale to study theology. Though he was not a minister, in 1780 Barlow departed for a chaplain's post in Washington's army where he whiled away most of his time reading and planning the writing of an epic poem. After leaving the army, the aspiring poet went to Hartford, Connecticut, where he became a member of the group called the Connecticut Wits, and fulfilled his dream by writing the *Vision of Columbus*. Although John Adams thought Barlow's poetry superior to John Milton's and despite the general acclaim of his countrymen, the Connecticut yankee could not make a living from his writing. Consequently, in late May, 1788, he boarded ship for a stormy voyage to France where he worked as an agent for the Ohio Company and the Scioto Associates, businessmen-speculators in Ohio lands. Among the prominent men involved in the great speculation were Jean Pierre Brissot de Warville, Étienne Clavière, William Duer, and Daniel Parker, who was "pleased with Barlow" because "he is a good man."[6]

Barlow lost interest in the Scioto project when revolution came to France in 1789. "It is really no small gratification to me to have seen two complete revolutions in favor of liberty," he happily wrote Ruth. Already possessing rather advanced ideas about society before he left America, the Connecticut native saw the French Revolution as a means to lift millions of people out of misery, poverty, and ignorance. As bloodshed marred the revolution and France went to war against almost all Europe, Barlow defended the great upheaval in various pamphlets and letters. After French citizenship had been conferred on him (along with Washington and Alexander Hamilton), he ran unsuccessfully for election to the National Convention in 1793.[7] Not all of Barlow's time and efforts were expended on

6. A month after his departure, proclaiming "my brain vibrates like a pendulum & my eye will scarcely follow my pen," Barlow described how "the Seasickness seized me the first day and continued to the last. The mouth of the Hudson claimed the first sacrifice of the contents of my stomach and that of the Seine was honored with the last. I hope the cup of Neptune has been sufficiently sweetened with the copious Libations of bile it received from my gall bladder, which I am sure was wrung to its last drop for more than a thousand times." Barlow to Duer, June 23, 1788, in William Duer Papers, New-York Historical Society; Parker to Craigie, August 6, 1788, in Craigie Papers.

7. Barlow to Ruth Barlow, July 28, 1789, Joel Barlow Papers, Beinecke Library, Yale University. Florence R. Fritz, "Joel Barlow's Early Deistic Liberalism: A Study of Radical Influences at Yale, 1774–1781" (Paper read before the Connecticut Historical Society, April 6, 1937, copy in Connecticut Historical Society), argues that Barlow's political liberalism antedated his French experiences. For another view, see Robert F. Durden, "Joel Barlow in the French Revolution," *William and Mary Quarterly*, Ser. 3, VIII (1951), 327–54; for Barlow's activities during the French Revolution, see Yvon Bizardel, *The First Expatriates: Americans in Paris During the French Revolution* (New York, 1975); Victor Clyde Miller, *Joel*

behalf of the Revolution, however. He dabbled in wartime commerce and sold foodstuffs to the French government, accumulating a small fortune. The versatile American also served the United States as a special emissary at the court of the Dey of Algiers and he lent his talents to healing the Franco-American split known as the Quasi-War.[8]

By any yardstick Joel Barlow was a success. He could have passed his life at ease among his circle of friends including Lafayette, Parker, and Robert Fulton. By the resumption of the Anglo-French war in 1803, however, Barlow was tired of the European scene, and he believed that the French Revolution had gone astray. Concerned about his cherished wife Ruth's health, approaching fifty, Barlow decided to return home; America, he told his brother-in-law, "tho' young, is growing old in wrong habits and prejudices, which have not yet become inveterate but will soon if not corrected."[9] Thomas Jefferson needed aid guiding the young nation and Barlow was ready to lend a helping hand.

Joel and Ruth Barlow wanted to settle in Connecticut upon their return to America. They discovered that their home state was a Federalist stronghold and that Barlow's participation in the French Revolution had turned friends into enemies. As Ruth later said, "had she known what reception they should have found in America, from their early and intimate friends— They should not have left Europe."[10] The Barlows were home, however,

---

Barlow: Revolutionist, London, 1791–92 (Hamburg, 1932); and M. Ray Adams, "Joel Barlow, Political Romanticist," *American Literature*, IX (1938), 113–52.

8. How much Barlow made is unknown. At his death he was worth a minimum of $80,000. See "Statement on Financial Affairs," October 26, 1812, in Barlow Papers; also Joseph Dorfman, "Joel Barlow: Trafficker in Trade and Letters," *Political Science Quarterly*, LIX (1944), 83–100; Milton Cantor, "Joel Barlow's Mission to Algiers," *The Historian*, XXV (1963), 172–94; see also Barlow's always interesting correspondence in Cantor (ed.), "A Connecticut Yankee in a Barbary Court: Joel Barlow's Algerian Letters to His Wife," *William and Mary Quarterly*, Ser. 3, XIX (1962), 86–109; William Stinchcombe, *The XYZ Affair* (Westport, Conn., 1980).

9. Barlow to Abraham Baldwin, January 3, 1801, in Barlow Papers, Harvard; also Leon Howard, "Joel Barlow and Napoleon," *Huntington Library Quarterly*, II (1938), 37–51; in an "Address to the Citizens of New Haven," given in October, 1805, Barlow declared that "our country must now be considered as the depository and the guardian of the best interests of mankind." Copy in Barlow Papers, Beinecke Library.

10. "The President keeps the marble bust of Barlow in his parlour—This is as disgusting to democratic as federal visitors." Unnamed and undated newspaper clipping, in Joel Barlow Papers, American Antiquarian Society, Worcester, Mass.; Ebenezer Sage to Henry P. Dering, January 16, 1810, in Dering Family Papers. The *National Intelligencer*, October 30, 1805, mentioned "a set of men pouring out a stream of billingsgate against the advocate of liberty [Barlow]," saying, "We perceive his writings tortured into meanings never intended." Still, the Barlows' reception was not completely hostile. See the "Address to the Citizens of New Haven," in Barlow Papers, Beinecke Library.

and so they located among newer and firmer friends in the new city of Washington. They built Kalorama, and they became fixtures in the Washington social scene. Life was pleasant for the childless couple; Ruth ran the household while Joel directed improvement on the grounds.[11] Occasionally he was called on to deliver a Fourth of July address or to write a rebuttal to a malcontent like Robert Smith after Smith's ouster from Madison's cabinet. In addition, Barlow revised the *Vision of Columbus*, calling it the *Columbiad*, and he gave considerable thought to writing a multivolume history of the United States, concentrating on the years since the Constitution, to refute the distortions of John Marshall and other Federalist literati. It seemed probable that the Barlows would pass the rest of their lives in Washington occupied with Kalorama and the company of their good friends, including the inseparable Fulton. "I am now in my own rural residence, which I consider as my last home and where I shall be happy to see you should I live till your return to your country," Barlow informed David Bailie Warden.[12]

Armstrong's resignation opened new vistas for "Homer," as some of his critics dubbed Barlow. At Barlow's urging, Fulton had suggested him for the leadership of the State or Navy departments in 1809.[13] Madison appointed others to these posts, but in 1811 the French vacancy seemed a natural position for Barlow. He was indubitably qualified and the only other candidate seriously mentioned for the Paris mission, Brockholst

11. "He has purchased a seat upon the summit of a high hill which overlooks George Town and 40 acres of farm. It is the handsomest seat I have seen in this part of the country, worth perhaps 40,000$," Congressman Sage wrote. "His home is surrounded by an oak forest except some avenues which give almost a birds view of Washington, George Town and many miles of the Powtowmak. He is making great improvements about his house and his plantation, his home is very richly furnished and his library which comes to about 4000 volumes, and which he has been 20 years collecting, I think must be a valuable one." Sage to Dering, Christmas [1809], in Dering Family Papers.

12. "It is now the great literary object of my life," Barlow to Elisha Babcock, October 25, 1809, Brainerd Collection, Connecticut Historical Society; see also Christine M. Lizanich, "'The March of this Government': Joel Barlow's Unwritten History of the United States," *William and Mary Quarterly*, Ser. 3, XXXIII (1976), 315–30; Barlow to Warden, April 28, 1808, in David Bailie Warden Papers, Library of Congress.

13. "He really considers himself as a new relation of Homer, though, judging from his Columbiad, I suppose in Elysium Homer will think Barlow's station sufficiently honorable as his boot-cleaner." Unnamed and undated newspaper clipping, in Barlow Papers, American Antiquarian Society; Barlow and Fulton thought very highly of each other. While Fulton was promoting Barlow (Fulton to Madison, January 28, February 17, 1809, in Madison Papers, LC), Barlow claimed national salvation on the high seas was through "the means of submarine attack, invented and proposed by one of our citizens [Fulton]." "Oration Delivered at Washington, July Fourth, 1809; at the Request of the Democratic Citizens of the District of Columbia," 13–14; see also Ruth Barlow to Cadwallader Colden, July 24, 1815, in Barlow Papers, Beinecke Library.

Livingston, was a member of the Livingston dynasty of which Madison was extremely wary. This being the case, the President asked Senate approval for the nomination of Joel Barlow as United States minister to France in February.

The Senate was full of surprises. Logically the Federalists should have been Barlow's major detractors; in fact, his nomination was warmly endorsed by the staunchest Federalist of all, Timothy Pickering. Barlow, he said, had been of "good character" before being seduced by France, "the Whore of Babylon which had polluted the World." Residence in France had enabled Barlow to master the French tongue and to acquire wealth which proved that "he understood the World as well as Poetry." While Pickering voted to confirm Barlow, Samuel Smith did not. Raging "like a madman," Smith overlooked Barlow's evident financial acumen and stormed that America needed a *"commercial man"* in France.[14] The Senate ignored Smith and an overwhelming number of Republicans joined a few Federalists to confirm Barlow.

The French were pleased with Barlow's appointment. They were happy to have a representative to their nation who knew its language, who had some standing in intellectual circles (a "new Franklin," Minister Sérurier speculated), and who obviously enjoyed high standing with Madison.[15] Consequently, anonymous tales questioning Barlow's beliefs made no impression on them. Some of the stories circulated about Barlow were inspired by Jonathan Russell in Paris where the ambitious Rhode Islander, embittered about being passed over for the ministerial post, denounced Barlow as

14. "Memorandum on Barlow's nomination," February 26, 1811, in Timothy Pickering Papers, Massachusetts Historical Society. William Lee claimed that he had helped persuade Pickering and his fellow Federalists James Lloyd and Nicholas Gilman to vote for Barlow. Lee to Mrs. Susan Palfrey Lee, March 6, 1811, in Mann, *A Yankee Jeffersonian*, 134–35; George W. Erving to James Bowdoin, March 11, 1811, in Bowdoin and Temple Papers. See also Charles Cutts to William Plumer, February 28, 1811, in Plumer Papers, LC; and Morier to Wellesley, March 3, 1811, in FOA 5:74, LC.

15. Sérurier to Cadore, March 1, 1811, and Sérurier to Cadore, n.d., but early 1811, in AMAE, LXV, LC; "Undoubtedly the best known American poet was Barlow." Echeverria, *Mirage in the West*, 233. The English generally regarded Barlow as an unrepentant Jacobin. A typical view was offered by William Playfair, a hack writer in London: "Returned to America he intrigued, and made his court to the president, whose hatred to England, and attachment to France, were not less than his own; and by that means he obtained his nomination as ambassador to Buonaparte." Playfair, *Political Portraits in the New Era*, I, 139. Playfair had helped Barlow organize the French end of the Scioto project. Amidst the troubles that wrecked the venture, according to Bizardel, *The First Expatriates*, 70, only Playfair "got out with his skin. Adept at pilfering and juggling the books, Playfair returned to England, where he soon became involved in counterfeiting, hoping that by ruining the value of French money, he could thereby undermine the Revolution."

"this pettifogging-canting cutthroat-fibbing doggerel philosopher . . . [who] stinks most rankly"; Russell alleged that aside from some old friends in France, "every report is said to be against him. He may be received but as to personal standing and personal influences he will be a non-entity."[16]

The validity of Russell's assertion was not tested immediately because Barlow remained in the United States another six months. The reason for the lengthy delay was simple: French actions and intent remained shrouded in mystery. Despite Cadore's August letter, American vessels were alternately seized or welcomed when they ventured into French ports. Disturbed by the inconsistency of the French, Madison decided even before Barlow's name was forwarded to the Senate for confirmation that the new envoy would remain home pending clarification of the status of the Berlin and Milan decrees. As weeks and then months went by, Russell on one side and the French on the other became increasingly upset by Barlow's absence from Paris. Russell fumed that Barlow's delayed arrival was "unaccountable" and "not only unkind and disrespectful to me but it affects injuriously the interests of the United States here." Through Minister Sérurier, the French asked how constructive negotiations could be conducted without a properly accredited diplomat in Russell's place. At this point, news from Paris indicated more generous treatment of American commerce and Sérurier voluntarily penned a favorable interpretation of French policy.[17] In light of these circumstances, Madison ordered Barlow to France.

As the first half of 1811 went by, Barlow became increasingly pessimistic about his mission. Aware of Napoleon's moodiness, the new envoy repeatedly expressed doubts about accomplishing anything. Moreover, in trying to achieve what probably was impossible, Barlow worried that he would sacrifice considerable personal wealth. Thoughts of death far from Kalorama and his new friends crossed his mind occasionally. The outlook

16. "Copie d'une Lettre ecrite par un Americaine a Son excellence le Duc de Bassano," June 20, 1811, in Russell Papers, Brown University. The letter may have been written by Russell's friend James Sloan; Sloan criticized Barlow in similar terms in a letter to Russell, December 14, 1811, *ibid*; Russell to Armstrong, June 27, 1811, *ibid*. Protesting the appointment of Benjamin Tupper (whom he deemed dishonest) as receiver of public monies at Marietta, Ohio, Russell linked Tupper with the Barlows—Mrs. Tupper and Ruth Barlow had been friends during Barlow's mission to Algiers. Russell to Albert Gallatin, May 31, 1804, in Jonathan Russell Papers, Massachusetts Historical Society.

17. Charles Cutts to Plumer, February 4, 1811, in Plumer Papers, LC; Monroe to Russell, June 8, 1811, in Russell Papers, Brown University; Samuel Welles to Russell, June 17, 1811, *ibid*. In another instance, Jefferson held up Robert Livingston's journey to France awaiting favorable action on the Convention of Môrtefontaine. Thornton to Grenville, March 28, 1801, in FOA 5:32, LC; Russell to John Spear Smith, August 9, 1811, in Russell Papers, Brown University; Sérurier to Bassano, July 10, 20, 1811, in AMAE, LXV, LC.

was bleak enough in April for him to confess that he was "heartily sick of the business before setting out, and wish I could retreat with honor." Doubt continued to fill Barlow's mind as he awaited his instructions. The chores and pleasures that filled his waking hours ranged from renting Kalorama to Sérurier (for $1,500 annually) to the gala festivities and parties in the Barlow home in the summer of 1811; none of these events dispelled the forebodings of Joel Barlow. From the deck of the U.S.S. *Constitution* in Hampton Roads, he continued ruminating. "The prospect of rendering any essential service to the public is by no means brilliant," he told Robert Fulton.[18]

Barlow carried instructions signed by the recently appointed secretary of state, his old friend James Monroe, who had given up the governorship of Virginia to join Madison's cabinet as Robert Smith's replacement. Smith's many deficiencies ranged from inadequacies in composing diplomatic correspondence to dissembling with the British and French ministers, but he had escaped Madison's censure thanks to the President's tolerance as well as Madison's apparent ignorance of Smith's deceitful nature.[19] Early in 1811, however, a Smith-Gallatin clash became inevitable when the majority of the Senate including Vice President Clinton rejected the rechartering of the Bank of the United States. An irate Gallatin ignored the various factors figuring in the vote and attributed defeat to Robert and Samuel Smith and their followers; briefly he submitted his resignation. Madison had to choose: he could release the hard-working, competent Gallatin and sacrifice the support of the Republican rank and file with whom the Pennsylvanian was most popular, or he could keep Gallatin and accept the loss of the Smith brothers and their allies.

In many ways the 1811 Smith-Gallatin squabble was a replay of what had transpired in 1809. Then Madison wanted Gallatin's service as secretary of state, but Virginia senator William Branch Giles, a violent oppo-

18. "It will be as nice a place to die in as any gentleman need to with, if I can be so lucky as to die here, & pretty soon, before it goes to decay, or into other hands," Barlow to Dearborn, August 14, 1809, in Fogg Collection; Barlow to Robert Fulton, April 8, 1811, in Joel Barlow Papers, Beinecke Library. See also Barlow to Henry Dearborn, April 11, 1811, in Henry Dearborn Papers, Massachusetts Historical Society; Barlow to Jefferson, May 2, 1811, in Jefferson Papers, LC; "Indenture" between Barlow and Sérurier, March 28, 1811, Barlow Papers, Beinecke Library; Barlow to Fulton, August 2, 1811, in Barlow Papers, Harvard University; Barlow to Dearborn, August 5, 1811, in Barlow Miscellaneous Manuscripts, New-York Historical Society.

19. "He wrote no part of the Correspondence with Mr. Jackson, I am sure," Benjamin Stoddert said of Smith. "Yet it is most likely he concealed from Madison, who is the Scribe in this Correspondence, the Knowledge he possessed of Erskine's Instructions and taught him to believe Erskine had other Instructions." Benjamin Stoddert to [?], December 6, 1809, copy in FOA 5:64, LC.

nent of the Swiss-born secretary, threatened "to raise the devil in [the] Senate and elsewhere and oppose the appointment." Informed sources claimed that Madison became "wrathy and declared he would nominate" Gallatin whatever the consequences. At this juncture, Gallatin enlisted Jefferson to reason with Madison, and the President judiciously sidestepped a confrontation by naming Robert Smith, a Giles favorite, to run the State Department.[20]

Ironically, Gallatin and Smith had been friendly once; indeed their families had been close socially. Robert Smith's inept handling of the Navy Department irritated Gallatin, however, and the treasury chief openly criticized Smith. Thus friendship turned into dislike and dislike into hatred; after one particular round of criticism from Gallatin, the infuriated Smith vowed that he would have "shot" his colleague "the next morning" except for circumstances.[21] Besides alienating Gallatin, Smith caused despair among Republicans who could not understand why Madison tolerated such a bungler. In 1809, Madison had kept Gallatin and Smith in the cabinet for harmony's sake; in 1811 the President chose Gallatin over Smith regardless of the consequences, telling the secretary of state that his conduct was no longer tolerable. For appearance's sake and to satisfy Smith, he was offered the ministry to Russia, but the stubborn and angry Marylander publicly rejected the position, announcing he would treat it "with silent contempt." Smith thereupon wrote an "Address to the People of the United States" intending to expose Madison as an incompetent French dupe.[22] The effort failed and Smith found he had committed suicide in the court of public opinion by attacking Madison, and he disappeared from public view until after the outbreak of the War of 1812 when he surfaced long enough to propose that "the *friends of peace*" organize themselves.[23] The suggestion attracted few if any followers and that was the last news of Robert Smith until his death in 1843.

20. Ebenezer Sage to Henry P. Dering, January 18, 1810, in Dering Family Papers. Sage almost certainly heard this story from Barlow. See also the entry of June 22, 1809, in Copy of Diary of John Randolph of Roanoke, Bruce-Randolph Collection, Virginia State Library.

21. Cited in Stagg, "James Madison and the 'Malcontents,'" 562.

22. "Smith's fall was complete, the Russian mission was a fiction to serve a few days as a parachute, and published in the intelligencer at his request." Barlow to Robert Fulton, April 8, 1811, in Barlow Papers, Beinecke Library. Barlow was a trusted confidant of Madison and is a more reliable source than Smith. See also Robert Smith to Samuel Smith, March 22, 1811, in Samuel Smith Papers, Library of Congress; "The mission to Russia was exactly like Madison," in Nathaniel Macon's opinion. "He cannot yet say no quite easy enough or go about your own affairs." Macon to Joseph H. Nicholson, September 21, 1811, in Nicholson Papers. The "address" appeared in the *National Intelligencer*, July 2, 1811.

23. Smith to Harrison Gray Otis, July 22, 1812, in Harrison Gray Otis Papers.

While Smith lived in obscurity, James Monroe ran the State Department and then the War Department before succeeding Madison as president in 1817. Yet when Senator Richard Brent of Virginia delivered Madison's offer to head the State Department, Monroe hesitated, professing that "the bias of my mind is against it" because it was probably too late to change the administration's foreign policy. Monroe feared he would be forced to support measures which he had already publicly disapproved, thereby damaging his reputation as a somewhat politically independent Republican and jeopardizing his political future.[24] Obviously the former envoy to Britain, who had been at odds with Madison since the rejection of the Monroe-Pinkney treaty, viewed the Virginia gubernatorial position as a better springboard to national office.

A cooler, more calculating mind prevailed in the person of Littleton Waller Tazewell, a young Virginian who possessed considerable political wisdom. As early as 1808 Tazewell advised Monroe that his political stock would be enhanced nationally if he opposed Senator Giles in the election that year. Now Tazewell urged his friend to accept Madison's offer of a cabinet position provided the President respected Monroe's judgment; Tazewell reasoned that if Madison refused, Monroe's independence would strengthen his prestige in "the community." Tazewell thought that the country was not in the dire straits many believed and that since Monroe could draw on a fund of goodwill in Great Britain, he might be the key to a settlement with that power. Assuming an Anglo-American accord caused war with France, Tazewell serenely forecast little discontent in the United States. Lest Monroe feel guilty about leaving the governorship, Tazewell consoled him "as to the government of Virginia which you occupy, it was confered [sic] upon you for the public benefit, and if the public good can be more promoted by your abandoning [it] than [remaining in] it, I consider it as your duty to resign it." Without further urging, the ambitious Monroe joined the Madison administration, telling a relative he did so because of the nation's critical problems and because he wanted to promote harmony in the Republican party.[25]

24. Monroe to Littleton Waller Tazewell, March 14, 1811, in Monroe Papers, LC.

25. Tazewell to Monroe, December 30, 1808, *ibid.*; Tazewell to Monroe, March 17, 1811, *ibid*; like Tazewell, Monroe's son-in-law favored a settlement with Britain "even at the hazard of an immediate war with France," thinking that there was nothing to lose as "we have no trade with France." George Hay to Monroe, April 22, 1811, *ibid.*; Monroe to Joseph Monroe, March 29, 1811, in Monroe Papers, New York Public Library. Samuel Smith offered another view of his brother's forced departure: "The object was it is believed to prepare the way for Mr. Monroe to be Successive to Mr. M." Samuel Smith to Mary Mansfield, April 1, 1811, in Carter-Smith Family Papers.

Monroe's appointment was generally well received around the nation. Federalists were happy because they believed Monroe would be civil to the new English minister, Augustus John Foster. Republicans were overjoyed because their party seemed strengthened. Even the ordinarily critical George Logan praised Monroe's selection because in Logan's mind the Virginian would protect the best interests of the United States.[26] Monroe did not have the high qualifications that former president John Adams established for a secretary of state, but few men did, and he proved to be a competent subordinate for Madison. Sérurier accurately characterized him as capable, honorable, and patriotic.[27] That was more than could be said of Robert Smith.

France also was changing diplomatic personnel in 1810 and 1811. Louis Turreau left Washington amidst rumors that the Emperor was disturbed about the general's relationship with Jerome Bonaparte's former wife, Elizabeth Patterson Bonaparte.[28] The truth was that Napoleon had decided that his longtime and faithful servant should be replaced during the winter of 1809–1810, just when Turreau was enjoying a modicum of popularity.

Louis-Barbé-Charles, comte Sérurier, was named Turreau's replacement on September 11, 1810. Although chosen for the American post in September, Sérurier did not sail for North America until December 30. In the interim, as he had done before assuming his post in Holland five years previously, Sérurier familiarized himself with the current status of Franco-American relations, learning that the Berlin and Milan edicts had been repealed conditionally but that the measures would remain in force until the Emperor was satisfied with reciprocity from the United States. He discovered from conversations with Russell that the Americans were obsessed

26. Logan to Monroe, May 14, 1811, in Gratz Collection, Historical Society of Pennsylvania. Jonathan Russell was outraged at the prospect of Monroe succeeding Smith: "I will not believe it. There can be no policy in taking up this heavy animal, he has fallen by the mere force of gravitation and it would be sinning against the laws of nature to attempt his elevation," Russell to Armstrong, December 7, 1810, in Russell Papers, Brown University. Years earlier, Senator John Cotton Smith had contemplated Monroe's career: "Yes, I shall not think it strange if Monroe, stupid and powerless as he is, should by the aid of this war . . . finish his diplomatic career with more eclat than any negotiator of modern times." John Cotton Smith to David Daggett, December 27, 1804, David Daggett Papers, Sterling Library, Yale University.

27. Sérurier to Cadore [March 5?], March 26, April 10, 1811, in AMAE, LXV, LC. The English diplomat Morier predicted Monroe's rise would not alter Anglo-American relations because Monroe "accepted of the Situation from Need, and not under any Condition to retain his Principles, which were at one Time friendly to us." Morier to Wellesley, May 9, 1811, in FOA 5:74, LC.

28. B. Smith to John Spear Smith, December 24, 1810, in Samuel Smith Papers.

with the status of these decrees, yet he could relay no more information on the subject after his arrival in America than Turreau had.[29] Despite this shortcoming and despite the lack of any fresh initiative, Sérurier readily understood that the central purposes of his mission were to parry any type of Anglo-American rapprochement and to promote a rupture between the two English-speaking countries.

A nephew of one of the Emperor's prominent field commanders, Sérurier moved to Washington from Holland. Only thirty-five years old, he had been schooled in Napoleon's diplomatic service; he had been successively secretary of the French mission in Cassel, then chargé and first secretary in Holland, and now envoy to the United States. "Your majesty has been very satisfied with his conduct," Champagny reminded Napoleon on the eve of Sérurier's American appointment. Sérurier continued to please the Emperor thereafter; he was a more charming, polished, and shrewd representative than Turreau. Like his predecessor, he was unquestionably loyal to Napoleon; as Jonathan Russell observed, Sérurier "is devoted to the service of his master and this devotion will form the rule of his conduct." Unlike Turreau, the youthful French diplomat was a popular figure in Washington throughout his tenure, "much esteemed by the President and by the officers of our Government," in striking contrast with another youthful minister, Augustus John Foster.[30]

Sérurier was also popular with members of the opposite sex, particularly Eliza Custis, a passionate Francophile who was separated from her husband. In one of her more astonishing letters, the thirty-four-year-old granddaughter of Martha Washington claimed "S must marry one of our ladies who can win his heart, and who has influences in our Country—this with the liberal treatment which I hope their great Emperor will show us, will make us all friends to the French." Reflecting for a moment, she added, "I know not where S will find a woman to engage his affections, but if *he* could

29. "Extrait des Ministres de la Secretaire d' Etat du Palais de St. Cloud," September 11, 1810, in AMAE, LXIII, LC, where Sérurier's name is misspelled Sérrurier; Cadore to Sérurier, October 4, 1810, and Sérurier to Cadore, November 7, 1810, March 4, 1811, all *ibid.*, LXIII–LXV. For reports on the Russell-Sérurier conversations, see Sérurier to Cadore, November 7, 1810, *ibid.*, LXIII; and Russell to Smith, November 17, 1810, in Russell Papers, Brown University.

30. Quoted in Whitcomb, *Napoleon's Diplomatic Service*. 55; see also *ibid.*, 54, 67–69, for details about Sérurier's career; Russell to Smith, September 27, 1811, in Despatches from France, NA; Eliza Custis to David Bailie Warden, July 29, 1811, in Warden Papers, Maryland Historical Society. Reflecting Sérurier's standing, Monroe asked *National Intelligencer* publisher Joseph Gales to print a favorable notice about him when Napoleon returned to power. Monroe to Gales, July 21, 1815, in Monroe Papers, New York Public Library.

be made happy by such an event, it would be desirable as it would unite our people to him." Reflecting a little longer, Eliza Custis decided she could win Sérurier's heart, although Ruth Barlow "constantly warns me against the dangers of loving S and urges me to shun his society, *I will not do this. I will be his friend, and do him all the service in my power.*"[31]

The second diplomatic personnel change occurred when Hugues-Bernard Maret, duc de Bassano, replaced Champagny, duc de Cadore, as foreign minister. Champagny opposed Napoleon's commercial policy and he was disturbed by the deterioration of Franco-Russian relations. Moreover, Napoleon found Champagny's administration of foreign affairs deficient. Consequently, Bassano moved into the foreign ministry on April 17. The forty-eight-year-old Bassano had been active in government since Napoleon's rise to power, participating in negotiations at Tilsit, Bayonne, Erfurt, and Vienna; during the Revolution he had also been involved in diplomacy. While Bassano had much diplomatic experience, he knew little of the United States. Thus Russell could write, "While he appears to be more affable and unreserved [than Cadore], it is equally difficult to collect from his conversation the real intention of his Government." Even if Bassano had been familiar or sympathetic with America's neutrality problems, there is no evidence he could have altered French policy.[32]

[II]

A month after acknowledging French compliance with Macon's Bill #2, President Madison delivered his second annual message. Alluding to the apparent repeal of the Berlin and Milan decrees, Madison told the Congress he had assumed sequestered American property would be restored immediately; "this expectation had not been fulfilled," he reported soberly. Madison chose not to divulge evidence which made the French position perfectly clear: Napoleon claimed that the non-intercourse law had damaged French commerce and the Emperor also alleged that French vessels had been seized in accord with the law's provisions. Indeed, Cadore had warned

31. See William D. Hoyt, Jr., "Self-Portrait: Eliza Custis, 1808," in *Virginia Magazine of History and Biography*, LIII (1945), 89–100; Eliza Custis to David Bailie Warden, July 29 and 31, 1811, in Warden Papers, Maryland Historical Society. Sérurier eventually wed the daughter of a refugee from San Domingo; Vice President Elbridge Gerry described her as "sensible, sprightly & pretty; with all delicate." Gerry to Mrs. Gerry, November 4, 1814, Elbridge Gerry Papers, Massachusetts Historical Society.

32. See Whitcomb, *Napoleon's Diplomatic Service*, 27–28, 140; Baron Ernouf, *Maret, Duc de Bassano* (Paris, 1878), 289; Albert Sorel, *L'Europe et la Révolution Française* (8 vols.; Paris, 1914), VII, 535–36; and Masson, *Le départment des affaires étrangères*, 242–43; Russell to Smith, April 25, 1811, in Despatches from France, NA.

Armstrong, "*If you confiscate French property under the law of non-intercourse, they will confiscate your property under their decree of Rambouillet.*" Of course, there had been no interference with Napoleon's flag vessels in international waters for the simple reason that the Royal Navy had swept the ocean clear of French merchant shipping. While privateers operated in American waters and entered American ports, none of these ships had been confiscated. In any case, the President knew that there was no basis for comparison between the millions of francs worth of American merchandise seized because of the numerous Napoleonic decrees and the damages reputedly suffered by the French.[33] Publicly the President said little about these contradictory actions; privately he was not so reserved, and he periodically vented his vexation with the French. Nonetheless, Madison was convinced that it was the British who caused America the most grief, and so he held fast to his plan for economic restrictions against the English unless the orders in council were relaxed.

The English did not relent, however. Instead, refusing to accept France's contention that the Berlin and Milan decrees could be partially abandoned, they demanded that the French unconditionally repeal their edicts. The British also wondered aloud why the Americans were still protesting against these measures if they no longer applied to the United States. "It is evident that the greatest Mortification is felt by this Government and its Adherents at the Conduct of their Friends the French," John Morier observed. Ridiculing America's military weakness, scorning the recent takeover of West Florida, and laughing at the general helplessness of the new nation, Morier, like many Englishmen, saw America's salvation in uniting "their Fate with that of Great Britain," not in resorting to commercial restrictions.[34]

By February, 1811, it was obvious that the British would not budge and that non-importation was in order. Seeing the handwriting on the wall, desperate Federalists denounced further economic restrictions as the fulfillment of a contract with France; it was more than coincidental, the Federalists charged, that non-importation should be considered just as Sérurier

33. "Second Annual Message," December 5, 1810, in Hunt (ed.), *Writings of Madison,* VIII, 123–24; Armstrong to Smith, September 12, 1810, in Despatches from France, NA; Daniel Parker to William Short, September 25, 1810, in Short Papers; Heath, *Napoleon I and the Origins of the Anglo-American War of 1812,* 128–29, estimates seizures valued at $10,000,000 under the Rambouillet decree alone.

34. Morier to Wellesley, February 14, 1811, in FOA 5:74, LC; Josiah Quincy, also assailed Madison's Florida policy: "We want West Florida. Our Western brethen will have West Florida. By G— we will take West Florida. By G— it is in the title deed." Quincy to William Sullivan, December 21, 1810, in Washburn Papers, Massachusetts Historical Society.

appeared in Washington. Lashing out at the new French envoy as the *"Minister of rapine and murder,"* they labeled non-importation legislation "the Sérurier Act" and they jeered Madison as Napoleon's faithful vassal. These verbal fireworks obscured a growing sentiment that something must be done, that even war must be risked because as an Ohio resident wrote, "a temporary warfare might have a Salutary influence on our Country."[35]

The Federalists were more accurate when they argued that American shipping in French ports was harried and that contrary to administration expectations, Franco-American trade had not grown. John Armstrong himself had pointed out that "the heavy Duties and the Fees will make it [Franco-American commerce] a total Loss to the Proprietors." Merchants rejected the French trade because of the First Empire's capricious treatment of neutrals, and skepticism was widespread that commerce would ever flourish in an atmosphere characterized by an "arrangement" with only one of the belligerents. This is not to say that vessels did not clear for France because many did despite the risks: some experienced no delays in unloading or loading cargoes and clearing ports immediately, while others encountered difficulties which involved lengthy delays and tiring battles with the ponderous Napoleonic bureaucracy. Sometimes the French would seize vessels and cargoes on the pretext that both were English. Since the British employed the American flag to penetrate the Continental System, the French regularly made mistakes when they sought to halt this traffic. Even if no troubles were encountered making the voyage to France and getting past the red tape and whims of Gallic officialdom, the French generally dictated what could be exported.[36] In light of these circumstances, Franco-American trade remained negligible.

At the end of February the Republicans overwhelmed the opposition and approved non-importation after a tumultuous House session lasting many hours. "I believe the house never approached nearer to being a riotous assembly," Charles Cutts, an incredulous witness, revealed. "The Speaker

35. Nathaniel Macon heard "that the new French [minister] would not give any information relating to repeal of [the] Berlin & Milan decrees." Macon to Nicholson, February 18, 1811, in Nicholson Papers; Sérurier to Bassano, April 20, 1811, in AMAE, LXII, LC; See also Georges de Caraman, "Les Etats-Unis il y a quarante ans," *Revue Contemporaine,* III (1852), 212; Samuel Finley to Thomas Worthington, February 2, 1811, in Richard C. Knopf (comp.), *Thomas Worthington and the War of 1812* (Columbus, Ohio, 1957), 4.

36. Morier to Wellesley, November 21, 1810, in FOA 5:70, LC; "That any prosperous commerce will proceed from any arrangement that had been or will be made with either of the Belligerents I do not believe—Any effect it may have in advancing the price of American exports will be temporary." David Winchester to James Winchester, November 4, 1810, in Winchester Papers, Tennessee Historical Society; "Decret," May 2, 1811, in AMAE, LXIV, LC.

could not keep order[.] Several times he ordered members down who told him they would not sit down[.] At length it became apparent that the opposition were determined to talk out the Session rather than let the bill pass and that they had made arrangements." Like earlier restrictive legislation, non-importation was ambivalent. Under the law which became effective on March 2, the importation of British goods in British bottoms was illegal, yet American ships could still sail to England carrying American merchandise and return with English manufactures, at least until April. If the law was imperfect, however, the intent was obvious: Britain was not respecting American neutrality as much as France was or professed to be. Therefore Great Britain would be penalized economically until she too was more considerate of the United States. If the British refused, the Congress would have to consider other options. "The United States must submit to abject, servile colonization, or call into action the national energies to vindicate the rights, and redress the wrong and insults which have been inflicted on us by that haughty and faithless government," Mississippian George Poindexter explained.[37] Poindexter and his colleagues then disbanded and returned to their respective homes, not to return to Washington until November.

[III]

As Congress adjourned, Jonathan Russell was midway through his yearlong stint as chargé d'affaires in Paris. The months had been difficult for the aspiring minister because he had been buffeted by both personal and public hardships. Russell's wife had died. Then the former merchant had been embarrassed and humiliated when the President chose Barlow as Armstrong's successor. His letters, some of which were read by the French police, reflected his disappointment and were increasingly filled with vitriolic denunciations of Barlow, Monroe, and Pinkney. Most distressing of all, though, was the state of his mission to France.

In September, 1810, Russell expressed a restrained optimism about Franco-American relations and the termination of the Berlin and Milan decrees. Thereafter the situation deteriorated. In October, Russell complained to Cadore about the French tariff schedule; in November, the

37. Cutts to Plumer, February 28, 1811, in Plumer Papers, LC. Morier's description of the proceedings was that "the Non-Importation Act against Great Britain was passed amidst the *drunken* Shouts of the Majority in the House of Representatives at five O'Clock in the Morning of the 28th of February," Morier to Wellesley, March 3, 1811, in FOA 5:74, LC; *Statutes at Large*, 651–52; Poindexter to [?], March 3, 1811, in J. F. H. Claiborne Collection.

Rhode Islander was uncertain about the repeal of the Berlin and Milan edicts; in December, he confessed to Armstrong that "we are still in the dark here with regard to the real intentions of this government as to the manner of performing the promise to you."[38]

Russell knew that Napoleon alone could settle outstanding issues, but the Emperor was usually absent from his capital. His subordinates could only assert what they thought their master meant or, like Bassano, obfuscate that a certain French pronouncement *"spoke for itself"* when, in fact, it did not. The foreign minister was certainly aware of American wishes, for Russell constantly bombarded him with notes as did Turreau and Sérurier from Washington. The theme of these messages was monotonously familiar: treat the United States fairly and the Americans would then be able to focus their full attention on Great Britain. Yet, Bassano was intimidated by Napoleon and, like many other members of the French government, fearful of an imperial outburst, shrank from asking unwanted questions or divulging unwanted information. As long as France was governed by an autocrat, the exasperated Russell warned Smith, Franco-American relations would be "precarious and uncertain." Typically Napoleon was indifferent or even hostile toward the United States, Russell recounted, but following news about the clash between H.M.S. *Little Belt* and the U.S.S. *President* on May 16, 1811, the French ruler heaped praise on America, telling Russell at a reception, "You are going to fight the English it seems." Russell replied coolly, "It seems so." Napoleon tried again, rephrasing his first comment, "You are going to have war with England." Russell offered an evasive "I don't know"; the Emperor, who disliked Russell, repeated a familiar theme: "Either you will be an English colony or you will defend your flag" and walked off. Angered by such an attitude and tired of French equivocation, Russell warned Bassano that as eager as Napoleon was for an Anglo-American war, "we are not sufficiently dull to be deceived by this kind of management." To a friend, Russell wondered "how long the representative of a great free & independent nation is—for the want of a proper manifestation of its strength—& spirit—to be exposed to such insolence[?]"[39]

Pessimism enveloped Russell in 1811. Consequently, though advised

38. Russell to Armstrong, December 7, 1810, in Russell Papers, Brown University. See also Russell to Armstrong, September 28, 1810, Russell to Cadore, October 1, 1810, and Russell to Pinkney, November 1, 1810, *ibid.*

39. Russell to Smith, December 4, 1810, *ibid*; Russell to John Spear Smith, August 2, 1811, in Samuel Smith Papers. For similar Napoleonic pronouncements concerning America's defense of its neutral rights, see Russell to Smith, April 4, 1811, in Russell Papers, Brown University; Russell to Smith, January 29, April 15, 1811, in Despatches from France, NA; *National Intelligencer*, June 6, 1811; Russell to Monroe, "private and confidential," July 13, 1811, in Russell Papers, Brown University.

that the collector in Bordeaux said the Berlin and Milan decrees were not applicable to American shipping, Russell suggested that property owners should proceed as if Franco-American relations were about to be broken. Late in March he advised Robert Smith that France's aim "at this moment is the entire destruction of our external commerce." To an intimate friend, Russell was even more candid: "For God's sake advocate vigorous measures be firm—decided—energetic and if possible haul up the drowning honor of our country by the locks." Not surprisingly the Rhode Islander dismissed as "hardly worth while" an Anglo-American war if it was designed to preserve trade with France. Russell predicted that Joel Barlow's arrival would make no difference. "I believe that our affairs will continue in the present uncertain—equivocal and non-descript situation."[40]

Russell's final frustration was Aaron Burr. The disgraced former vice president had fled to Europe using an alias during the summer of 1808. Burr's intentions are still not understood: his defenders claim that he arrived in Paris with dreams of freeing Spanish America; his critics believe his aim was to plot the dismemberment of the Western Hemisphere among Britain, France, and Spain.[41] Like so many of the activities that involved the enigmatic New York politician, shadows obscure what Burr referred to as his "projects." While surviving French records indicate that Burr was thinking about freeing Spanish-controlled territory adjoining the United States, Armstrong discovered in June and July, 1810, that Burr's acquaintance, the powerful minister of police, Joseph Fouché, had been dismissed from his office by Napoleon for participating in a plan to make peace with Britain. What particularly interested Armstrong was that the central feature of the peace proposal, the splitting of North and South America between the two great belligerents, sounded like something inspired by Burr.[42]

40. Russell to Samuel Smith, February 16, 1811, in Russell Papers, Brown University; Russell to Robert Smith, March 26, 1811, *ibid*; Russell to George Blake, March 28, 1811, *ibid*. "I am riding here on rather a tempestuous sea—but it is not exactly the sea of liberty." Russell to Armstrong, March 26, 1811, *ibid*; Russell to Samuel Smith, June 29, 1811, *ibid*. Russell to Sylvanus Bourne, June 2, 1811, in Sylvanus Bourne Papers, Library of Congress.

41. See Julius W. Pratt, "Aaron Burr and the Historians," *New York History*, XXVI (1945), 447–70. For examples of recent pro-Burr writings, see Samuel Engle Burr, Jr., *Napoleon's Dossier on Aaron Burr: Proposals of Col. Aaron Burr to the Emperor Napoleon* (San Antonio, 1969); and Walter Flavius McCaleb, *New Light on Aaron Burr* (Austin, 1963).

42. "Colonel Burr's project," March 1, 12, 19, 1810, in AMAE, LXIII, LC; Armstrong to Smith, June 7, July 15, 1810, Despatches from France, NA; Brant, *James Madison: The President, 1809–1812*, 180. In a journal entitled "Retrospect of Sixteen happy days followed by sorrow much after the fashion of life" at Armstrong's home, Rokeby, is the following entry: "The veteran [Armstrong] said that Fouche, who was very candid, acquainted him with all Burr's overtures to the French Government. The object of these, it seems, South America."

Following Fouché's fall, the penniless Burr lost hope for his grandiose schemes and he requested a passport to return home to New York.[43] The document was not forthcoming; as he told his daughter, he received "fair promises and civil words . . . but nothing more." At first Burr thought the Emperor was seriously considering his projects and the lack of a passport did not bother him. As the fall and then the winter came, Burr became desperate and he implored David Bailie Warden, Alexander McRae, and then Russell to expedite his passport request. Warden was brusque, McRae cool, and Russell moralistic as each diplomat in turn spurned Burr. "The man who evades the offended laws of his country abandons for the time the right to their protection," Russell lectured Burr.[44]

Russell was actually in a predicament concerning Burr. He knew the former New York Republican chief and he had corresponded with Vice President Burr on patronage affairs. The two men had been close enough for Burr to pen a letter of introduction on Russell's behalf. Then came Burr's famous duel with Alexander Hamilton and this episode was followed by Burr's bizarre adventures in the West, culminating in his treason trial before Chief Justice John Marshall in Richmond. Russell had had nothing to do with Burr during these affairs and the Rhode Islander, believing he might be made minister to France, was not about to alienate Madison or Jefferson by accommodating Burr in the winter of 1810–1811. Suddenly and inexplicably and before Russell knew of the Senate's confirmation of Barlow, Burr received his passport. Russell did not disclose why the document was issued, but it appears that he feared public disclosure of his relationship with a Frenchwoman by Bassano, another Burr acquaintance; given the choice of granting Burr his passport and avoiding mortifying revelations about his private life, or risking Jefferson's and Madison's wrath, Russell chose the former course.[45]

43. When Barlow alluded to Burr's plan for the division of the Western Hemisphere two years later, Madison remarked, "If such a plan was really favored by the two powers, was it not with a view in each to dupe the other into a war with the U.S. a successful and satisfactory division of the spoil could not be seriously counted on by either." Marginalia on Barlow to Madison, September 26, 1812, Madison Papers, LC.

44. Burr to Theodosia Burr, November 10, 1810, in Mark Van Doren (ed.), *Correspondence of Aaron Burr and His Daughter Theodosia* (New York, 1929), 314; McRae had been active at Burr's Richmond trial; in 1812 he told John Sevier that Burr was acquainted with Fouché and drawing an income of $2,000 from the French, that Burr was really a British spy, and that Burr had proposed the division of America. "Memo," written between January 8–12, 1812, in John H. DeWitt, "Some Unpublished Letters of John Sevier to his Son, George Washington Sevier," *Tennessee Historical Magazine*, VI (1920), 62; "Correspondence with Burr," November 4, 1810, in Russell Papers, Brown University.

45. Jonathan Russell to Aaron Burr, June 26, 1801, in Worthington C. Ford (ed.), "Some Papers of Aaron Burr," *American Antiquarian Society Proceedings*, n.s., XXIX (1919), 105–106; Burr to Dr. Dumont, August 1, 1803, in Russell Papers, Brown Univer-

Because of other problems Burr did not return to America until the eve
of the declaration of war against Britain in June, 1812. By that time
Jonathan Russell had forgotten the frustrations of his year in France and was
suffering through the trying task of representing the United States in Britain. In France, Joel Barlow was pressing the French for a far-reaching settlement of Franco-American differences.

sity; Burr to Russell, August 1, 1803, *ibid*; McCaleb, *New Light on Aaron Burr*, 155–56;
and Nathan Schachner, *Aaron Burr: A Biography* (New York, 1937), 488. While McCaleb
and Schachner were zealous Burrites, I have found nothing to indicate that they erred in
discussing Burr's acquisition of a passport.

SEVEN

Neither Peace nor War

Congressmen hoping for and expecting a clarion call for action by President James Madison when the First Session of the Twelfth Congress gathered in November, 1811, were sorely disappointed by his Third Annual Message. Instead of denouncing the great belligerents, Madison delivered a scholarly analysis in which he dispassionately discussed the state of Anglo-American and Franco-American relations: Great Britain refused to lift her orders in council and British warships were prowling American waters. Continuing his familiar tale, Madison explained that while America acted in good faith toward France, the French were not as generous to the United States. Indeed, at the moment it seemed that France intended to retain seized American property.

Although lacking flair and devoid of any startling announcement, it was obvious that, barring a diplomatic breakthrough, Madison expected Congress to recognize the inevitability of hostilities with the English. Thus more time was devoted to America's troubles with Britain than with France, and the President mentioned Joel Barlow's French mission in a manner suggesting that a settlement with Napoleonic France was attainable. Madison reminded the assembled legislators that "no independent nation can relinquish" its rights, and he expressed confidence that the "Congress will feel the duty of putting the United States into an armor and an attitude demanded by the crisis, and corresponding with the national spirit and expectations."[1]

1. "Third Annual Message," November 5, 1811, in Richardson (comp.), *Messages and Papers of the Presidents*, I, 476–79. Sérurier observed that some onlookers felt the message a declaration of war against Britain. Sérurier to Bassano, November 5, 1811, in AMAE, LXVI, LC.

The "*Congress will feel the duty.*" This was a statement of pure Madisonian philosophy. The executive branch would not usurp the legislative branch's authority and responsibility; rather, in a democratic republic, the representatives of the people deliberated and decided. If the populace saw war as the only solution remaining, then their delegates would agree with the President and vote for hostilities. "I wish much that we made a mild, calm, firm stand from 1792 against all deviations from the Law of Nations," one citizen wrote in 1807.[2] In 1811, the time had come. The United States could be pushed no further. It was the moment for congressional action.

The Congress was not of one mind, however. True, there were men like thirty-two-year-old John Adams Harper from New Hampshire who were positive that there would be an "*arrangement,* or an actual *war* with Great Britain" before adjournment. There were also representatives like Peleg Tallman from the coastal town of Bath, Maine, who were appalled by these warlike attitudes. "They seem willing to take a violent stand against any land, in contempt of the consequences," he complained of men like Harper. Prowar zealots, Tallman explained on another occasion, lived in a dream world. They assumed that in case of war Britain's North American possessions would be easy pickings and that trade with France would mushroom, with the duties from this traffic offsetting revenue lost from the collapse of Anglo-American commerce. The majority of congressmen were like Kentuckian Joseph Desha, more upset with Britain than France, but extremely wary of war. Familiar with this hesitancy, George Poindexter, a delegate from Mississippi Territory, noted that "all agree *that something must be done.*" Knowledgeable also of the snaillike pace of the Congress, and recalling the nation's propensity for economic coercion, Poindexter feared "we shall have non-intercourse until the nation will be overrun with *Old maids* and witches."[3] Poindexter's worry was groundless. The Congress would act, but not in a hasty fashion. Much like the President himself, most congressmen wanted peace. Like Madison, they too would conclude eventually there was no alternative to armed conflict, and a little less than seven months after hearing the President's less than stirring speech, the Twelfth Congress would be considering a declaration of war against Great Britain.

[I]

As observed earlier in this study, historians have not been kind to James Madison. From John Bach McMaster to Bradford Perkins the Virginian has

2. Tench Coxe to Albert Gallatin, August 11, 1807, quoted in Richard J. Mannix, "The Embargo: Its Administration, Impact, and Enforcement" (Ph.D. dissertation, New York University, 1975), 31.

3. Harper to William Plumer, December 2, 1811, in Clifford L. Egan (ed.), "The Path

been characterized generally as a colorless, meek, and vacillating states-man. A commonly accepted view holds that Madison was cajoled, threat-ened, even forced to accept hostilities in 1811 – 1812. "The ridiculous agi-tation of the War Hawks on the subject was too much for his enfeebled constitution; he gave way and went to war in most unfavorable circum-stances," one unfriendly critic has explained. Among the historians exam-ining the war's origins, only Roger Brown portrays Madison as a forceful leader; in fact, Brown maintains that the President "made up his mind to recommend war measures" between August 23 and September 6, 1811.[4] Brown may be accurate narrowing the time of decision to this two-week period. On the other hand, Madison may have decided even earlier but waited to discuss his conviction until James Monroe visited him during that fortnight. Whatever the precise time, strong circumstantial evidence exists to support Brown's contention that almost a year before war was declared and two to four months before the Twelfth Congress met, Madison accepted the inevitability of conflict.

Certainly the President sensed the widespread discontent permeating the country. His favorite reading matter, Joseph Gales's *National Intel-ligencer* (which began displaying an American eagle at the top of its editorial column in late 1810) flayed the nation's diplomacy in March, 1811, declar-ing it lacked "definition." Arguing that "embarrassments" would continue until the adoption of a "definite policy," the editorial complained that "we have mixed up the ingredients of a warlike and pacific policy into a com-pound, which has proved in the end, to use a vulgar phrase, neither one thing or the other." Given the links between the *National Intelligencer* and the administration, these comments may well have been a trial balloon testing public opinion about a more determined foreign policy.

Two months later, the *National Intelligencer* spoke again. This time its message was that American rights were "absolute," and that as the country had taken a stand, it could no longer allow one belligerent to justify its actions by citing what the other belligerent was doing. The duty of the British and French was simple: "Let both do us justice, we will be the friend of both." Otherwise, "if both countries continue aggressiveness, we must

---

to War in 1812 Through the Eyes of a New Hampshire 'War Hawk,'" *Historical New Hampshire*, XXX (1975), 153; Tallman to William King, November 6 and 21, 1811, in William M. Emery, *Honorable Peleg Tallman, 1764 – 1841* (n.p.: n.p., 1935), 49, 50; "War is waged on our legitimate commerce not at the ports of France, nor on the high Seas, only but on the coast of the U.S., our coasts and the mouths of our harbors," Desha to James Winchester, November 16, 1811, in Winchester Papers; Poindexter to Cowles Mead, No-vember 11, 1811, in J. F. H. Claiborne Collection.

4. Anthony Steel, "Impressment in the Monroe-Pinkney Negotiation, 1806 – 1807," 369; Roger H. Brown, *The Republic in Peril: 1812* (New York, 1964), 29.

eventually set them both at defiance." In short, in May, 1811, the time for a settlement was at hand; Secretary of State Monroe, keenly aware of public frustration, hinted at things to come when he suggested to William Short that "the present summer" might see a resolution of existing difficulties. "If it does not, the whole subject will be before the Congress at the next session much indispleased as it and the nation will be by the experience."[5]

Political pressure was certainly a factor in Madison's calculations during the summer of 1811. He had alienated the Smiths when he sided with Gallatin; immediately the brothers from Maryland went on the attack criticizing administration foreign policy. American commerce, Samuel Smith charged, was "almost a dead letter," and Baltimore's wharves were "full of ships."[6] Brother Robert, meanwhile, unleashed an assault on Madison in the form of his *Address to the People of the United States*, stressing that more forceful and dynamic leadership was needed to safeguard America's neutral rights. Besides these men, the President noticed the activities of DeWitt Clinton in New York State; stories reached Madison that Clinton had seen Armstrong and that Armstrong, in turn, was in contact with the Smiths. There was also factional strife in the Pennsylvania Republican movement with Albert Gallatin and his supporters skirmishing with opponents led by Senator Michael Leib and publisher William Duane. There were troubles in Virginia as well with such quixotic figures as John Randolph and William Branch Giles. The Smiths, Clinton, Armstrong, Leib, Duane, and Giles were united in common thinking that Madison was inept and that it was time to confront the belligerents.

Madison has been accused of buckling under the pressure of prowar congressmen, the War Hawks, when they demanded that he lead the nation into war in return for their support for his candidacy in 1812. This tale is untrue, and it is equally false to allege that Madison accepted the inevitability of war in the summer of 1811 to defuse disillusioned and discontented Republicans. Certainly he and Monroe knew, as one informant wrote the secretary of state, that "the people are not only dissatisfied but disgusted" with the "effects of the weak and juvenile policy by which the affairs of the nation . . . have been governed" and that "a change of some sort seems inevitable."[7] The administration could not ignore such views; it was

5. *National Intelligencer*, March 21, May 18, 1811; Monroe to Short, June 4, 1811, in Short Papers. It was no coincidence that the *National Intelligencer*, June 27, 1811, warned the great powers that adherence to "their obnoxious edicts" would lead to "an appeal . . . to the wisdom of the Congress and of this nation at the next session."

6. Samuel Smith to John Spear Smith, July 31, 1811, in Samuel Smith Papers.

7. Stagg, "James Madison and the 'Malcontents,'" 583, argues that "Madison was in an intolerable position in the summer of 1811" and that he "could regain the initiative at home

beyond dispute also that many Americans remained to be convinced that a change was necessary. In the summer of 1811 Madison and Monroe aimed to placate advocates of a vigorous course with promises of action. They hoped that those skeptical about altering the nation's position would be enlightened by the negotiations about to commence in Washington between Monroe and the new English minister, Augustus John Foster.

Foster had already spent three years in America during Thomas Jefferson's presidency. The young Briton had not been impressed by the new nation's people or leaders; like many of his fellow countrymen, he believed Americans to be boorish, materialistic hypocrites. More troublesome than Foster's personal beliefs was the continuing deadlock in Anglo-American diplomatic relations. The British had announced that they were not about to rescind their orders in council; they categorically rejected as a sham the conditional repeal of the Berlin and Milan decrees. Foster's instructions reflected this mood. He was empowered to settle the four-year-old *Chesapeake-Leopard* affair, and that was about all. Given the years of frustration the American nation had undergone, considering the political pressures on Madison, and bearing in mind the rigidity that characterized Anglo-American relations in mid-1811, Foster's mission was doomed before it started.

Foster's arrival in the United States coincided not only with the publication of Robert Smith's *Address* but with the return of William Pinkney from London where the American minister despaired of success. Within a month it was clear to Foster that he, like Pinkney, could not succeed. Conversations with Monroe yielded nothing; the American was as determined as Foster was to defend his country's interests. "War," Monroe wrote an English correspondent, "dreadful as the alternative is, could not do us more injury than the present state of things, and it would certainly be more honorable to the nation, and gratifying to the public feelings."[8]

French Minister Sérurier was besieged throughout this period by Monroe's complaints about the Emperor's mode of operations and lack of sensitivity for the neutral United States. When the U.S.S. *Essex* returned from France early in July without definitive information on French policy and the true status of the Berlin and Milan decrees, the infuriated secretary of state stormed that France had left the Republicans vulnerable to Federalist charges that Napoleon had tricked Madison with the Cadore letter. "The

---

and abroad by moving toward the positions advocated for so long by his Republican opponents." Clarke to Monroe, April 15, 1811, in Monroe Papers, New York Public Library.

8. Monroe to [Holland?], n.d., but probably late September or early October, 1811, quoted in Perkins, *Prologue to War*, 282; for information on Foster and his mission, see Perkins, 274–82.

revocation of the Berlin and Milan decrees has become a personal affair," Sérurier explained to Bassano, because the "English" party was insisting that Madison had been deceived.[9] Although Sérurier tried to soothe Monroe and Madison, and although Napoleon was now willing to sacrifice the Floridas to America, the atmosphere was sufficiently poisoned for Sérurier to cancel a visit to Madison's Virginia home.

This was a crucial moment in the early history of the United States. For years the young republic had been abused by the great powers; in July, 1811, it seemed that all the humiliations the nation had undergone were more starkly visible than ever. Pinkney's mission had collapsed, the Monroe-Foster conversations were fruitless, and the Royal Navy was as vigilant as ever off the American coast. With their outrageous laws, onerous restrictions, and outright hostility, the French were almost as obnoxious as the English.

At this gloomy juncture the 560-ton corvette *John Adams* arrived with heartening news from France. Merchantmen sequestered since the previous November were being released. Furthermore, ships with properly certified cargoes were being admitted to French ports subject to payment of duties and the acceptance of export controls. Monroe meanwhile secured from the harried and eager-to-please Sérurier a statement "that America may confide in the inviolable intention of the Emperor to fulfill with fidelity his part of the conditional engagements contracted by the letters of his minister of foreign affairs to Genl. Armstrong, and that the decrees of Berlin and Milan will remain repealed as to America, under the sole condition for her, either to obtain the repeal of the orders in council of England, or to cause her rights to be respected by that power."[10] Sérurier was not announcing anything new, of course. Yet the timing of his letter coupled with the information brought by the *John Adams* indicated that the French were less dogmatic than the English. That was all Madison needed to summon the Twelfth Congress into an earlier than normal meeting. Keeping in mind the sequence of events, it is unlikely that the President asked congressmen to assemble for yet another anouncement of failure. Instead, it is most probable that Madison had decided that the country must be made ready for war.

If there was to be war with Britain, there must be peace with France. Thus Madison and Monroe limited themselves to vigorous protests against Napoleonic high-handedness. When an armed clash occurred between Americans and French sailors in Savannah and two French privateers were

9. Sérurier to Bassano, July 24, 1811, in AMAE, LXV, LC; see also Sérurier to Bassano, June 30, July 5, 10, 1811, *ibid.*

10. Sérurier to Monroe, July 19, 1811, Notes from the French Legation, NA. See also Sérurier to Bassano, July 20, 1811, AMAE, LXV, LC.

burned in mid-November, Monroe moved expeditiously to settle the incident.[11] Other irritations plagued Franco-American relations, but Madison and Monroe were guardedly optimistic that Joel Barlow could negotiate a sweeping settlement of outstanding differences.

[II]

Early in August, 1811, the Barlows, Ruth Barlow's sister, Clara Baldwin, Joel's seventeen-year-old nephew, Thomas, and David Bailie Warden sailed from Annapolis on the U.S.S. *Constitution*, Isaac Hull commanding. As the voyage took a month, there was ample time for Barlow to tutor Tom and to banter with Ruth and Clara. What he thought or speculated about the future remains unknown. On the eve of the long trip, though, he was still pessimistically writing Robert Fulton that "I go with an ardent wish, but without much hope of doing good."[12]

Besides tutoring Tom and bantering with Ruth and Clara, Barlow also perused Monroe's extensive instructions. Dated July 26, just two days after the issuance of the proclamation calling the Twelfth Congress into early session, Monroe's guidelines reflected the exasperation existing in the United States in general and Washington in particular. Ranging over Franco-American relations, the Secretary of State assailed the Bayonne and Rambouillet decrees, terming them in effect pure theft; he denounced French rationales that the Rambouillet edict was proper retaliation for injuries allegedly sustained as a consequence of non-intercourse. Criticizing the impediments France placed on American trade, Monroe wrote: "It is indispensable that the trade *be free*; that all American citizens engaged in it be placed on the same footing" and "that their system of carrying it on by licenses granted by French agents be immediately annulled." Attacking the outrages of French corsairs on the high seas, Monroe requested indemnities for American merchants and he repeated his demand for the opening of French ports "on a fair and liberal scale." Restating the familiar theme that France benefited from America's neutral trade, Monroe summarized his instructions with the message that if France "wishes the profit of neutral commerce she must become the advocate of neutral rights, as well by her

11. See my "Fracas in Savannah: National Exasperation in Microcosm, 1811" *Georgia Historical Quarterly*, LIV (1970), 79–86.

12. The *Columbian Museum and Savannah Advertiser*, September 12, 1811, reported that the *Constitution* had been boarded by an officer from a British warship. There is no mention of this in Warden's "Journal of a Voyage from Annapolis to Cherbourg on Board the Frigate Constitution, 1 Aug. to 6 Sept., 1811," *Maryland Historical Magazine*, XI (1916), 127–41, 204–17; Barlow to Fulton, August 2, 1811, in Barlow Papers, Harvard University.

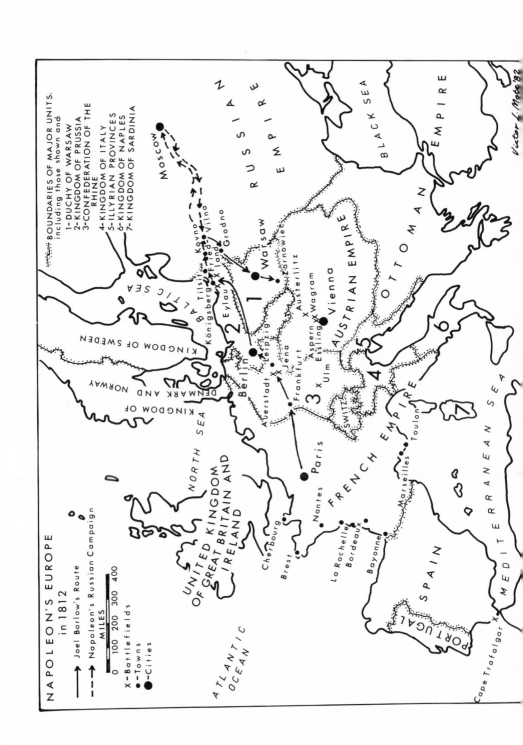

NAPOLEON'S EUROPE
in 1812

→ Joel Barlow's Route

- - - Napoleon's Russian Campaign

MILES

0   100   200   300   400

X—Battlefields
●—Towns
●—Cities

BOUNDARIES OF MAJOR UNITS.
including those shown and:
1- DUCHY OF WARSAW
2- KINGDOM OF PRUSSIA
3- CONFEDERATION OF THE
   RHINE
4- KINGDOM OF ITALY
5- ILLYRIAN PROVINCES
6- KINGDOM OF NAPLES
7- KINGDOM OF SARDINIA

ATLANTIC
OCEAN

NORTH SEA

UNITED KINGDOM
OF GREAT BRITAIN AND
IRELAND

Cherbourg

Brest

Nantes

La Rochelle
Bordeaux

Bayonne

PORTUGAL

Cape Trafalgar X

SPAIN

FRENCH EMPIRE

Paris

Frankfurt

Auerstadt

Berlin

Jena

Leipzig

Marseilles
Toulon

MEDITERRANEAN SEA

SWITZ.

Ulm X
Aspern
X Essling

Wagram
X Austerlitz

Vienna

AUSTRIAN EMPIRE

KINGDOM OF
DENMARK AND NORWAY

KINGDOM OF SWEDEN

BALTIC SEA

Königsberg

Eylau X

Tilsit

Friedland X

Kovno

Vilna

Grodno

Warsaw

Zarnowiec

OTTOMAN EMPIRE

BLACK SEA

RUSSIAN EMPIRE

Moscow

Victor L. Motz '82

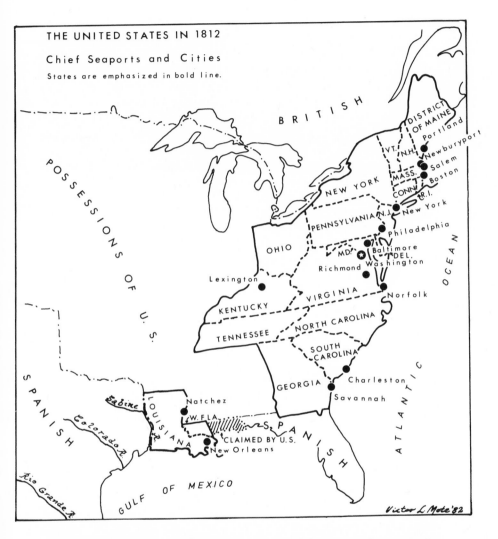

THE UNITED STATES IN 1812

Chief Seaports and Cities

States are emphasized in bold line.

practice as her theory." Significantly, Monroe did not specify how Barlow was to secure indemnities, the opening of French ports, and protection of American shipping from French attacks; the secretary stipulated only that the settlement must be "without delay" and should meet American claims "to their fullest extent."[13] Considering Armstrong's inability to reach any

13. Monroe to Barlow, July 26, 1811, in Diplomatic Instructions of the Department of State, NA. Monroe told Foster of Barlow's instructions shortly after Congress met. "Mr.

kind of mutually satisfactory agreement in his years in Paris, not to mention the nature of the Napoleonic regime, these were formidable goals.

The *Constitution* put into Cherbourg early in September, and the Barlow entourage left immediately for Paris. Joel and Ruth were soon housed in their former home between the Invalides and Rue Luxembourg, welcoming old friends and visiting with members of the Franco-American community; on the twentieth Barlow called on Russell and Jean Baptiste Petry at Daniel Parker's estate, Draveil. Happy to be back in his old haunts, Barlow jokingly told Alexander Wolcott that everyone was greeting Ruth and himself enthusiastically "& even the old coach horses which we gave to a friend in the country . . . would certainly try to come back to us if they were not dead."[14]

In a more serious vein, Barlow discussed his first days in Paris. He was being greeted with "fair words & good promises as to public concerns & personally with flattering attention." As pleasant and enjoyable as his reception was, Barlow remained level-headed and cautious in his outlook. Thus after meeting with Turreau and Bassano and receiving more friendly assurances, he warned Monroe that his favorable reception might be misleading: a settlement remained to be arranged. *"You know, sir, that the French Government has always been wonderfully ignorant of the American character, policy & habits of feeling: and in this relation it has never understood its own interest."*[15]

Being privy to administration secrets and perhaps its plans as well, Barlow was fully aware of Madison's hopes for a speedy agreement with the French, and Monroe's instructions reemphasized the American desire for a rapid settlement. Unfortunately for Madison, Monroe, and Barlow, negotiations could not commence before Barlow had presented his credentials to Napoleon, and the day that Barlow arrived in Paris the Emperor left for a lengthy visit to Holland. To Barlow's dismay, serious conversations were delayed for two months. In the best of times, with Napoleon present in Paris, an acceptable accord would have taken months to negotiate; when the

---

Barlow has been instructed to demand of The French Government a fair and open Trade between the two Countries and to send an early answer by The Constitution Frigate, which is not like it's [*sic*] Predecessors to be plying about from Shore to Shore like Ulyses [*sic*] receiving only Mortifications and hard Blows (as were the Expressions of Mr. Monroe)." Foster to Wellesley, November 5, 1811, "Secret," in FOA 5:77, LC.

14. Barlow to Wolcott, September 26, 1811, in Barlow Papers, Harvard University; also Barlow to Benjamin H. Latrobe, n.d., but late 1811, *ibid.*

15. Barlow to Wolcott, September 26, 1811, *ibid.*; Barlow to Monroe, September 29, 1811, in Despatches from France, NA; the italicized wording is quoted in Heath, *Napoleon I and the Origins of the Anglo-American War of 1812*, 277. The *National Intelligencer*, November 14, 1811, obviously based on this despatch, reflected Barlow's wariness.

Augustus John Foster

Reproduced from the Huntington Library
publication *Jeffersonian America: Notes on the United
States of America Collected in the Years 1805–6–7
and 11–12 by Augustus John Foster, Bart.*

Napoleon, by Vigneron (1809)
From the Collection of H. De Béarn

Talleyrand in the costume of vice grand chancellor of the Empire, by Prud'hon (1809)

Maret, Duc de Bassano
Courtesy of the French Cultural Services,
New York

Louis-Marie Turreau
From Adrien Carré, "La Vendée ses bourreaux et
l'Armée française," *Revue du Souvenir Vendéen*
(December, 1969), 14.

Emperor was in and out of his capital in 1800, the Convention of Môrtefontaine took almost seven months to conclude.

Barlow was not idle while awaiting Napoleon's return. He reestablished contacts with the many friends he had not seen since 1804. Then there were the endless obligatory protocol visits to various First Empire functionaries (and more had to wait until the Emperor had formally received him), where Barlow tried to create an understanding of America's position. The Barlows entertained frequently, producing a favorable impression with their warm and lavish hospitality. Young John Spear Smith was graciously received by the minister and his wife and said the new envoy was determined to "make an Ambassadorial splash."[16] Indeed, Barlow had spent his year's salary within three months and he suggested a major increase in the compensation of American representatives.

William Lee and David Bailie Warden assisted Barlow. Technically Lee was consul in Bordeaux, but, because of his close friendship with Barlow, he was living and working in Paris, aiding the minister in the conduct of diplomacy and, for his own account, trying to arrange profitable voyages for ships he owned; thus on one occasion he asked Barlow to intervene on his behalf with Napoleon's ex-wife, Josephine, thinking a word from the poet-diplomat would win him participation in the sugar trade from Martinique.[17]

Warden, also Barlow's friend, was American consul and agent for prize cases in Paris. His real interest, however, was in socializing with the French elite; the Irish-born revolutionary was thrilled to be accepted by the ersatz aristocracy of the First Empire. Lee and Warden were capable men operating within their appointed spheres; in fact, they complemented Barlow. Each worked diligently promoting and explaining the American cause, even writing books for French audiences. After Barlow's death, the two subordinates unfortunately became embroiled in a bitter quarrel, wrecking their careers in France.[18] That was in the future, however; in 1811–1812 Warden and Lee were as hopeful as Barlow that some kind of an accord would settle Franco-American difficulties.

Napoleon's return from Holland gave the Americans a chance to convert

16. John Spear Smith to Samuel Smith, December 22, 1811, in Samuel Smith Papers. In this letter Smith described Barlow as "unpolished," Ruth Barlow as "pretensious," and Clara Baldwin as "vulgar."

17. "He thinks it would be a fortune to him." Barlow to Ruth Barlow, June 18, 1812, in Jonathan Bayard Smith Family Papers, LC. Lee had been involved in brokering firearms for Virginia in 1802 with Barlow writing Governor James Monroe on Lee's behalf, March 17, 1802, in Gratz Collection. For another example of Lee's business activities, see Lee to Fulwar Skipwith, April 2, 1805, in Skipwith Papers.

18. "There will be a hell of a blow up amongst the Demo's before long," Nathan Haley told Jonathan Russell, May 28, 1812, in Russell Papers, Brown University.

hope into reality. Receiving Barlow on November 17, the Emperor was relaxed, talkative, and arrogant. "I am great enough to be just," he told the American when Barlow brought up the treatment of commerce. "But on your part you must defend your dignity against my enemies & those of the continent. Have a flag, and I will do for you all that you can desire." [19] At a ball marking the seventh anniversary of Napoleon's coronation a fortnight later, the Emperor again spoke to Barlow, this time referring to the clash of the U.S.S. *President* with H.M.S. *Little Belt* the previous May. "Well, Monsieur, you know how to oppose the English." When Barlow affirmed "Sire, we know how to make them respect our flag," the French ruler commented on a note recently presented to Bassano: "It is going to be answered immediately and satisfactorily."

Barlow was delighted with the turn of events. The Emperor and other dignitaries, he told Madison, "have taken pains to signalize their attentions to me in a manner they have rarely done to a foreign minister, & never to an American." He could foresee a gradual lowering of tariffs on American produce, minimal duties on American goods transiting France, a change in the license system, the release of American ships, and indemnities for property already sold. Lest Barlow's expectations seem misplaced and the man-of-letters-turned-diplomat appear naïve, let it be said that members of the Franco-American community concurred with Barlow's favorable interpretation of the reception. [20]

Still, translating Napoleonic rhetoric into reality was Barlow's task. Through November and December, therefore, the American representative conversed with Bassano. He reminded his French friend that France could benefit economically both short term and long term with a more lenient and just commercial policy. Doubtless he stressed to the Foreign Minister that amicable Franco-American relations would outline Anglo-American differences more clearly even though Barlow abhorred the idea of a conflict with Great Britain. Certainly Barlow appealed for justice for neutral America

19. Barlow to Monroe, November 21, 1811, in Despatches from France, NA. Before Napoleon's departure for Egypt in the 1790s, Barlow described the youthful Corsican as "unsocial"; in "mixed companies he would not talk unless he could get someone into a corner, and he would converse on more serious and important subjects than usually are discussed in such circles." "Recollections of Joel Barlow, August 9, 1809," in the *Daily National Intelligencer*, May 25, 1819. Ironically, Barlow was viewed as aloof and detached. See William Plumer's manuscript "Biographical Sketches," in Plumer Papers, New Hampshire State Library, and Petry to Bassano, November 15, 1811, in AMAE, LXVI, LC.

20. Barlow to Madison, December 19, 1811, in Madison Papers, LC; compare Henry Blumenthal, *France and the United States: Their Diplomatic Relations, 1789–1914* (Chapel Hill, 1970), 26: "The emperor exposed Joel Barlow, the American poet-diplomat who pleaded his country's cause, to many personal indignities."

and invoked international law where applicable (according to Petry, Barlow carried learned commentaries on neutral rights), pointing out that French generosity would be recognized by appreciative Americans.[21] In brief, Barlow shared the sentiments of many of his influential countrymen: France had everything to gain and nothing to lose from harmony with the United States.[22]

Barlow's hopes for an early resolution of outstanding problems were dashed by French inaction. "He always treats the subject with apparent candor and solicitude," Barlow said of Bassano, "seems anxious to gain information, declares that neither he nor the Emperor had before understood American affairs in the light in which they now appear, and always assures me that he is nearly ready with an answer." Napoleon was the stumbling block, the Foreign Minister claimed, for the Emperor had to reconcile his Continental System with any agreement with America.[23] In addition, the Corsican-born ruler was preoccupied with Franco-Russian relations. Presumably when France's European troubles were under control then and only then could a definitive Franco-American accord be struck.

Barlow was severely criticized by members of the Smith-Armstrong faction for his inability to bargain successfully with France. "*'Tis the old system of humbugging*," a correspondent wrote Jonathan Russell, with "ministerial dinners . . . invitations to Imperial fetes . . . verbal promises" tricking the American diplomat. John Spear Smith predicted failure for Barlow's mission from the start. By January, 1812, Smith gleefully reported Barlow the "picture of woe" because his expectations of a treaty had not been fulfilled. The lesson was clear: "Never send us again a doggerel poet. The canting quackery of Jefferson, the imbecile and miserable politics of his pupils—have dug a grave for the honor and the wealth of the Country—and another four years will suffice for the death & burial." Russell, who had heard of the flattering reception accorded Barlow, contented himself with expressions of pity for anyone imagining himself to be "the lucky mortal . . . destined to restore the relations between France & the United States."[24]

21. See Barlow to Bassano, November 10, 1811, enclosed with Barlow to Monroe, November 21, 1811, in Despatches from France, NA, and Petry to Bassano, November 15, 1811, in AMAE, LXVI, LC. Years before Barlow had collaborated with Fulwar Skipwith and Thomas Paine writing *Pacte Maritime*, a proposal for neutral nations to guarantee neutral rights. Echeverria, *Mirage in the West*, 211.

22. William Lee observed, "Had the policy of the [French] Government been tinctured with the least wisdom we should have measured with England long since." Lee to Mrs. Susan Lee, n.d., but late 1811, in Lee-Palfrey Family Papers.

23. Barlow to Monroe, December 19, 1811, in Despatches from France, NA. See also Barlow to Russell, December 19, 1811, in Russell Papers, Brown University.

24. Leonard Jarvis to Russell, February 16, 1812, in Russell Papers, Brown University;

French delay discouraged but did not deter Barlow from seeking an agreement. He knew that success in diplomacy sometimes required months, even years of effort; on the Barbary coast in the 1790s, it had taken him two years to complete his mission. As an interested observer, Barlow had witnessed the protracted negotiations preceding the Convention of Môrtefontaine in 1800. He also knew that the Louisiana Purchase agreement had not materialized overnight in 1803. As 1812 dawned, Barlow had been in France less than four months, and it had been less than two months since his meeting with the Emperor. In light of his experience, Barlow not unwisely chose to pursue negotiations.

There were other reasons for Barlow's persistence. He believed that peace must be preserved and that a treaty with France would give the United States leverage in negotiations with Britain, helping to preserve peace with that nation. Having lived in embattled Europe for so many years and having seen the devastation wrought by war, Joel Barlow would do almost anything to prevent the tide of war from engulfing his homeland. It should be recalled that Barlow viewed the young republic as mankind's last hope. War would unleash unimaginable and uncontrollable currents, perhaps fatally disrupting the American experiment. The emissary also knew that success in France would enhance his reputation in the United States. As William Lee observed, a treaty would "do wonders" for Barlow, "perhaps make him President."[25] Lesser men than Barlow would have been influenced by the possibilities arising from a meritorious treaty.

The French, meanwhile, relaxed some of their restrictions. For example, Napoleon decided to allow American rice and flour into his ports without certificates of origin and to allow the ships bringing those commodities to depart carrying whatever they wished. The French also started returning vessels sequestered under the Rambouillet decree of 1810, prompting optimism about increased trade with Europe. Minor pinpricks such as the seizure and condemnation of American shipping in the Baltic still continued, but it was believed that a nod from Napoleon could and would halt such depredations.

At this point Barlow made a crucial decision and chose to seek a commercial treaty with the French. This was a controversial as well as a signifi-

---

John Spear Smith to Samuel Smith, January 26, 1812, in Samuel Smith Papers. See also Smith's letters to his father dated November 27, December 2, 8, 30, 1811, and February 2, March 2, 1812, all *ibid.*; Russell to Armstrong, January 21, 1812, in Russell Papers, Brown University. Yet Russell had written Petry that he could "be jealous of no man who contributes to the rapprochement of my country and its earliest ally." Russell to Petry, December 12, 1811, *ibid.*

25. Lee to Mrs. Susan Palfrey Lee, February 5, 1812, in Mann, *A Yankee Jeffersonian*, 152.

cant departure from Monroe's directions, but Barlow believed such an agreement was an ideal way to end the long-standing problems clouding relations between the two countries. In Algiers in 1796, he had "found . . . it . . . necessary to make engagements which are very likely to be disapproved." Now in 1812 it seemed that through a commercial treaty Franco-American trade would be promoted and past difficulties erased, ends desired by Madison and Monroe alike. On January 17 Barlow sent Madison a nineteen-page draft of a treaty which incorporated many details of the defunct 1800 Convention with France.[26]

As Barlow tried to hammer out an accord, he thought of various courses open to him. He could stay in France, protest violations of America's neutral rights, and work for a settlement as he was doing. He could remain in France, dismiss negotiations as futile, and complain as Armstrong had to Napoleon, Cadore, and Cadore's subordinates. He could leave the First Empire's court and retreat to some other capital (as Charles Cotesworth Pinckney had done fifteen years earlier prior to the XYZ Affair) in hopes of forcing the French government to respect the rights of the United States. Still another alternative was to emulate William Pinkney and return to Washington, leaving Warden or Lee in charge. Looking over these choices, if Barlow were to stay in Paris, it made sense to attempt an accommodation with the French. To adhere rigidly to a policy of protestations would have proven futile, as John Armstrong had already discovered. In all probability a retreat to another capital would have been equally fruitless, for Napoleon felt no overriding need to woo the United States.

It is interesting to speculate what would have happened had Barlow appeared in Washington in February or March, 1812, announcing that his mission was a failure. Doubtless the Federalists would have been ecstatic, convinced that an Anglo-American war was now improbable. An embarrassed Madison and an upset Monroe would have been forced to reassess their war policy. Denunciations of France would have filled the halls of Congress. Yet Britain would still have remained the chief culprit in the minds of most citizens. The orders in council were still in force and impressment continued. With the Battle of Tippecanoe in November, 1811, the British also appeared guilty of conspiring with the Indians. In short, King George's realm seemed permanently at odds with its offspring. Given the very serious differences besetting Anglo-American relations, even if Barlow had returned to Washington it seems likely there would have been a war against England at some point.

Madison and Monroe were disturbed enough without Barlow's presence

26. Barlow to Oliver Wolcott, April 27, 1796, in Wolcott Papers, Connecticut Historical Society; Barlow to Madison, January 17, 1812, in Madison Papers, LC. See also Barlow to Bassano, January 17, 1812, in AMAE, LXIX, LC.

on the Potomac. They had expected some kind of an agreement with France during the winter; instead, all they had received was notice of their friend's impressive reception and word that the French were favorably disposed toward America. Their reaction to Barlow's proposal for a commercial treaty, then, was understandably negative: "I am at a loss for the necessity of it [a treaty], or the motives of F[rance] to set it on foot, if it be not meant to gain time, and be guided by events," Madison informed Barlow. The President did not direct his representative to break off talks, however, nor did he suggest an alternative course for Barlow. One can imagine the weariness with which Madison wrote: his hopes for a settlement had been dashed before, but this time an agreement was particularly desirable. The United States had accepted the Cadore note and an emissary familiar with France and the French had been sent to Napoleon's court. Finally, the administration had publicly stated that it deserved and expected more just treatment from France.[27]

It was during these months that the French began attacking American grain shipments to the Iberian peninsula, where French divisions were engaged in bloody encounters with the Spanish, Portuguese, and English.[28] Angered at this commerce, and confident that interdicting it would cripple their opponents, the French allowed their corsairs to make "good prizes" of vessels engaged in trade with Spain and Portugal.[29] What the French viewed as profiteering at their expense and vital support of the enemy's lifeline, President Madison deemed a neutral right, and as expedient on two grounds. Grain exports originated in Pennsylvania, Maryland, and Virginia, all of which were Republican bastions. Halting this trade would not help the Republicans or Madison in those crucial states. There is also reason to believe that the President thought food exports to the British-led forces in the peninsula would keep the conflict alive, occupying a large number of Britain's troops in Spain rather than in North America in the event of Anglo-American hostilities. Therefore the trade continued (even after the outbreak of the War of 1812) and so did French attacks.[30]

27. Madison to Barlow, February 24, 1812, in Hunt (ed.), *Writings of James Madison*, VIII, 179. See also Monroe to Barlow, February 24, 1812, in Diplomatic Instructions of the Department of State, NA; Sérurier to Bassano, January 2, March 2, 1812, in AMAE, LXVII, LC.

28. A typical case was the experience of the brig *Factor* out of Newburyport, Massachusetts. Returning home from Lisbon, the *Factor* was stopped by the frigate *Lorient*; a boarding party from the *Lorient* seized $4,000 and all provisions "except two Barrels of Beef and one & a half of Bread." The *Factor's* crew subsisted on this remnant from September 19 to October 29, 1811. Barlow to Bassano, January 8, 1812, in Despatches from France, NA.

29. Bonnel, *La France, les Etats Unis et la guerre de course*, 301; and for Sérurier's protests, Sérurier to Bassano, October 23, 1811, January 2, March 23, 1812, in AMAE, LXVII, LC.

30. Sérurier to Bassano, March 23, 1812, *ibid.*; and Monroe to Barlow, March 21, April

Because of slow communications, Barlow was unaware of Madison's discontent with negotiations for a commercial treaty until April. A restrained optimism appeared in his letters; on January 2 he speculated to an old friend that his mission might "be more successful than I expected." Notifying Monroe in February of Napoleon's preoccupation with the affairs of Europe and Russia, the poet-diplomat pointed out that "I cannot count upon their getting on very fast with ours." At the end of the month, Barlow warned Benjamin Latrobe about undue expectations. "It is a very difficult thing to produce a change in a system combined with so many circumstances of revenge & other strong positions arranged against an enemy as is the anticommercial system of Napoleon." Still, Barlow's optimism was evident: he delayed the return passage of the sloop *Hornet* so it could convey the text of a treaty. Talks were going slowly, he admitted to Jonathan Russell, "but I think [they] will be done pretty well."[31]

Seven weeks later, toward the end of April, 1812, Barlow was still without his treaty when messages arrived from Madison and Monroe. Clearly French inaction irked the two Virginians; the President questioned the necessity for a commercial treaty and he commented on the lack of clarity in Bassano's reply to Barlow's initial note. Supporting Madison, Monroe suggested that France must settle accounts or expect to suffer the consequences. Recognizing the necessity for action, seeing that his friends' patience was exhausted, and perhaps feeling chagrined that he was being stalled by the French, Barlow explained to Madison that "the polestar from which I have all along graduated my compass was to remove the causes of war with England." At the same time, he appealed to the French to "make

---

23, 1812, in Diplomatic Instructions of the Department of State, NA. For further discussion of the grain trade see Lawrence S. Kaplan, "France and the War of 1812," *Journal of American History*, LVII (1970), 38, and the various studies of the late W. Freeman Galpin including, "The Grain Trade of Alexandria, Virginia, 1801–1815," *North Carolina Historical Review*, IV (1927), 404–27, and "The American Grain Trade to the Spanish Peninsula, 1810–1814," *American Historical Review*, XXVIII (1922), 24–44. Concerning French attacks on the grain trade, John Graham, a Department of State clerk, wrote Warden: "Great dissatisfaction is felt here about the Conduct of France and there is no saying what effect a Change of measures in England might produce." Graham to Warden, n.d., 1812, Warden Papers, Maryland Historical Society. See, too, Sérurier to Bassano, April 9, 15, 1812, in AMAE, LXVII, LC.

31. Barlow to Alexander Wolcott, postscript dated January 2, 1812, in Barlow Papers, Yale University. Barlow added, "How useful it will be is another question." Barlow to Monroe, February 8, 1812, in Despatches from France, NA; Barlow to Latrobe, February 29, 1812, in Barlow Papers, Yale University; Barlow to Russell, March 3, 1812, in Russell Papers, Brown University. Daniel Parker shared Barlow's confidence in the eventual outcome. The work would be "soon finished without any material alteration," he wrote Russell, March 3, 1812, *ibid.*

and publish an authentic act declaring the Berlin & Milan Decrees as relative to the United States, to have ceased in November, 1810."[32] The French accommodated the American, doing so through the "St. Cloud decree," a measure ostensibly in existence since late April, 1811.

The French were as surprised by the Americans' lack of familiarity with this document as the Americans were by the decree's sudden appearance.[33] Bassano professed incredulity that there were no copies of the year-old measure in American hands. Learning of the existence of the St. Cloud edict on May 10, 1812, Barlow described it as "remarkable." Informing Madison that legation files were absent of any reference to this important law, he added, "If you have no knowledge of it, the suspicion I have will be confirmed, that it was created last week expressly for this purpose & in consequence of my note [to the French] of the 1st of May." Reflecting on the turn of events, the man-of-letters turned diplomat confessed, "I know not, in state ethics by what name such management is called."[34]

Other Americans were equally skeptical at the sudden appearance of the decree. In London, Russell said the British were unconvinced by Napoleon's latest stroke. Then he cynically implored Barlow to continue pressing the French. "If you could only now make them find some other decree, which undoubtedly has been passed a twelve-month at least, making the revocation *total*, our work would be done." Russell's friend John Spear Smith compared the unpublished April 28 measure to "Nero's laws, written in small characters at the top of lofty columns." Summing up American opinion, almost a year later the *National Intelligencer* termed the strange April 28 instrument "an act of diplomacy, call it duplicity if you will, of a most extraordinary character."[35]

32. See Barlow to Madison, May 2, 1812, in Madison Papers, LC, and his letter to Bassano, May 1, 1812, enclosed with Barlow to Monroe, May 2, 1812, in Despatches from France, NA.

33. A split exists about the legitimacy of the St. Cloud decree. Ulane Bonnel (*La France, les Etats-Unis et la guerre de course*, 302, 442) notes that the measure is in proper chronological sequence in the archives of the Ministry of Foreign Affairs, and she reprints the text. On the other hand, Georges Lefebvre (*Napoleon: From Tilsit to Waterloo, 1807–1815*) does not even mention it. On the American side, the most detailed probing of French archival material relating to the St. Cloud decree has been done by Phoebe Heath (*Napoleon I and the Origins of the Anglo-American War of 1812*, 304–306) and she writes that "fairly conclusive evidence exists to show that the measure of April 28, 1811, was not decreed at the period indicated by the date" (*ibid.*, 304).

34. Bassano to Sérurier, April 30, 1812, and Bassano to Barlow, May 10, 1812, in AMAE, LXIX, LC; Barlow to Madison, May 12, 1812, in Madison Papers, LC.

35. Russell to Barlow, May 29, 1812, in Russell Papers, Brown University, responding to a Barlow letter of May 11, 1812, *ibid.*; Russell asked Barlow to secure proof of repeal in a

However valid the decree, Joel Barlow continued negotiating, hoping that an Anglo-American war could be avoided. Unhappily for Barlow, the empire's chief actors were leaving the Paris stage for Central Europe in late April and early May because Napoleon was preparing to launch his great offensive against Russia. One of Bassano's underlings, Emmerich, duc de Dalberg, was placed in charge of negotiations. Of course, this arrangement meant further delays, more inconvenience, and added frustration for Barlow. "*Homer* now begins to discover that they have made a complete fool of him," chortled Russell's friend Nathan Haley.[36] While Barlow labored in Paris, redoubling his efforts for a Franco-American settlement, the Twelfth Congress was moving unsteadily down the path to war.

[III]

Seven and one-half months elapsed between President Madison's annual message and the declaration of war against Great Britain. While the Congress considered enlarging the army, upgrading the navy, and levying new taxes in the months immediately after the address, decisive action was not taken until the second quarter of 1812. During these months, congressional opinion ran the gamut from despair to hope as the clasp of war was closed. The impatient George Poindexter, for example, fumed that "words, words, words appear still to be the rage." Nathaniel Macon was more charitable about the seeming congressional procrastination when he said that war was probable although "at this time there is some diversity of opinion as to the measure which ought to be now adopted." In contrast to Poindexter and Macon, Richard Mentor Johnson of Kentucky claimed that he had "never seen the war spirit up before in this house," and Felix Grundy from neighboring Tennessee was confident that "the Rubicon is pass'd." Ebenezer Sage from New York stated categorically "that this government will go on from step to step to . . . war, nothing will avert them but justice from the other side [of] the water." English diplomat Foster, relying on his Federalist friends, however, reported that "most sensible men felt the government would not be pushed into war." Benjamin Tallmadge, one of these sensible men, derided "the noisy, blustering Speeches of our Kentucky & Tennesee [*sic*] Bro'thers." According to the Connecticut Federalist, "the

letter dated March 25, 1812, *ibid.*; John Spear Smith to Samuel Smith, May 18, 1812, in Samuel Smith Papers; *National Intelligencer*, March 8, 1813.

36. Nathan Haley to Russell, May 28, 1812, in Russell Papers, Brown University. Even before the St. Cloud episode, another of Russell's correspondents told him he was needed in Paris: "My good friend we want some of your energy here. Milk & water wont do." L. Jarvis to Russell, April 16, 1812, in Russell Papers, Massachusetts Historical Society.

more Sober & reflective sort of folks think that the war party must fail for want of two most essential ingredients [viz?] *Men & Money*."[37]

Representative Macon observed correctly that the ebb and flow apparent in Congress would continue until the *Hornet* returned with positive information from Barlow. With a Franco-American agreement in hand, the war drive against Britain would gather momentum. While everyone knew that Barlow was engaged in important negotiations, Madison wanted all news from Paris kept strictly confidential, fearful that untimely revelations would undermine the war spirit building in the nation. Secrets in Washington were hard to keep, though, and Barlow's mission was the object of much speculation. Foster, who heard much of the gossip, was serenely confident that Barlow would not secure a mutually satisfactory accord and he advised his government to avoid any provocative actions, certain that a do-nothing policy would foil budding war schemes.[38]

Foster's advice was given shortly before the Henry affair became public knowledge. As a British agent, John Henry had toured New England checking public opinion during Jefferson's second term. This was not particularly noteworthy; British authorities used others for the same task as far back as George Washington's administration. Henry's "intelligence" was of little value, for New Englanders openly proclaimed their distaste for Jefferson and his embargo. Dissatisfied with the sum of money he received for his services, Henry decided to sell his reports to the Americans through an intermediary named Edouard de Crillon. Although four years had passed since Henry's mission, he and Crillon convinced the receptive Republicans

37. Quoted in order are Poindexter to Cowles Mead, December 12, 1811, in J. F. H. Claiborne Collection; Macon to [?], January 2, 1812, in Personal Papers Miscellaneous, Library of Congress; Johnson to James Barbour, December 9, 1811, in Barbour Papers, New York Public Library; Grundy to Jackson, November 28, 1811, in Bassett (ed.), *Correspondence of Andrew Jackson*, I, 208; Sage to William Van Deurson, April 27, 1812, in Beinecke Library, Yale University; Foster to Wellesley, December 28, 1811, "Most Secret," in FOA 5:77, LC; Tallmadge to [?], January 16, 1812, in War of 1812 Collection, William L. Clements Library. Sérurier compared the plight of the Americans to Ulysses on the rocks of Calypso; they did not know what to do. Sérurier to Bassano, March 2, 1812, in AMAE, LXVII, LC.

38. Dolley Madison cautioned Ruth and Joel Barlow that information passed to Postmaster-General Gideon Granger was appearing in newspapers. Dolley Madison to the Barlows, n.d., 1811, in *Memoirs and Letters of Dolly Madison*, 96–97. Nonetheless, in mid-April Harper said he had seen a letter from Barlow to Granger dated March 3 promising an "honorable Treaty" with France. Harper to Plumer, April 13, 1812, in Egan, "The Path to War in 1812," 167. Granger was distressed at the prospect of war, frightened that hostilities would retard "the growth of the nation," endanger "republican principles," and incur "all the evils of federal spending Systems & internal Taxes." Gideon Granger to John Tod, December 24, 1811, in Gideon and Francis Granger Papers, Library of Congress; Foster to Wellesley, March 6, 1812, "*Separate and Secret*," in FOA 5:84, LC.

that they had vital and revealing details of Federalist disloyalty available. Consequently Madison and Monroe paid $50,000, the proceeds of the American secret service fund, to Henry-Crillon for the story. What appears to have been a foolhardy venture occurred because Madison saw the promised revelations as a means to hurt the Federalist opposition politically and to heighten war fever among his countrymen.[39]

No time was wasted in transmitting documents relating to the Henry-Crillon affair to the Congress. The Federalists were confused and embarrassed by Henry's reports; in Representative Harper's words, Timothy Pitkin "began to kick and *squirm*" while Josiah Quincy "looked pale— walked the floor in haste and was much agitated as was Tallmadge." The most upset appeared to be "Deacon [John] Davenport on whose face I actually saw, not only great drops of sweat, but it really ran down copiously on his face." When Henry's reports proved devoid of any sensational disclosures, the Federalists thought that the episode would redound to their favor. "Madison will lose much more than he will gain by giving Henry $50,000," Abijah Bigelow predicted. Bigelow was wrong, however. The Henry affair did not damage Madison at all and if John Adams Harper was right, the populace "approve[d] of the conduct of the executive."[40]

As the Henry story receded into the background, a ninety-day embargo was placed on American shipping through the combined effort of the executive and the legislature. Enactment of the measure offered a classic case of government operation under Madison. Late in March, Representative Peter Porter, a prominent New York Republican and a member of the House Foreign Affairs Committee, questioned Secretary Monroe about the President's thinking on again resorting to commercial warfare. Monroe returned with the response that "the Executive was of the Same Opinion that it entertained at the beginning of the Session, 'that without an accommodation with G[reat] B[ritain] Congress ought to declare war before adjourning.'" At this meeting Monroe told Harper also that Madison would recommend a sixty-day embargo if such an act would be welcomed in the House. On April 1 Madison made this recommendation; on April 4, to accommodate the Senate's desire for a longer period of coercion, a ninety-day em-

39. Samuel Eliot Morison, *By Land and by Sea* (New York, 1953), 265–86; Albert Gallatin speculated that the Henry case would crush "the spirit of the Essex junto," and dampen the ardor of New York's Clintonians. Gallatin to Jefferson, March 10, 1812, in Jefferson Papers, LC.

40. Harper to Plumer, March 11, 1812, in Egan, "The Path to War in 1812," 160; Bigelow to Hannah G. Bigelow, March 25, 1812, in Brigham (ed.), "Letters to Abijah Bigelow," 333; Harper to Plumer, April 7, 1812, in Clifford L. Egan (ed.), "Additional Letters of John Adams Harper," *Historical New Hampshire*, XXXI (Spring–Summer, 1976), 55.

bargo became law. Recalling Roman history, John Adams Harper thought that "the Rubicon is passed—war is inevitable."[41]

Some observers wondered against which power war would be declared, even at this late date. While the administration was angry with Britain, French aggravations continue to infuriate American opinion. As French corsairs pillaged America's Iberian commerce, Nathaniel Macon wrote that the "Devil himself would not tell which Government England or France is the most wicked."[42] Then on April 9, the *National Intelligencer* indicted the British for taking "the lead" in heaping insults on America; given nautical superiority, France would not hesitate to treat the United States in even more cavalier fashion. Five days later, however, in an anonymous *National Intelligencer* editorial, Monroe explained why the administration was singling out Britain as its target: Barlow seemed on the verge of successful negotiations in France while Anglo-American relations were deadlocked. If the French continued plaguing the United States, "we shall be at liberty to pursue the course which circumstances may require."[43] When he wrote the editorial, Monroe was convinced that the *Hornet* would duly arrive with positive news from Paris, clearing the way for war against Great Britain. To Monroe's and Madison's annoyance, the *Hornet* did not return; the exasperated Madison complained to Jefferson that "the delay of the Hornet is inexplicable." With the ship still absent three weeks later, Madison believed that Barlow was dealing with "matters which will work great embarrassment & mischief here." Then blaming the French for the *Hornet's* nonappearance, the President minced no words about the situation to Sérurier. "I do my best to calm things," the hapless Sérurier told Bassano, "but the next day discontent flares anew."[44]

Only on May 22 did the eagerly awaited vessel return. Hardly had rumors begun circulating about the contents of messages aboard the *Hornet*

41. Quoted in Ronald L. Hatzenbuehler, "The War Hawks and the Question of Congressional Leadership in 1812," *Pacific Historical Review*, XLV (1976), 16. Compare Perkins, *Prologue to War*, 383–84; *Statutes at Large*, II, 700–701; Harper to Plumer, April 7, 1812, in Egan (ed.), "Additional Letters of John Adams Harper," 55.

42. Macon to Nicholson, March 24, 1812, in Nicholson Papers.

43. *National Intelligencer*, April 9, 1812. This impartiality dumbfounded Randolph's friend James Garnett. He wondered if the administration had moved to the position that a case for war existed against both powers, making hostilities impractical against either. Garnett to Randolph, April 7, 1812, Correspondence of John Randolph and James M. Garnett, in Bruce-Randolph Collection; *National Intelligencer*, April 14, 1812. "I still think we shall have war with G.B. and if France does not behave herself well, I should not be surprised that we give both a [touch?] at the same time." Macon to Nicholson, March 30, 1812, in Nicholson Papers.

44. Madison to Jefferson, April 3, 24, 1812, in Hunt (ed.), *Writings of James Madison*, VIII, 187, 188–89; Sérurier to Bassano, May 4, 1812, in AMAE, LXVII, LC.

when word spread that Barlow's negotiations had been futile. "I have this day been confidentially informed that Mr. Barlow had completely failed in negotiations," Foster gloated. On May 26 the despondent Madison sent Barlow's most recent correspondence to the Congress. That same day the *National Intelligencer* detailed the administration's position on the troubled state of American diplomacy. Deeply disappointed at the lack of progress in Paris, the *Intelligencer* indicated that the public would soon have new information to form "a correct judgment" about relations with the belligerents. Four days later, the newspaper carried the clearest statement yet on the dilemma confronting the United States, restating what Monroe had written over six weeks before. "The comparative injustice of France cannot in any degree palliate the unremitted infractions of our rights by Great Britain; and whatever impression may have been made by the evasions of France, let not our measure" against Britain be eased. France would be attended to as soon as justice had been obtained from Britain.[45] Two days after this important editorial, on June 1, Madison asked Congress to approve a declaration of war against Britain because of numerous violations of American neutrality.

[IV]

Some observations are in order about the decision for war. A declaration of war was not the miraculous event some historians have portrayed it to be; rather the miracle was that American patience with the belligerents lasted so long. The influential Baltimore editor Hezekiah Niles wondered if "future ages" would be able to understand why "America had submitted to such indignities."[46] One hundred and seventy years later this forbearance appears to have been a mistake; a strong case for hostilities existed at the time of the *Chesapeake-Leopard* affair and war should have been declared in 1807. Still, the youthful democracy called the United States of America exhibited tremendous intrinsic strength in surviving the vicissitudes of neutrality for so many years.

The primary causes of the War of 1812 were the issues of American national honor, the sense of humiliation suffered at the hands of Great Britain in the forms of impressment and the violation of neutral rights. In the 1790s citizens were outraged by British activities: "A happy moment

45. Foster to Castlereagh, May 23, 1812, in FOA 5:86, LC. Also Sérurier to Bassano, May 27, 1812, in AMAE, LXVII, LC; *National Intelligencer*, May 26, 30, 1812.

46. *Niles' Weekly Register*, December 7, 1811. "At length the patience and forbearance of the country were exhausted," reminisced another editor years later, John Binns, *Recollections of the Life of John Binns* (Philadelphia, 1856), 199.

for America to be revenged the Millions of insults," Joshua Barney cried in 1794. Eighteen years later continued insults could be tolerated no longer. "War alone can furnish a remedy for this deplorable malady of the body politic & chastisement for insufferable insults daily heaped upon us by the enemy," a Virginian informed Madison. Governor William Plumer summed up the prevailing attitude when he told the New Hampshire House of Representatives that "a state of humiliation [was] incompatible with national dignity." When Congress finally approved war after months of hope, waiting, and debate, many citizens breathed a collective sigh of relief. "We are beginning now to hold up our heads and boast that we are Americans," William Wirt wrote Monroe from Virginia. "There is not a man here who is not an inch taller since congress has done its duty."[47]

Impressment and maritime restrictions only began the list of American grievances. Madison mentioned British intrigue with the Indians; for Kentuckians and other westerners warfare commenced in November, 1811, when General William Henry Harrison's small army clashed with the red men at the Battle of Tippecanoe. The fight at Tippecanoe accentuated already strong feelings of Anglophobia. American independence had been declared in 1776. Thirty-five years later, many citizens believed the nation too dependent on Britain and Europe. A war would sever ancient ties, making America truly free. We would have "to *look to ourselves*, estranging us from accursed Europe," Hezekiah Niles proclaimed. In Western Pennsylvania, nationalism laced with Anglophobia was of fundamental importance in the development of war spirit.[48]

The British seemingly went out of their way to anger Americans. Some of them admitted that Britain aimed at "*the Universal monopoly of Commerce*" through the orders in council. To many Britons, Americans were cowards,

---

47. Joshua Barney to his brother, December 21, 1794, cited in Bernard Mayo, *Henry Clay: Spokesman of the New West* (Boston, 1937), 33; J. G. Jackson to Madison, March 30, 1812, in Madison Papers, LC. "I fully believe the national spirit & the national honor demand it [war]," Jackson to Madison, April 13, 1812, *ibid*. No one wanted war, but the people were tired of the continued "wrongs inflicted and unredressed by England." Jefferson to Madison, March 26, 1812, *ibid*.; Lynn W. Turner, *William Plumer of New Hampshire, 1759–1850* (Chapel Hill, 1962), 206–207; Wirt to Monroe, June 21, 1812, in Monroe Papers, LC.

48. James W. Hammack, Jr., *Kentucky and the Second American Revolution* (Lexington, 1976), 8; and Mary Lou Conlin, *Simon Perkins of the Western Reserve* (Cleveland, 1968), 75–76: "Documents of the period validate that the principal—indeed—almost the only—concern of the settlers was the Indians and their savagery." Niles to D. Chambers, May 16, 1812, in Miscellaneous Manuscript Collection, Library of Congress; "*A plague on both your houses*," *Niles' Weekly Register* thundered July 31, 1813; Kaufman, "War Sentiment in Western Pennsylvania: 1812," 443.

the United States *"a nation of cheats"* that *"sprang from convicts."* Astonished by the scathing remarks Englishmen reserved for the new country, an American who traveled extensively in that island nation concluded that the "english are the greatest fools in the world," for instead of conciliating the United States, "they quarrel with their own bread and butter—they ought to make every sacrifice in the world to remain at peace, for that is the only state in which they can thrive." Even some Federalists were alienated by the British air of superiority and spirit of self-righteousness. Convinced that their country was defending Western Civilization, many Britons equated American criticisms with a pro-French policy. "It is hardly fair to infer that because the Americans disapprove of the conduct of G[reat] Britain, they should necessarily become the lovers of France," Thomas Reid protested to Robert Saunders Dundas, 2nd Viscount Melville. Reid's reminder fell on deaf ears; the ruling elite of Great Britain was convinced of an overpowering French hold on the United States. Thus Robert Stewart, Viscount Castlereagh, wrote to Foster that the "internal Politicks of America have so much connected the interests of the Party in power with the French Alliance, that I cannot encourage much expectation, whatever they may in their hearts feel, that they will be induced to assume any authoritative tone against France."[49] Subservience might have changed the views of Castlereagh, Francis James Jackson, and others from contempt to pity, and precipitated better treatment of America, but it seems fair to conclude that such meekness would have intensified English haughtiness.[50]

Augustus Foster reflected the prevailing attitude toward America. His dispatches were filled with misinformation mirroring his biases, and he never really took the Twelfth Congress or public sentiment seriously. When the *National Intelligencer* reported a Philadelphia meeting supporting war with Britain, Foster airily dismissed the event. "I am told the Assembly who agreed to the latter amounted to but 2,000 persons principally com-

49. Samuel F. B. Morse to Mr. and Mrs. Jedediah Morse, January 1, 1813, August 6, 1812, in Edward L. Morse (ed.), *Samuel F. B. Morse: His Letters and Journals* (2 vols.; Boston and New York, 1914), I, 91–92, 81–82; John Rodman to Harmanus Bleecker, September 18, 1811, in Bleecker Papers; Reid to Melville, March 5, 1812, in Melville Papers, William L. Clements Library, University of Michigan; Castlereagh to Foster, April 10, 1812, in Bernard Mayo (ed.), *Instructions to the British Ministers to the United States, 1791–1812*, American Historical Association, *Annual Report, 1936* (3 vols.; Washington, 1941), III, 363.

50. A Federalist blamed British attitudes on America itself because "We have exhibited so much of the *flatulency* of the national vanity, and have made so many arrogant demands." Entry of April 19, 1806, in Benjamin Silliman, *Journal of Travels in England, Holland, and Scotland, and of Two Passages over the Atlantic in the Years 1805 and 1806* (2 vols.; Boston, 1812), II, 337.

posed of Irishmen of the lowest order, Negroes and Boys." Although Foster spent a small fortune on lavish receptions (and was amused by the crude manners he witnessed), he relied excessively on Federalists in interpreting American policy.[51]

Foster's major shortcoming was misjudging events in the winter and spring of 1811–1812. When Barlow failed in his quest for a speedy agreement with France, the Briton reported the possibility of some kind of new arrangement with the United States, this less than two months before Madison's war message. He portrayed Monroe as sympathetic to England when evidence indicates that the Secretary of State was taking an increasingly harder line toward that nation. Foster simply dismissed or overlooked hints of hostilities, reasoning perhaps that the war threat would evaporate if he ignored it.[52] A discerning individual would not have been misled by the erratic conduct of the Americans, for there were numerous signs that the country was drifting toward war. Foster did not see these warnings, however, and his sense of complacency did nothing to lessen the intransigent attitudes of his superiors.

Englishmen and partisans of Britain were astonished by the outbreak of war and were given to wondering how the United States could fight the one country standing resolutely against Bonaparte.[53] Ignoring abundant evidence concerning causation, these supporters of George the III's realm believed a conspiracy existed between Madison and Napoleon; how else could one explain America's declaring war on England while Napoleon's legions were crossing the Niemen River into Russia? Doubtless Madison took the efficient French war machine into his calculations, gambling that Britain would be involved with Napoleon and unable to check American military operations in North America.[54] It was sheer coincidence, however,

---

51. Foster to Castlereagh, May 26, 1812, in FOA 5:88, LC; see also Foster to Wellesley, February 2, 1812, "Separate and Secret," and March 12, 1812, "*Secret*," in FOA 5:84, LC; and Foster's messages in FOA 5:86, LC.

52. Foster to Wellesley, April 3, May 3, 1812, in FOA 5:85, LC, and Davis, *Jeffersonian America*, 91–92; Foster to the Duchess of Devonshire, April 18, 1812, in Foster, *The Two Duchesses*, 360, spoke of France and Britain being the object of an American declaration of war in which case Sérurier talked of consulting with him.

53. Madame de Staël asked this question of Jefferson, November 10, 1812, in Kimball, "Correspondence of Mme. de Staël with Jefferson," 66. Jefferson answered her on May 28, 1813, citing British ambitions for "*permanent dominion of the ocean and the monopoly of the trade of the world*," ibid., 67–68. According to John Quincy Adams, Madame de Staël was "better conversant with rhetoric than with logic." Witnessing one of her monologues with Lord Cathcart, Britain's ambassador in Russia, Adams related that when she finished another Englishman cried out, "Thank God! That's over!" John Quincy Adams to John Adams, March 22, 1813, in Ford (ed.), *Writings of John Quincy Adams*, IV, 452–53.

54. See Richard Glover's explanation of the War of 1812 in "The French Fleet,

that the Franco-Russian conflict erupted simultaneously with the Anglo-American war.

Just as clarification has been needed about the existence of a secret Franco-American understanding, so James Madison's leadership deserves comment. Madison was not a charismatic figure, and he did not galvanize Congress into war with spirited leadership or stirring rhetoric. Rather, employing his friend Monroe, he worked quietly but diligently with the Congress to defend American rights and honor.[55] He had a sympathetic audience in the legislative branch, overwhelmingly controlled by faithful Republicans. Among the Republicans were a small band of men who supported all warlike measures. These were the fabled "War Hawks" of 1812, but they were a tiny minority of the party. The majority accepted war as a last resort, something forced on the United States by the intractability of the British. They filled their speeches and writings with words such as *liberty, honor, patriotism*, and *freedom*, and most Republicans, however reluctantly, believed that war was America's sole recourse.[56] Through Henry Clay, speaker of the house, and the House Foreign Affairs Committee, the Republicans demonstrated their solidarity with the administration; the declaration of war in June, 1812, then, was a joint endeavor, not the work of war-crazed westerners and southerners who blackmailed Madison into cooperation by threatening to withhold the nomination for the presidency in the upcoming election.[57]

1807–1814: Britain's Problem, and Madison's Opportunity," 249: "The problem with Madison is the problem of diagnosing all his motives. The evidence in this paper shows that in 1812 he had an opportunity like that facing Mussolini in June 1940—an apparent chance to gain territory by attacking a power whose eventual defeat was certain whether he attacked or not." Consul Isaac Barnet noted the French army's prowess in a letter to James Monroe, March 22, 1812, in Monroe Papers, New York Public Library, and said the army should be very successful in the upcoming campaign.

55. Edward Coles to W. C. Rives, January 21, 1856, in "Letters of Edward Coles," *William and Mary Quarterly*, Series 2, VII (1927), 163–64.

56. Rudolph M. Bell, "Mr. Madison's War and Long-Term Congressional Voting Behaviour," *William and Mary Quarterly*, Series 3, XXXVI (1979), 373, 374, 382; Robert L. Ivie, "The Republican Dramatization of War in 1812" (Paper presented at the annual meeting of the Western Speech Communication Association, San Francisco, November, 1976), 6.

57. The War Hawks have been an enduring historiographical issue. See Egan, "The War of 1812: Three Decades of Historical Writing," 74–75. Recent papers about the War Hawks include Harry W. Fritz, "The War Hawks of 1812: An Historical Reality" (Paper presented at the annual meeting of the Western Social Science Association, Denver, Colorado, May, 1975); Hatzenbuehler, "The War Hawks and the Question of Congressional Leadership in 1812," 1–22; Donald R. Hickey, "To the Editor," *Pacific Historical Review*, XLV (1976), 642–44; and Hatzenbuehler's response to Hickey's criticisms, "To the Editor," *ibid.*, 644–45.

More than three quarters of those voting for war in the House came from Pennsylvania and the areas to the south and west of the Keystone State. There has been a tendency to overlook opposition to hostilities in those presumably rabidly prowar areas just as there has been a tendency to ignore support for war in the New England states. In Virginia, certainly a strong war state, antiwar opposition existed in scattered portions of the Old Dominion; those who voiced opposition to the war were worried about slave revolts, they believed that the French were as odious as the British, they feared the impact of hostilities on American institutions, they wondered what would happen to Virginia's economy, and they thought that war was simply futile.[58] The Ohio General Assembly passed a resolution about foreign affairs in January, 1812, flaying the belligerents, Britain especially. "The flag of freedom and impartial neutrality has been wantonly insulted. Tears of the widows and orphans of murdered Americans, have flowed in vain." Clearly Ohio was a hotbed of anti-British sentiment. Yet Ohio's tiny three-man congressional delegation split its vote: Representative Jeremiah Morrow voted for war, Senator Thomas Worthington voted against the war, and Senator Alexander Campbell absented himself at voting time. The highly respected Worthington voted negatively because of Ohio's exposed and vulnerable settlements and because of the nation's military unpreparedness.[59] Residents of Michigan Territory were outraged with Britain's violations of America's neutral rights, but the closer war came, the more the ardor of the citizens cooled, again because of exposed frontier settlements.[60] Even Henry Clay's Kentucky, where Anglophobia flourished, where nationalism thrived, and where expectations of military glory were widespread, furnished the anitwar vote of Senator John "One-Arm" Pope.[61]

As the War Hawk tale has persisted, so has the legend that the United States was "dragged at the wheels of Napoleon's chariot in a constant dust of mystification until he had finally achieved the end of his scheming and landed them in a war." Actually, French diplomatic aims were an open book; long before June, 1812, it was evident that Napoleon wanted an

58. Myron F. Wehtje, "Opposition in Virginia to the War of 1812," *Virginia Magazine of History and Biography*, LXXVII (1970), 67–72.

59. "Resolution of the General Assembly of the State of Ohio, relating to the Foreign Affairs of the United States," January, 1812, Miscellaneous Letters of the Department of State, NA; William R. Barlow, "Ohio's Congressmen and the War of 1812," *Ohio History*, LXXII (1963), 176; and diary entry of June 16, 1812, Thomas Worthington Papers, Library of Congress.

60. William R. Barlow, "The Coming of the War of 1812 in Michigan Territory," *Michigan History*, LIII (1969), 92–93, 102.

61. Hammack, *Kentucky and the Second American Revolution*, 13–15. It was years before Pope recovered from the public's disfavor.

Anglo-American war. Madison recognized French desires as secretary of
state and as president. In case he forgot, divergent sources including John
Quincy Adams, agrarian philosopher John Taylor of Caroline, and Monroe's son-in-law, George Hay, dissected French motives for him.[62]

Madison, Monroe, and the Republican-controlled Congress knew exactly what they were doing when they accepted war in 1812. Britain was
not only more obnoxious to the United States than France, it was also more
vulnerable because of its control of Canada. Occupied by an American
army, Canada would serve as a lever for extracting pledges of Britain's good
behavior in the future. If the English proved reluctant to reform their ways,
Canada could be added to the national domain. In no sense can the War of
1812 be interpreted as a war of conquest or aggrandizement, however.[63]

There was considerable sentiment for a triangular war, America versus
Britain and France. Such an undertaking would have been foolish, of
course, and the idea was rejected, although by a surprisingly narrow mar-
gin. More cautious men argued that France could be thrashed after Britain.
That consideration was even given to warring with both powers simultaneously is graphic proof of national anguish in the spring of 1812. No
wonder the *National Intelligencer* warned, "If ample atonement be not made

62. Alfred Thayer Mahan, *Sea Power in Its Relations to the War of 1812* (2 vols.; Boston,
1905), I. 278–79; Adams to Monroe, October 3, 1811, in Ford (ed.), *Writings of John
Quincy Adams*, IV, 233; Taylor to Monroe, November 24, 1811, in Monroe Papers, New
York Public Library; George Hay to Monroe, January 22, 1812, *ibid.*; Hay to Monroe,
October 12, 1811, in Monroe Papers, LC.

63. This view reflects current historical judgment. Contemporaries displayed mixed
emotions about Canada: "We can make War, and perhaps take Canada at the expense of
$100,000,000 of dollars & it will be a curse to us when we have got it and as for Nova Scotia,
we should be making a wretched bargain to take it as a gift, unless the British would remove
all the tories it contains to Botany Bay, we have enough of this species of gentry already."
Ebenezer Sage to Henry P. Dering, January 25, 1810, in Dering Family Papers. "I have
been unable to discover on what quarter the British could do the U.S. any material injury and
we could at least conquer Canady & humble their over bearing pride," James Caldwell wrote
Worthington, December 14, 1811, in *Thomas Worthington and the War of 1812*, 18. Representative Harper, however, could not contemplate "a war for years to conquer the British
Provinces then surrender them by negociation[;] unless we can have a pledge that conquered,
they shall be retained.ĭ' Harper to Plumer, May 13, 1812, in Egan, "The Path to War in
1812," 174. Foster heard of Harper's views: "A Mr. Harper of the Foreign Committee is said
to have declared that in his opinion it would be advisable to go to war for Canada alone, that
he would be for never laying down arms until Canada should be taken." Foster to Castlereagh, June 9, 1812, in FOA 5:86, LC. See also Brown, *The Republic in Peril*, 125–30;
Lawrence S. Kaplan, "France and Madison's Decision for War, 1812," *Mississippi Valley
Historical Review*, L (1964), 652–71; and J. C. A. Stagg, "James Madison and the Coercion
of Great Britain: Canada, the West Indies, and the War of 1812," *William and Mary Quarterly*, Series 3, XXXVIII (1981), 3–34.

by France for these outrages, we trust in God she will be made to feel, by a vigorous retaliation of her flagrant injustices, the resentment of a national and spirited people for affrontful and unwarrantable injuries committed on their rights and commerce."[64]

[V]

The outbreak of war intensified American pressure on France for more just and equitable treatment. Madison and Monroe confronted Sérurier repeatedly with stories about French vessels burning American merchantmen headed for Spain and Portugal, and they complained frequently about the obstacles impeding the expansion of Franco-American commerce. Barlow was also apprised of the widespread discontent and disappointment with France existing in the United States, and he so informed Dalberg and through Dalberg, Bassano. Even the English unwittingly lent the Americans a helping hand in applying further pressure on the French when, too late to affect the American declaration of war, they curbed their orders in council in June, 1812. "You see that this Government, altho' rather late & with a bad grace, gives up its offending orders in council," Jonathan Russell pointedly reminded a French diplomat. "I hope that this measure may quicken a disposition on your side of the channel to cultivate friendship & commercial intercourse between our two countries."[65]

According to Barlow, news of the limited revocation "produced a great & agreeable sensation," in Paris and the poet-diplomat used the information to prod the French for more equitable treatment of America. Weary of French procrastination, dismayed by the outbreak of the War of 1812, and concerned it might appear that he was failing his friends, Barlow unceasingly demanded that America be given proper attention, and he asked that the Emperor "devote a few moments of his thoughts to our affairs & that he will consent that his minister should answer to some of the notes I have had the honor to present him within the last six months." He also discussed the American case to anyone in earshot: to ex-Empress Josephine at her estate Malmaison, to his friend Parker at Draveil, to Jean-Jacques Regis, Prince de Cambacérès, in Paris. While Barlow's message was familiar, he added some new facts derived from letters of Monroe and Madison: responding to the inflamed national mood, Barlow might be summoned home, largely severing diplomatic channels; furthermore, the American

---

64. *National Intelligencer*, June 20, 1812. The *National Intelligencer* was still discussing the folly of a triangular war on June 22, 1814.

65. Russell to Petry, June 30, 1812, in Russell Papers, Brown University.

people might demand war against France unless she altered her policy toward the United States. Reiterating this message and showing the French one of Madison's letters dated August 11, the envoy reported some progress had been made and that "several innocent men" had been frightened by the letter. Cambacérès assured him that if Napoleon had even a half hour to familiarize himself with America's current situation, he would approve a settlement. Though much remained to be done, Barlow became "pretty confident of success & great success." In mid-October, as progress was being made in negotiations, Bassano invited Barlow to Napoleon's advanced base at Vilna, Lithuania. The endless delays, the many wearisome conversations, and the tedious bureaucratic inconveniences would be swept aside and forgotten when a mutually acceptable treaty of commerce was agreed upon.[66]

There were good reasons for Bassano's invitation to Barlow. Dalberg had been instructed to stall negotiations, and had faithfully done so. Barlow's insistent demands had worn the duc down, however, and the time had arrived for Bassano himself to handle the American. The journey to Vilna would consume almost a month, giving the French further leeway. In any case, if a Franco-American agreement was to be signed, obviously someone of greater stature than Dalberg, whose greed and politics prompted his fall from favor, would have to conclude the work.[67]

Barlow understood that he was undertaking a hazardous journey to a distant city on the edge of a war zone on the eve of winter. He believed that he had no alternative to the risky trip because a treaty of commerce with indemnifications hung in the balance; to spurn Bassano's invitation to Vilna might mean further lengthy delays. The potential adventure of the travel strongly appealed to Barlow. Sixteen years previously he had sought an appointment for a mission in Turkey and the Italian states with the explanation that "what might be seen in such a tour would increase my little stock of knowledge."[68] Barlow therefore accepted Bassano's offer. He would take

66. Barlow to Russell, July 14, 1812, *ibid.*; Barlow to duc de Dalberg, August 26, 1812, in AMAE, LXIX, LC; Barlow to Madison, September 26, 1812, in Madison Papers, LC. Irving Brant, "Joel Barlow, Madison's Stubborn Minister," *William and Mary Quarterly*, Series 3, XV (1958), 446–47, points out that the French obtained a copy of this letter; Barlow to Ruth Barlow, September 26, 1812, in Jonathan Bayard Smith Family Papers.

67. Duc de Dalberg to Bassano, May 28, 1812, in AMAE, LXIX, LC; Emile Dard, *Napoleon and Talleyrand* (New York, 1937), 78, 89, 294–95; Bonnel, *La France, les Etats Unis et la guerre de course*, 301.

68. Barlow to Wolcott, April 27, 1796, Wolcott Papers. Some confusion exists about Barlow's goals on this journey. He was adamant that indemnities be paid and agreement on this issue was a prerequisite to a commercial treaty. As the French would under no circumstances pay cash to settle damages, Barlow was apparently willing to accept a complicated

his nephew, Thomas, and travel to Vilna, 1,400 miles to the east, via Frankfurt-on-the-Main, Berlin, and Königsberg. While Jean Baptiste Petry would follow the Barlows in three or four days, no armed escort or other protection was extended to the Americans until they were seventy miles from Vilna. In short, except for their driver, Joel and Thomas Barlow would be traveling across war-torn Europe on their own. No doubt Barlow had these things in mind when he made out his will the day before his departure.

On October 27 the Barlows left their residence at 100 rue Vaugirard. Despite heavy rains, they made good time journeying across eastern France. In central Germany they took time to visit Martin Luther's grave at Wurttenberg, and they passed the battlefield of Jena, site of a Napoleonic victory six years earlier. On November 5, 675 miles from Paris, the Barlows entered Berlin.[69] There was no time to enjoy the Prussian capital, for Vilna was still 725 miles distant.

Conditions deteriorated east of Berlin. The constant rain had turned all of Saxony into a "quagmire," and with no frost the roads were terrible. Still the Barlows reached the ancient city of Königsberg on the twelfth, and there they made ready for the winter. On the seventeenth they reached Kovno, the staging point for Napoleon's chief invasion force the preceding June, and now a rear area on the Russian front; the town was jammed with soldiers and filled with the debris of war. An escort of four dragoons joined the Americans for the final seventy-mile leg of the trip. Between Kovno and Vilna, the two Americans were confronted by the carnage of war: dead horses and broken wagons were strewn by the wayside while wounded men in open wagons moved in endless cavalcade to the west. Twenty-two days and 1,400 miles from Paris, the Barlows reached Vilna the evening of November 18.

Vilna was an old university town and probably a pleasant place in normal times. The French had striven to make the community appear normal by organizing cultural events and carrying on with everyday life. Maret, duc de Bassano, was present as were the representatives of Austria, Baden, Denmark, Prussia, and Saxony. Rumors of disaster in the East circulated

---

formula whereby France would pay claims from licensed export earnings to the United States. See "Historical Anecdotes and Observations, committed to paper by William Lowndes," November 10, 1819, in William Lowndes Papers, Library of Congress, and Chase C. Mooney, *William H. Crawford 1772–1834* (Lexington, 1974), 57. Volume LXIX of the AMAE, LC, contains relevant information.

69. Barlow's itinerary can be followed in Clifford L. Egan (ed.), "On the Fringe of the Napoleonic Catastrophe: Joel Barlow's Letters from Central and Eastern Europe, 1812," *Early American Literature*, X (1975–1976), 251–72.

freely, but Barlow was confident that Napoleon would be triumphant. Once the Russians had been crushed, the treaty would be completed.

The Barlows stayed in Vilna a little over two weeks. There were dinners with Bassano, dances with Polish ladies, tutoring sessions with Tom, conversations with other diplomats, gloomy reports from Ruth about the war on the home front, and sad news about the death of his friend Mark Leavenworth. Amidst all these things, Barlow continued sending Bassano notes. "I cannot penetrate the cause of this neglect," he complained to the Frenchman on one occasion. "It is inconceivable to my government especially as it has long since been informed that I had taken the liberty more than once of inviting your Excellency's attention to the subject as a matter of very serious importance."[70] Even as Barlow penned these lines a courier was bringing orders from Napoleon that Vilna must be evacuated.

Unknown to those present in Vilna, the *Grande Armée* had been dealt mortal blows by the Russians and their ally, winter. Though the French had occupied Moscow, capture of the important Russian city did not curtail national resistance. The French realized belatedly that they were deep in enemy country late in the year. As Barlow was preparing to leave Paris for Lithuania, the French abandoned Moscow. All went well for the French and their allies as they retraced their steps until they were west of Smolensk. Crossing the Beresina River, military catastrophe overtook Napoleon; the disaster was compounded by the arrival of winter. As Barlow was closing on Vilna, the *Grande Armée* disintegrated.

On December 6 the Barlows, accompanied by Petry, left Vilna. The American diplomat was disappointed that a treaty still eluded him; he wrote his wife that he had "done no good" and that he would have to complete an agreement when he returned to Paris. As his sled sped toward Warsaw via Grodno on the Niemen River, Barlow contemplated the fate of Napoleon's once mighty force—or what was left of it—buried in an ocean of whiteness with temperatures below zero. Scarcely four years before Barlow had written that the "best place to cure the . . . French disease is in the swamps of Poland, & their physicians are the Cossacks."[71] Whether the poet-diplomat remembered these lines as he approached Warsaw is unknown; however, disgust with the war and the terrible human suffering it had brought inspired Barlow to write one of his better known poems, "Advice to a Raven in Russia."

In Warsaw Barlow decided to swing to the south, driving for Paris through Cracow, Vienna, and Munich rather than returning home through

70. Barlow to Bassano, December 4, 1812, in AMAE, LXIX, LC.
71. Barlow to Coxe, September 11, 1808, in Tench Coxe Papers, Historical Society of Pennsylvania.

Berlin. He believed that the weather and the roads might be better; besides, he would be able to visit some old friends including Louis Guillaume Otto, the French ambassador in Vienna and a man very familiar with the United States, and Benjamin Thompson, Count Rumford, a loyalist living in Munich. Throughout his trip Barlow's health had been excellent and as he left Warsaw he wrote Ruth Barlow that he would be with her in twenty-five days. Between Warsaw and Cracow, however, he became ill suddenly and he was forced to stop at the small town of Zarnowiec. A physician was summoned, but it was too late to help Barlow. Lamenting that "my uncle is no more," Tom Barlow told Ruth that "an inflamation of the lungs with a violent fever" had caused death.[72] The diplomatic mission that Barlow had accepted with so much foreboding ended with his death on the plains of Poland; in a very real sense he was one of the casualties of Napoleon's great Russian offensive. Like many soldiers of the invading army, Barlow was buried far from his native country.

Time proved that Barlow had died uselessly. William H. Crawford, his successor as minister to France and a loyal Jeffersonian from Georgia, was to spend almost two years in Paris vainly seeking a settlement of the same tiresome problems that had taken Barlow to Vilna. As Napoleon's preoccupation with non-American affairs had thwarted Barlow, so the collapse of the First Empire in 1813–1814 held the Emperor's attention. In April, 1814, Napoleon finally lost control of France and was exiled to the island of Elba. With his defeat the reasons for Anglo-American conflict and Franco-American differences ceased and the War of 1812 ended in December, 1814. At long last, after years of national humiliation, a more powerful and respected United States was free to devote its energies to more constructive pursuits than war. Yet the past did not die, for the claims of American citizens for losses incurred in the early 1800s were still outstanding almost a generation later.

72. Thomas Barlow to Ruth Barlow, December 27, 1812, in Barlow Papers, Harvard University.

Epilogue

Word of Joel Barlow's death in Po-
land did not reach Paris until mid-January. Even then Ruth Barlow had to
wait for Daniel Parker to provide her with more complete information
about her husband's last days between Warsaw and Zarnowiec, because
Thomas Barlow found "the subject . . . too painful for me to repeat to
you." Jean Baptiste Petry also provided some details about Barlow's death;
he did not appear seriously ill, Petry told Ruth, and Barlow believed that
"he could cure himself." Terribly distressed, Ruth Barlow remained in
Paris until the summer of 1813 when she sailed for America. Living in New
York with Robert Fulton and his wife, Ruth confessed to Dolley Madison
that "the sight of Kalorama would recall too painful ideas."[1] In 1814 she
returned to Washington, haunted with memories of the happy life she had
shared with her husband of three decades, living at Kalorama with her sister
Clara. Barlow's body was never returned to the United States, and he lies
today in the churchyard where he was buried during the terrible winter of
1812–1813. Before her death in 1817, Mrs. Barlow had a marble tablet
honoring her fallen husband placed in Zarnowiec.

The question of who should act in Barlow's place ignited a simmering
dispute between William Lee and David Bailie Warden. Ignoring Warden,
Lee claimed that the Paris legation was in chaos and he argued that Thomas
Barlow was too young to transact diplomatic business. Warden challenged
Lee's authority, however, announcing, "I am acknowledged in my quality

1. Thomas Barlow to Ruth Barlow, December 27, 1812, in Barlow Papers, Harvard
University; Petry to Ruth Barlow, January 8, 1813, in Barlow Papers, Yale University; Ruth
Barlow to Dolley Madison, December 16, 1813, *ibid.*

of consul general as the only commissioned agent and organ of our Government at Paris." The "hell of a blow up" predicted by Russell's friend Nathan Haley in 1812 thus had finally materialized, intensifying Ruth Barlow's grief. Warden's conduct, she complained to Madison, was so "indelicate . . . & I think incorrect" that she had asked Thomas Barlow to "protect the private papers which regard the negotiation [for a commercial treaty]."[2]

As he had done before in his campaigning for an appointment, Warden enlisted the support of influential friends in America and Europe. Joseph Carrington Cabell had spoken to Jefferson on Warden's behalf in 1811; in 1813 he discussed Warden and the American colony in Paris with William H. Crawford when the new minister to France stopped at Cabell's Virginia estate en route from Washington to Georgia before embarking for France. "Fortunately he already knew most of them," Cabell informed Warden, and "I believe he contributed to your restoration to your present office."[3] Prominent foreign intellectuals also came to Warden's assistance. Portuguese botanist Joseph Francis Correa de Serra wrote Madison and Jefferson while Prussian educator-explorer Baron Wilhelm von Humboldt wrote Madison twice and Gallatin at least once, emphasizing Warden's talents.

Warden proceeded to act as the official representative of the United States, attending functions at Bassano's and referring to himself as the "sole agent accredited to and recognized by the French government." Lee was not persuaded by Warden's claim and, noting the technical responsibilities of Warden, argued that Armstrong's one-time friend was not only exceeding his authority, but was being disrespectful to Ruth Barlow. His words falling on deaf ears, Lee retreated to Bordeaux, chiding Warden because "there is nothing so disgraceful to public officers as to be disputing and quarelling [*sic*] in a foreign country." In what was meant as a final salvo, Lee described Warden as one "of those upright Gentlemen who are so very straight that they bend backwards."[4]

Into this acrimonious atmosphere stepped Crawford. It took the Georgia politician only a short time to grow weary of Warden and sick of the squabbling. Finding Warden "ignorant and arrogant, full of duplicity, obsequious to his superiors, and insolent to his inferiors," Crawford dismissed him. Although Warden's champions beseeched Crawford to rescind the

2. Warden to Lee, January 19, 1813, in Lee to Monroe, January 20, 1813, in Despatches from United States Consuls in Bordeaux, NA; Ruth Barlow to Madison, February 10, 1813, in Gratz Collection.

3. Cabell to Warden, May [?], 1813, in Warden Papers, Maryland Historical Society.

4. "Au Directeur de *la Revue Des Deux Mondes*," October–November, 1830, copy in Warden Papers, LC; Lee to Warden, July 17, 1813, *ibid*.

dismissal, the new minister refused to reinstate the Irish-born Warden. Not even Jefferson, who had once praised Warden as "perfectly modest & good & of a delicate mind," was able to change Crawford's mind.[5]

Warden chose to remain in Paris, the intellectual center of his universe. Over the next three decades he wrote frequently about his adopted homeland, collected a large library (which he sold to the State of New York), and was an unsuccessful office seeker from President Andrew Jackson—despite authoring a brief adulatory account of the general, *Notice Biographique Sur Le General Jackson* (Paris, 1829). He died in Paris on October 9, 1845. His nemesis William Lee, who had escaped Crawford's wrath by being in Bordeaux, served in that city on the Bay of Biscay until 1816 when, presumably pleased that Warden had been humbled, he returned to America. Lee worked for the treasury department until he was swept out of office by the same Andrew Jackson who ignored Warden. Lee died in Massachusetts at the end of February, 1840.

Crawford's tenure in France lasted less than two years. While the Warden-Lee clash distressed him, he was most unhappy because of his inability to resolve Franco-American differences. As Crawford's predecessors had discovered, France's European problems overshadowed American affairs, and this was especially true amidst the collapse of the First Empire in 1813–1814. Gradually Crawford immersed himself in American matters

---

5. Entry of September 16, 1813, in Knowlton (ed.), *The Journal of William H. Crawford*, 44–45; Jefferson to Madison, December 8, 1810, in Madison Papers, LC. Jefferson's inability to help Warden is an interesting example of Madison's independence while president. Defending Warden in a lengthy letter to Madison, Jefferson claimed Crawford "has sound sense, but no science, speaks not a word of the [French] language, and has not the easy manner which open[s] the doors of the polite circle. I have as little doubt," Jefferson continued critically, "that if Crawford could suppress the little pride & jealousy which are beneath him, he might often make Warden the entering wedge for accomplishing with that Government, what will be totally beyond his own faculties. I fear his experience has not yet taught him the lesson, indispensable in the practical business of life, to consider men as other machines to be used for what they are fitted, that a razor should be employed to shave our beards and an axe to cut our wood, and that we should not throw away the axe because it will not shave us, nor the razor because it will not cut our wood." Jefferson to Madison, October 13, 1814, in Jefferson Papers, LC. Madison answered Jefferson ten days later. He defended Crawford as "a man of strong intellect . . . but of a temper not perhaps sufficiently pliant." Denying that Crawford was jealous of Warden, Madison argued that Warden's "apparent modesty & gravity cover ambition [,] vanity [,] avidity (from poverty at least) [,] & intrigue." In Paris, the real Warden had mistreated Ruth Barlow, "seized" a "station for which he had as little of qualifications as of pretensions." Finally, Warden had cleverly ingratiated himself with erudite scientists ("to whom he has paid court"), the Irish, and those in government. Madison to Jefferson, October 23, 1814, in Madison Papers, LC. On the Jefferson-Madison relationship, see Roy J. Honeywell, "President Jefferson and His Successor," *American Historical Review*, XLVI (1940), 64–75.

instead of international problems and it was with relief that he returned home in 1815. A rising political star, Crawford's career was cut short when illness forced him out of the 1824 presidential race; he died a decade later.

Jonathan Russell was a vocal opponent of Crawford in 1824. That should not have surprised anyone, for Russell, having served inconspicuously with John Quincy Adams, James A. Bayard, Henry Clay, and Albert Gallatin, through the negotiations culminating in the Treaty of Ghent, had attached himself to the politically ambitious Clay, one of Crawford's adversaries in 1824.[6] After the peace settlement, Russell was minister to Norway and Sweden until 1818; returning home, he ran for and was elected to the House of Representatives. The former chargé d'affaires in France seemed to be in an enviable position in the early 1820s: he was in his political prime and he enjoyed Clay's support. Unfortunately for the ambitious Russell, he became embroiled in a dispute with Adams about certain passages in correspondence during the Ghent negotiations. Adams emerged triumphant in the war of words, Clay abandoned Russell, and Russell's promising post-diplomatic career ended.[7] He died in Milton, Massachusetts, in mid-February, 1832.

By the mid-1830s most of the Americans who had served in France during the Napoleonic era or who had been active in government prior to 1812 had passed from the scene. Robert R. Livingston of Louisiana Purchase fame died in 1813. James Bowdoin, Armstrong's foe in Paris in 1806 and 1807, died in 1811. James Monroe moved up to the presidency in 1817, served two terms, and retired to a farm in Loudon County, Virginia. Monroe spent his last years an impoverished claimant seeking compensation for expenses incurred serving the United States on diplomatic missions abroad. He died in New York City on the Fourth of July, 1831. Thomas Jefferson also had died on the Fourth of July five years previously. Like Monroe, Jefferson's last years were filled with financial difficulties; constantly admonishing his countrymen about the evils of the public debt, private citizen Jefferson was unable to live within his means. James Madison, Jefferson's alter ego and collaborator, died a decade after his friend, scarcely a week from the Fourth of July.

Daniel Parker, the wealthy friend or acquaintance of Barlow, Jefferson, Monroe, and others, died in dire circumstances in France early in 1829. A century and a half after his death, his career remains shrouded in mystery.

---

6. Crawford's biographer has written that "Russell apparently was a peevish, petulant, pestering, carping type who never seemed satisfied with the actions of an individual against whom he had a pique." Mooney, *William H. Crawford*, 230–31, n43.

7. Samuel Flagg Bemis, *John Quincy Adams and the Foundations of American Foreign Policy* (New York, 1956), 498–508.

Draveil, Parker's magnificent estate, provided a beautiful setting for the wedding of Thomas Barlow and Francis Anica Preble (whose mother was rumored to have been Parker's mistress) on July 28, 1817. The couple remained in France until after Parker's death when they returned to America, settling in Washington, Pennsylvania, where Thomas Barlow died in October, 1859.

John Armstrong mended his differences with Madison and he supported the Virginian in the presidential election of 1812. In the early phases of the War of 1812 Armstrong rendered important service in the New York City area and when Secretary of War William Eustis resigned his post in December, 1812, Armstrong, while not Madison's first choice for the office, was named to the position. As secretary of war, Armstrong turned in a credible performance; however, he was made a scapegoat for the burning of Washington in 1814 and removed. Armstrong spent most of the next three decades at "Rokeby," his estate overlooking the Hudson River, pondering and writing about the crucial events he had witnessed or in which he had been a participant. He died on April 1, 1843.[8]

Fulwar Skipwith, once described by Armstrong as a "block-head," settled in West Florida where he grew cotton on a 1,300-acre plantation "on the Montesano Bluffs near Baton Rouge."[9] Although he claimed not to be involved in the revolt that delivered West Florida to the United States, Skipwith drew up the constitution for the briefly independent Republic of West Florida and he served as its elected leader. Like his friend Monroe, Skipwith memorialized Congress for debts owed him for service overseas until his death in 1839.

By the late 1830s, most of the French ruling elite known to Armstrong, Barlow, Lee, Skipwith, and Warden had passed from the scene. Napoleon survived his downfall by six years, dying in exile on the remote South Atlantic island of St. Helena in 1821, having uttered a few gratuitous remarks about the United States. Talleyrand enjoyed a much happier ending; he helped restore Louis XVIII to the throne of France and he was a key figure at the peacemaking in Vienna at the end of the Napoleonic Wars. Before his death in 1838, Talleyrand was ambassador to Britain. His successors at the Foreign Ministry, Champagny, duc de Cadore, and Maret, duc de Bassano, died respectively in 1834 and 1839.

Turreau survived until December 15, 1816. Despite his involvement in controversial and significant events during the French Revolution and under Napoleon, he has not had a biographer. Sérurier lived into the 1850s;

8. Skeen, "Mr. Madison's Secretary of War," *passim*.
9. Abernethy, *The South in the New Nation*, 344–45.

early in that decade he was writing a detailed account of his tenure in Washington. Certainly Sérurier, as an eyewitness to the War of 1812, with his knowledge of the events preceding that conflict, and because of his familiarity with American statesmen, had much of value to relate. He never completed the manuscript and his dispatches from Washington, which are filled with useful information about the second Anglo-American war, have generally been overlooked by historians of the War of 1812. Sérurier returned to the United States as a diplomat in the early days of Andrew Jackson's presidency, when, ironically enough, relations between the two nations were strained by American claims for shipping losses sustained a quarter century before. Like Turreau, Sérurier does not have a biographer; like Turreau, he deserves one. D'Hauterive died in 1830; Louis André Pichon survived until 1850.

When Pichon died in 1850, France was witnessing the rise of another Napoleon; once in power, like his relative, Napoleon III followed policies that seriously strained Franco-American relations. In the United States in 1850 the turmoil and troubles of the Age of Jefferson seemed remote and irrelevant to Americans concerned with the threat slavery posed to the Union. Jefferson and Madison had guided "the Ark of Our liberties to a safe repose"; now another generation was charged with the same responsibility.[10]

10. Levi Bartlett to Josiah Bartlett, June 15, 1812, in Bartlett Papers.

Appendix: A Chronology

1799

November 9   Napoleon seizes power in the coup d'état of 18 *Brumaire.*

1800

September 30   Convention of Môrtefontaine signed.

October 1   The Treaty of San Ildefonso transfers Louisiana from Spain to France.

1801

March 1   Louis André Pichon arrives in America to serve as chargé d'affaires.

March 4   Thomas Jefferson succeeds John Adams as president.

November 12   Robert R. Livingston arrives in France to serve as minister to France.

1802

March 25   Peace of Amiens ends Franco-British war (preliminary articles signed on October 1, 1801).

June, 1802   Thomas Sumter observes Livingston and Daniel Parker discussing the Floridas.

1803

April 30   The Louisiana Purchase agreement officially signed.

May 19   Breakdown of the Peace of Amiens.

June 3   Great Britain issues first order in council of the new war.

June 20   The French order the confiscation of British products.

1804

February 24   Congress passes the Mobile Act.

September 20   François Marbois tells Livingston that France will expect money if the United States is to obtain the Floridas.

October   John Armstrong arrives in France to succeed Livingston as minister to France.

November   Louis Turreau arrives in Washington as minister to the United States.

November–December   James Monroe in Paris seeking French help to obtain the Floridas from Spain.

December 2	Napoleon crowned emperor.
December 14	Spain joins France in the war against Britain.

1805

January–June	Monroe-Pinckney negotiations in Madrid.
January 4	Spain and France conclude a treaty in effect guaranteeing the integrity of Spanish colonial possessions.
March 3	Haitian port clearance bill becomes law.
May–June [*date unknown*]	*Essex* decision.
August	General Jean Moreau begins his American exile.
September 14	Armstrong approached about money for the Floridas.
October 20	Battle of Ulm.
October 21	Battle of Trafalgar.
October 21	*War in Disguise* published.
November 12	Jefferson's cabinet gives approval to use money for a Florida settlement.
December 2	Battle of Austerlitz.

1806

February 28	Congress approves further legislation affecting trade with Haiti.
March	Senate approves Armstrong to negotiate for West Florida with Bowdoin.
April 13	Andrew Gregg's amended and changed bill becomes law (not effective until December, 1807).
May 16	Fox's blockade.
October 14	Battles of Jena and Auerstadt.
November 21	Berlin decree.
December 31	Monroe-Pinkney treaty.

1807

January 7	British order in council issued.
February 8	Battle of Eylau.
June 14	Battle of Friedland.
June 22	*Chesapeake-Leopard* affair.
Late June	Franco-Russian negotiations at Tilsit.
August	Talleyrand leaves the Foreign Ministry, succeeded by Champagny.
October 10	*Horizon* case.
November 11	British order in council issued.

December 17	Napoleon responds to the order in council of November 11 with the Milan decree.
December 22	The embargo law becomes effective.

1808

January 9	Supplemental embargo legislation.
March 12	Supplemental embargo legislation.
April 17	Bayonne decree.
April 25	Supplemental embargo legislation.
May 2	Spanish rebellion begins.

1809

January 9	Embargo Enforcement Act.
March 1	Non-intercourse act replaces the embargo.
March 4	James Madison inaugurated as Jefferson's successor.
March–July	The Coles mission to France.
April 21	Erskine agreement proclaimed.
April 26	Britain redefines its blockade of Europe.
May–July	Armstrong-d'Hauterive talks.
May 21–22	Battles of Aspern-Essling.
July 6	Battle of Wagram.
July 21	Madison learns of Britain's disavowal of the Erskine agreement.
December–January, 1810	Napoleon pressured for an accommodation with the United States; Armstrong and Lee expect an agreement.

1810

1810	License trade at its zenith.
March 23	Rambouillet decree.
May 1	Macon's Bill #2 supersedes non-intercourse (published in Paris on June 24).
July 5	St. Cloud decree allows imports from America under license system.
Late July	Napoleon decides to revoke the Berlin and Milan decrees as they pertain to the United States.
August 5	The Cadore letter conveys Napoleon's decision about the Berlin and Milan decrees to Armstrong.
August 5	Trianon tariff fixes rates on imports from America; provision made for the disposition of sequestered American merchandise.
September 12	Armstrong leaves France; Jonathan Russell becomes chargé d'affaires.

September 26   Independence of West Florida proclaimed.

October 18   Fontainebleau decree attempts to curb smuggling and
                    movement of unwanted goods into France.

November 2   Madison proclaims French compliance with Macon's bill
                    #2; Britain has three months to respond.

December 31   Russia abandons the Continental System; Russian ports
                    are opened to American ships.

1811

February 13   Sérurier arrives in Washington replacing Turreau as min-
                    ister to the United States.

Late February   The Senate approves Barlow as minister to France.

March 2   Non-importation goes into effect against Britain.

March   Robert Smith ousted as secretary of state and is suc-
                    ceeded by James Monroe in April.

April 17   Duc de Bassano becomes foreign minister.

April 28   Date of the specious St. Cloud decree revoking the
                    Berlin and Milan decrees against the United States.

May 16   H.M.S. *Little Belt* and the U.S.S. *President* clash.

Early July   Augustus John Foster arrives in Washington and talks
                    with Monroe deadlock immediately.

Mid–July   Madison interprets favorably a message from Sérurier and
                    news brought by the *John Adams*.

July 24   Twelfth Congress summoned to meet early in November.

July 26   Monroe draws up Barlow's instructions.

July–August   Madison decides on war with Britain.

August 5   Barlow sails for France aboard the *Constitution*.

Mid–September   Barlow arrives in Paris and receives a warm welcome;
                    Napoleon departs for Holland.

November 5   Madison delivers his annual message to the newly as-
                    sembled Twelfth Congress.

November 7   Battle of Tippecanoe.

November 17   Napoleon receives Barlow.

1812

March   The Henry affair.

April–May   Napoleon and Bassano leave Paris for Germany; Barlow
                    negotiates with Dalberg.

April 4   Ninety-day embargo laid.

April 14   Monroe's prowar editorial appears in the *National
                    Intelligencer*.

May 22	The *Hornet* returns from Europe without favorable news.
June 1	Madison submits his war message to Congress.
June 18	The United States declares war on Great Britain.
June 24	Napoleon launches his Russian campaign.
September–October	French in Moscow; they begin leaving the Russian capital on October 19.
October 27	Joel and Thomas Barlow depart Paris for Vilna.
November 18	The Barlows reach Vilna.
November 26–29	French catastrophe on the Beresina River.
December 6	The Barlows and Petry leave Vilna.
December 26	Joel Barlow dies at Zarnowiec.

Bibliography

Most books concerning Franco-American relations have been authored by Americans. Indeed, the works of Henry Adams, Albert H. Bowman, Alexander De Conde, and Lawrence S. Kaplan have no equivalents in French historiography, and it does not appear that any significant French-authored works about France's relations with the United States in the Napoleonic period will be forthcoming soon. While books by Adams, Bowman, De Conde, and Kaplan do examine Franco-American diplomacy, none of these historians except Adams have thoroughly explored the post-Louisiana Purchase period, and Adams' multivolume masterpiece is almost a century old. This book, then, is the first modern study of Franco-American relations in the era of the Emperor Napoleon.

Heavy reliance has been placed on manuscript sources, and I have culled archives from Mississippi to Nova Scotia looking for relevant information; I believe that the many collections I have examined have strengthened my presentation. Still, certain holdings were more important than others; they include the Jonathan Russell Papers at Brown University; the Joel Barlow Papers at Harvard University; the photoduplications of the Archives du Ministère des Affaires Étrangères and the Foreign Office Archives of the Public Record Office as well as the Thomas Jefferson Papers, the James Madison Papers, the James Monroe Papers, and the Joseph H. Nicholson Papers, all in the Manuscript Division of the Library of Congress. The Despatches from France and the Diplomatic Instructions of the Department of State: All Countries, both in The National Archives, are a must.

The *National Intelligencer*, linked as it was to Jefferson's and Madison's administrations, is also an indispensable source. On the French side, the *Correspondance de Napoléon Ier* (32 vols.; Paris, 1858–1870) is a necessary primary source, while an important secondary work is François Crouzet, *L'Economie britannique et le blocus continental, 1806–1813* (2 vols.; Paris, 1958). Two decades after its publication, Crouzet's thorough investigation deserves translation into English.

The period from 1800 to 1815 in American history has attracted major scholarly writing. Warren H. Goodman ("The Origins of the War of 1812: A Survey of Changing Interpretations," *Mississippi Valley Historical Review*, XXXIII [1941], 171–86), and Clifford L. Egan ("The War of 1812: Three Decades of Historical Writing," *Military Affairs*, XXXVIII [1974],

72–75) are good guides to the relevant literature. Two books not included in these historiographical articles, which should not be overlooked, are Frank E. Melvin, *Napoleon's Navigation System* (New York, 1919) and James Woodress, *A Yankee's Odyssey: The Life of Joel Barlow* (Philadelphia and New York, 1958). Melvin's work is old and awkwardly written, but he provides a gold mine of useful information. The Woodress biography deftly sketches Joel Barlow's career through such tumultuous episodes as the French Revolution, the rise of Napoleon, and service to the early American Republic.

MANUSCRIPT SOURCES

Connecticut

Beinecke Library, Yale University, New Haven
 Joel Barlow Papers
 Pequot Collection
Connecticut Historical Society, Hartford
 Brainerd Collection
 Oliver Wolcott Papers
Sterling Library, Yale University, New Haven
 David Daggett Papers

District of Columbia

Library of Congress Manuscript Division
 Archives du Ministère des Affaires Étrangères, Correspondance Politique, États-Unis, Vols. LIII–LXXII
 Josiah Bartlett Papers
 Nicholas Biddle Papers
 Sylvanus Bourne Papers
 George Washington Campbell Papers
 William Eustis Papers
 Foreign Office Archives, Public Record Office, 5
 Augustus John Foster Diary
 Gideon and Francis Granger Papers
 John Holker Papers
 Thomas Jefferson Papers
 James Kent Papers
 Lee-Palfrey Family Papers
 William Lowndes Papers
 James Madison Papers
 James McHenry Papers
 Miscellaneous Manuscript Collection
 James Monroe Papers
 Daniel Mulford Diary
 Wilson Cary Nicholas Papers

Joseph H. Nicholson Papers
Personal Papers Miscellaneous
William Plumer Papers
Rodney Family Papers
William Short Papers
Fulwar Skipwith Papers, Causten-Pickett Collection
John Cotton Smith Papers
Jonathan Bayard Smith Family Papers
Samuel Smith Papers
Joseph Story Papers
David Bailie Warden Papers
Thomas Worthington Papers
National Archives, Department of State Archives (microfilm)
Despatches from United States Consuls in Bordeaux
Despatches from United States Consuls in La Rochelle
Despatches from United States Consuls in Marseilles
Despatches from United States Consuls in Nantes
Despatches from United States Consuls in Paris
Despatches from United States Ministers to France
Diplomatic Instructions of the Department of State: All Countries
Miscellaneous Letters of the Department of State
Notes from the French Legation
National Archives, Department of War Archives (microfilm)
Letters Received by the Secretary of War

Maine

Maine Historical Society, Portland
J. S. H. Fogg Collection
William King Papers

Maryland

Maryland Historical Society, Baltimore
David Bailie Warden Papers

Massachusetts

American Antiquarian Society, Worcester
Andrew Craigie Papers
Joel Barlow Papers
Houghton Library, Harvard University, Cambridge
Joel Barlow Papers
Massachusetts Historical Society, Boston
Bowdoin and Temple Papers
Henry Dearborn Papers
Elbridge Gerry Papers
Thomas Jefferson Papers

Harrison Gray Otis Papers
Timothy Pickering Papers
Jonathan Russell Papers
Saltonstall Family Papers
Washburn Papers
Peabody Museum, Essex Institute, Salem
Crowninshield Family Papers

Michigan

William L. Clements Library, University of Michigan, Ann Arbor
Dering Family Papers
Melville Papers
War of 1812 Collection

Mississippi

Mississippi Department of Archives and History, Jackson
J. F. H. Claiborne Collection

The Netherlands

Gemeente-Archief, Amsterdam
Peter Stadnitski Papers

New Hampshire

New Hampshire State Library, Concord
William Plumer Papers
William Plumer Biographical Sketches

New York

New-York Historical Society, New York City
Barlow Miscellaneous Manuscripts
William Duer Papers
Albert Gallatin Papers
Robert R. Livingston Papers
Miscellaneous Manuscripts T.
Naval History Collection
John Smith of Mastic Papers
United States Military Philosophical Society Papers
New York Public Library
James Barbour Papers
James Madison Papers
James Monroe Papers
New York Public Library Annex
William Constable Papers
New York State Library, Albany
Harmanus Bleecker Papers

Rokeby Collection, Barrytown-on-Hudson, New York
  John Armstrong Miscellaneous Collection

Nova Scotia

Public Archives of Nova Scotia, Halifax
  Letters to the Secretary of State
  Letters of the Secretary of State
  Gideon White Papers

Ohio

Kent State University Library, Kent
  Sérurier Papers (microfilm from the Centre de Microfilm des Archives de Seine et
    Oise, France)

Pennsylvania

Historical Society of Pennsylvania, Philadelphia
  Tench Coxe Papers (microfilm)
  Gratz Collection
  Dreer Collection
  George Logan Papers
  Robert Vaux Papers

Rhode Island

John Hay Library, Brown University, Providence
  Jonathan Russell Papers

Tennessee

Tennessee Historical Society, Nashville
  John Overton Papers
  Rhea Family Papers
  Winchester Papers

Virginia

Alderman Library, University of Virginia, Charlottesville
  Joseph Carrington Cabell Papers
  Carter-Smith Family Papers
  James Madison Papers
Bruce-Randolph Collection, Virginia State Library, Richmond
  Copy of Diary of John Randolph of Roanoke (microfilm)
  Correspondence of John Randolph and James Mercer Garnett (microfilm)
College of William and Mary, Williamsburg
  Tucker-Coleman Papers

NEWSPAPERS

[Lexington] *Kentucky Gazette*
Niles' Weekly Register
[Washington] *National Intelligencer*

PUBLISHED SOURCES

Adams, Charles Francis, ed. *Memoirs of John Quincy Adams.* 12 vols. Philadelphia: J. B. Lippincott, 1874–1877.
Adams, Henry, ed. *Documents Relating to New England Federalism, 1800–1815.* Boston: Little, Brown, 1905.
——— ed. *The Writings of Albert Gallatin.* 3 vols. Philadelphia: J. B. Lippincott, 1879.
American State Papers: Class I, Foreign Relations. 6 vols. Washington, D.C.: Gales and Seaton, 1832–1861.
Annals of the Congress of the United States. 42 vols. Washington, D.C.: Gales and Seaton, 1834–1856.
Barlow, Joel. *Oration Delivered at Washington, July Fourth, 1809; at the Request of the Democratic Citizens of the District of Columbia.* Washington City: R. C. Weightman, 1809.
Bassett, John Spencer, ed. *Correspondence of Andrew Jackson.* 7 vols. Washington, D.C.: Carnegie Institution of Washington, 1926–1935.
Battle, Kemp P., ed. *Letters of Nathaniel Macon, John Steele and William Barry Grove.* Chapel Hill: University of North Carolina, 1902.
Beaujour, Felix de. *Aperçu des États-Unis au commencement du XIXe siècle, depuis 1800 jusqu'en 1810.* Paris: L. G. Michaud, 1814.
Bernard, John. *Retrospections of America, 1797–1811.* New York: Harper and Brothers, 1887.
Binns, John. *Recollections of the Life of John Binns.* Philadelphia: Parry and M'Millan, 1856.
Bowdoin and Temple Papers. Massachusetts Historical Society *Collections*, VI, Ser. 7. Boston: n.p., 1907.
Boyd, Julian P., *et al.*, eds. *The Papers of Thomas Jefferson.* 19 vols. to date. Princeton: Princeton University Press, 1950–.
Brown, Everett Somerville, ed. *William Plumer's Memorandum of Proceedings in the United States Senate, 1803–1807.* New York: Macmillan, 1923.
Brunhouse, Robert L., ed. *David Ramsay, 1749–1815: Selections from His Writings.* American Philosophical Society *Transactions*, New Series, LV (August, 1965).
Burr, Samuel Engle, Jr. *Napoleon's Dossier on Aaron Burr: Proposals of Col. Aaron Burr to the Emperor Napoleon.* San Antonio: Naylor, 1969.
Cantor, Milton, ed. "A Connecticut Yankee in a Barbary Court: Joel Barlow's Algerian Letters to His Wife." *William and Mary Quarterly*, Series 3, XIX (January, 1962), 86–109.

Caraman, Georges de, Comte. "Les États-Unis il y a quarante ans." *Revue Contemporaine*, III (1852), 208–34.

Cary, Thomas G., ed. *Memoir of Thomas Handasyd Perkins; Containing Extracts from His Diaries and Letters*. Boston: Little, Brown, 1856.

Cauthen, Charles E., ed. *Family Letters of the Three Wade Hamptons, 1782–1901*. Columbia: University of South Carolina Press, 1953.

Channing, William Henry, ed. *Memoir of William Ellery Channing*. 3 vols. Boston: Wm. Crosby and H. P. Nichols, 1851.

Chinard, Gilbert. *Jefferson et les Idéologues d'après Sa Correspondance Inédite avec Destutt de Tracy, Cabanis, J. B. Say et Auguste Comte*. Baltimore and Paris: Johns Hopkins Press, 1925.

Coggeshall, George. *Voyages to Various Parts of the World Made Between the Years 1799 and 1844*. New York: D. Appleton, 1851.

Coles, Edward. "Letters of Edward Coles." *William and Mary Quarterly*, Series 2, VII (July, 1927), 158–73.

Davenport, Francis Gardner, and Charles Oscar Paullin, eds. *European Treaties Bearing on the History of the United States and Its Dependencies*. 4 vols. Washington, D.C.: Carnegie Institution of Washington, 1917–1937.

Davis, Richard Beale, ed. *Jeffersonian America: Notes on the United States of America Collected in the Years 1805–6–7 and 11–12 by Sir Augustus John Foster, Bart*. San Marino, Calif.: The Huntington Library, 1954.

DeWitt, John H. "Some Unpublished Letters of John Sevier to His Son, George Washington Sevier." *Tennessee Historical Magazine*, VI (April, 1920), 62–68.

Du Pont, Victor Marie. *Journey to France and Spain, 1801*. Edited by Charles W. David. Ithaca: Cornell University Press, 1961.

Fitzpatrick, John C., ed. *The Writings of George Washington from the Original Manuscript Sources, 1745–1799*. 39 vols. Washington, D.C.: Government Printing Office, 1931–1944.

Ford, Paul Leicester, ed. *The Works of Thomas Jefferson*. 12 vols. New York: Putnam's, 1905.

Ford, Worthington Chauncey, ed. "Letters of William Vans Murray to John Quincy Adams, 1797–1803." American Historical Association *Annual Report, 1912*. Washington, D.C.: Government Printing Office, 1914.

———, ed. "Some Papers of Aaron Burr." American Antiquarian Society *Proceedings*, New Series, XXIV (1919), 43–128.

———, ed. *Thomas Jefferson Correspondence Printed from the Originals in the Collections of William K. Bixby*. Boston: n.p., 1916.

———, ed. *Writings of John Quincy Adams*. 7 vols. New York: Macmillan, 1913–1917.

Foster, Vere, ed. *The Two Duchesses*. London: Blackie and Son, 1898.

Hamilton, J. G. de Roulhac, ed. "Letters of John Rust Eaton." *The James Sprunt Historical Publications*. Raleigh, N.C.: Commercial Printing Co., 1910.

Hamilton, Stanislaus Murray, ed. *The Writings of James Monroe*. 7 vols. New York and London: Putnam's, 1898–1903.

Hammond, Hans. "Letters of John Taylor of Caroline." *Virginia Magazine of History and Biography*, LII (April, 1944), 121–34.

Hémardinquer, Jean-Jacques, ed. "Une correspondance de banquiers parisiens (1808–1815): aspects socio-politiques." *Revue d'histoire moderne contemporaine*, XVII (July–September, 1970), 514–39.

Hopkins, James F., ed. *The Papers of Henry Clay.* 5 vols. to date. Lexington: University Press of Kentucky, 1959–.

Hunt, Gaillard, ed. *The Writings of James Madison.* 9 vols. New York: Putnam's, 1900–1910.

Huntington, Samuel. *Letters from the Samuel Huntington Correspondence, 1800–1812.* Cleveland, Ohio: Western Reserve Historical Society, 1915.

Huth, Hans, and Wilma J. Pugh, eds. and trans. *Talleyrand in America as a Financial Promoter, 1794–96.* American Historical Association *Annual Report, 1941.* 3 vols. Washington, D.C.: Government Printing Office, 1942.

Innis, H. A., and A. R. M. Lower, eds. *Select Documents on Canadian Economic History, 1783–1885.* Toronto: University of Toronto Press, 1933.

Jackson, Lady, ed. *The Bath Archives. A Further Selection from the Diaries and Letters of Sir George Jackson, K. C. H., from 1809 to 1816.* 2 vols. London: Richard Bentley and Son, 1873.

The Jefferson Papers. Massachusetts Historical Society *Collections*, I, Ser. 7. Boston: n.p., 1900.

Kimball, Marie G. "Unpublished Correspondence of Mme de Staël with Thomas Jefferson." *North American Review*, CCVIII (July, 1918), 63–71.

King, Charles R. *The Life and Correspondence of Rufus King.* 6 vols. New York: Putnam's, 1894–1900.

Knopf, Richard C., comp. *Thomas Worthington and the War of 1812.* Vol. III of *Document Transcriptions of the War of 1812 in the Northwest.* 10 vols. Columbus, Ohio: Ohio Historical Society, 1957–1962.

Knowlton, Daniel Chauncey, ed. *The Journal of William H. Crawford.* Northampton, Mass.: n.p., 1925.

Knox, Dudley W. *Naval Documents Related to the United States War with the Barbary Powers.* 6 vols. Washington, D.C.: Government Printing Office, 1939–1944.

Lecestre, Léon, ed. *Lettres inédites de Napoléon Ier.* 2 vols. Paris: E. Plon, Nourrit et Cie, 1897.

Lizanich, Christine M. "'The March of the Government': Joel Barlow's Unwritten History of the United States." *William and Mary Quarterly*, Series 3, XXXIII (April, 1976), 315–30.

Lodge, Henry Cabot. *Life and Letters of George Cabot.* Boston: Little, Brown, 1877.

Madison, Dolley. *Memoirs and Letters of Dolly Madison.* Boston and New York: Houghton Mifflin, 1886.

Madison, James. *Letters and Other Writings of James Madison, Fourth President of the United States.* 4 vols. Philadelphia: J. B. Lippincott, 1865.

Mann, Mary Lee, ed. *A Yankee Jeffersonian: Selections from the Diary and Letters of William Lee of Massachusetts, Written from 1796–1840.* Cambridge: Harvard University Press, 1958.

Marshall, Thomas Maitland, ed. *The Life and Papers of Frederick Bates*. 2 vols. St. Louis: Missouri Historical Society, 1926.

Mayo, Bernard, ed. *Instructions to the British Ministers to the United States, 1791– 1812*. American Historical Association *Annual Report, 1936*. 3 vols. Washington, D.C.: Government Printing Office, 1941.

Méneval, Claude-François de. *Memoirs Illustrating the History of Napoleon I from 1802 to 1815*. 3 vols. New York: D. Appleton, 1894.

Miller, David Hunter, comp. *Treaties and Other International Acts of the United States of America*. 8 vols. Washington, D.C.: Government Printing Office, 1931– 1948.

Morse, Edward L., ed. *Samuel F. B. Morse: His Letters and Journals*. 2 vols. Boston and New York: Houghton Mifflin, 1914.

Napoleon. *Correspondance de Napoléon Ier publiée par ordre de l'Empereur Napoléon III*. 32 vols. Paris: H. Plon and J. Dumaine, 1858–1870.

Niemcewicz, Julian Ursyn. *Under Their Vine and Fig Tree: Travels Through America in 1797–1799, 1805*. Edited and translated by Metchie J. E. Budka. Elizabeth, N.J.: Grassman Publishing Co., 1965.

Nolte, Vincent. *Fifty Years in Both Hemispheres or Reminiscences of the Life of a Former Merchant*. London: Redfield, 1854.

Pitkin, Timothy. *A Statistical View of the Commerce of the United States of America*. Hartford: Charles Hosmer, 1816.

Playfair, William. *Political Portraits in the New Era*. 2 vols. London: C. Chapple, 1814.

Public Statutes at Large of the United States of America. 79 vols. Boston and Washington: Little, Brown and Co., Government Printing Office, 1848–.

Reynolds, Mary Robinson, comp. "Letters of Samuel Taggart, Representative in Congress, 1803–1814." American Antiquarian Society *Proceedings*, New Series, XXXIII (1923), 113–226, 297–438.

Richardson, James D., comp. *A Compilation of the Messages and Papers of the Presidents*. 10 vols. Washington, D.C.: Bureau of National Literature, 1912.

Rives, George L., ed. *Selections from the Correspondence of Thomas Barclay*. New York: Harper and Brothers, 1894.

Sawvel, Franklin B., ed. *The Complete Anas of Thomas Jefferson*. New York: Round Table Press, 1903.

Seybert, Adam. *Statistical Annals . . . of the United States of America*. Philadelphia: Thomas Dobson and Son, 1818.

Silliman, Benjamin. *Journal of Travels in England, Holland, and Scotland, and of Two Passages over the Atlantic in the Years 1805 and 1806*. 2 vols. Boston: T. B. Wait and Co., 1812.

Stewarton, [?]. *The Secret History of the Court and Cabinet of St. Cloud*. New York: Brisban and Brannan, 1807.

Syrett, Harold C., and Jacob E. Cooke, eds. *The Papers of Alexander Hamilton*. 26 vols. New York: Columbia University Press, 1961–1979.

Talleyrand. *Memoires du Prince Talleyrand*. 5 vols. Paris: Calmann Levy, 1891–92.

Tatum, Edward H. Jr., and Marion Tinling, eds. "Letters of William Henry Allen, 1800–1813." *Huntington Library Quarterly*, I (October, 1937, January, 1938), 101–32, 203–43.

Turreau, Louis Marie, Baron de Linières. *Aperçu sur la situation politique des États-Unis d'Amérique.* Paris: Chez Firmin Didot, 1815.

———. *Memoirs for the History of the War of La Vendée.* London: Baylis, 1796.

Van Doren, Mark, ed. *Correspondence of Aaron Burr and His Daughter Theodosia.* New York: Stratford Press, 1929.

Wagstaff, H. M., ed. *The Papers of John Steele.* 2 vols. Raleigh, N.C.: Edwards and Broughton, 1924.

Warden, David Bailie. "Journal of a Voyage from Annapolis to Cherbourg on Board the Frigate Constitution, 1 Aug. to 6 Sept., 1811." *Maryland Historical Magazine*, XI (June and September, 1916), 127–141, 204–217.

Washington, H. A., ed. *The Writings of Thomas Jefferson.* 9 vols. New York: J. C. Richie, 1854–1856.

HISTORICAL STUDIES

Abernethy, Thomas Perkins. *The South in the New Nation, 1789–1819.* Baton Rouge: Louisiana State University Press, 1961.

Abraham, James Johnston. *Lettsom: His Life, Times, Friends and Descendants.* London: William Heinemann Ltd., 1933.

Adams, Henry. *History of the United States During the Administrations of Jefferson and Madison.* 9 vols. New York: Scribner's, 1889–1891.

Adams, M. Ray. "Joel Barlow, Political Romanticist." *American Literature*, IX (January, 1938), 113–52.

Ames, William E. *A History of the National Intelligencer.* Chapel Hill: University of North Carolina Press, 1972.

Ammon, Harry. *The Genet Mission.* New York: W. W. Norton, 1973.

Anderson, M. S. "The Continental System and Russo-British Relations During the Napoleonic Wars." *Studies in International History.* Edited by K. Bourne and D. C. Watt. Hamden, Conn.: Archon Books, 1967.

Auguste, Yves. "Jefferson et Haiti (1804–1810)." *Revue d'histoire diplomatique*, LXXXVI (October–December, 1972), 333–48.

Baldwin, Simeon E. *Life and Letters of Simeon Baldwin.* New Haven: Tuttle, Morehouse and Taylor, n.d.

Banner, James M., Jr. *To the Hartford Convention: The Federalists and the Origins of Party Politics in Massachusetts, 1789–1815.* New York: Knopf, 1970.

Barker, Richard J. "The Conseil Général des Manufactures under Napoleon (1810–1814)." *French Historical Studies*, VI (Fall, 1969), 185–213.

Barlow, William R. "The Coming of the War of 1812 in Michigan Territory." *Michigan History*, LIII (Summer, 1969), 91–107.

———. "Ohio's Congressmen and the War of 1812." *Ohio History*, LXXII (July, 1963), 175–194, 257–59.

Bell, Rudolph M. "Mr. Madison's War and Long-Term Congressional Voting Behavior." *William and Mary Quarterly*, Series 3, XXXVI (July, 1979), 373–95.

Bellot, H. Hale. "Thomas Jefferson in American Historiography." Royal Historical Society *Transactions*, Series V, IV (1954), 135–55.

Bemis, Samuel Flagg. *John Quincy Adams and the Foundations of American Foreign Policy*. New York: Knopf, 1956.

———. "Thomas Jefferson," in Vol. II of *The American Secretaries of State and Their Diplomacy, 1776–1925*. 10 vols. Edited by Samuel Flagg Bemis. New York: Knopf, 1927–1929.

Biographie Universelle. 45 vols. Paris: Chez Madame L. Desplaces, n.d.

Bizardel, Yvon. *The First Expatriates: Americans in Paris During the French Revolution*. New York: Holt, Rinehart and Winston, 1975.

Blumenthal, Henry. *France and the United States: Their Diplomatic Relations, 1789–1914*. Chapel Hill: University of North Carolina Press, 1970.

Bohlen, Charles E. *Witness to History, 1929–1969*. New York: W. W. Norton, 1973.

Bolkhovitinov, N. N., and S. I. Divil'kouskii. "Russian Diplomacy and the Anglo-American War of 1812–1814." *Soviet Studies in History*, I (Fall, 1962), 19–30.

Bonnel, Ulane. *La France, les États-Unis et la guerre de course (1797–1815)*. Paris: Nouvelles Editions Latines, 1961.

Borden, Morton. *Parties and Politics in the Early Republic, 1789–1815*. New York: Thomas Y. Crowell, 1967.

Bowman, Albert H. "Louis A. Pichon and the French Perception of the United States." Paper read at the 41st Annual Meeting of the Southern Historical Association, Washington, D.C., November 15, 1975.

Boyd, Julian P. "Thomas Jefferson's 'Empire of Liberty.'" *Virginia Quarterly Review*, XXIV (Autumn, 1948), 538–54.

Brant, Irving. "James Madison and His Times." *American Historical Review*, LVII (July, 1952), 853–70.

———. *James Madison: Commander in Chief, 1812–1836*. Indianapolis and New York: Bobbs-Merrill, 1961.

———. *James Madison: The President, 1809–1812*. Indianapolis and New York, Bobbs-Merrill, 1956.

———. "Joel Barlow, Madison's Stubborn Minister." *William and Mary Quarterly*, Series 3, XV (October, 1958), 438–51.

———. "Madison and the War of 1812." *Virginia Magazine of History and Biography*, LXXIV (January, 1966), 51–67.

Brinton, Crane. *The Lives of Talleyrand*. New York: W. W. Norton, 1930.

Brodie, Fawn M. *Thomas Jefferson: An Intimate History*. New York: W. W. Norton, 1974.

———. "Jefferson Biographers and the Psychology of Canonization." *Journal of Interdisciplinary History*, II (Summer, 1971), 155–71.

Brown, Roger H. *The Republic in Peril: 1812*. New York: Columbia University Press, 1964.

Bruchey, Stuart Weems. *Robert Oliver, Merchant of Baltimore, 1783–1819.* Baltimore: Johns Hopkins Press, 1956.

Buist, Marten G. *At Spes Non Fracta: Hope & Co. 1770–1815.* The Hague: Martinus Nijhoff, 1974.

Butel, Paul. "Crise et mutation de l'activité économique à Bordeaux sous le consulat et l'Empire." *Revue d'histoire moderne et contemporaine,* XVII (July–September, 1970), 546–58.

Cantor, Milton. "Joel Barlow's Mission to Algiers." *The Historian,* XXV (February, 1963), 172–94.

Carré, Adrien. "La Vendée ses bourreaux et l'Armée française." *Revue du Souvenir Vendéen,* n.v. (December, 1969), 3–22.

Casey, Richard P. "North Country Nemesis: The Potash Rebellion and the Embargo of 1807–1809." *New-York Historical Society Quarterly,* LXIV (January, 1980), 31–49.

Cassell, Frank A. *Merchant Congressman in the Young Republic: Samuel Smith of Maryland, 1752–1839.* Madison: University of Wisconsin Press, 1971.

Chabert, A. *Essai sur les mouvements des revenus et de l'activité économique en France de 1798 à 1820.* Paris: Libraire de Medicis, n.d.

Checkland, S. G. "American versus West Indian Traders in Liverpool, 1793–1815." *Journal of Economic History,* XVII (June, 1958), 141–60.

Childs, Frances S. "A Secret Agent's Advice on America, 1797." *Nationalism and Internationalism: Essays Inscribed to Carlton J. H. Hayes.* Edited by Edward Mead Earle. New York: Columbia University Press, 1950.

———. "Citizen d'Hauterive's 'Questions on the United States.'" Institut Français de Washington *Bulletin,* 5–6 (1957), 34–44.

———. "The Hauterive Journal." *New-York Historical Society Quarterly,* XXXIII (April, 1949), 69–86.

Coatsworth, John H. "American Trade with European Colonies in the Caribbean and South America, 1790–1812." *William and Mary Quarterly,* Series 3, XXIV (April, 1967), 243–66.

Conlin, Mary Lou. *Simon Perkins of the Western Reserve.* Cleveland: Western Reserve Historical Society, 1968.

Copp, Walter Ronald. "Nova Scotian Trade During the War of 1812." *Canadian Historical Review,* XVII (June, 1937), 141–55.

Cox, Henry Bartholomew. "To the Victor: A History of the French Spoliation Claims Controversy, 1793–1955." Ph.D. dissertation, George Washington University, 1967.

Cox, Isaac Joslin. *The West Florida Controversy, 1798–1813.* Baltimore: Johns Hopkins Press, 1918.

Crouzet, François. *L'économie britannique et le blocus continental, 1806–1813.* 2 vols. Paris: Presses Universitaires de France, 1958.

Cunningham, Noble E., Jr. *The Jeffersonian Republicans in Power: Party Operations, 1801–1809.* Chapel Hill: University of North Carolina Press, 1963.

Cuthbertson, Brian Craig Uniacke. "The Old Attorney General: Richard John Uniacke, 1753–1830." M.A. thesis, University of New Brunswick, 1970.

Dangerfield, George. *Chancellor Robert R. Livingston of New York, 1746–1813.* New York: Harcourt, Brace, 1960.

Dard, Emile. *Napoleon and Talleyrand.* New York: D. Appleton-Century, 1937.

De Conde, Alexander. *The Quasi-War: The Politics and Diplomacy of the Undeclared War with France, 1797–1801.* New York: Scribner's, 1966.

———. *This Affair of Louisiana.* New York: Scribner's, 1976.

Dorfman, Joseph. "Joel Barlow: Trafficker in Trade and Letters." *Political Science Quarterly*, LIX (March, 1944), 83–100.

Dunan, M. "Un adversaire du système continental." *Revue des études napoléoniennes*, VII (January–June, 1915), 262–75.

Durden, Robert F. "Joel Barlow in the French Revolution." *William and Mary Quarterly*, Series 3, VIII (July, 1951), 327–54.

Earl, John L. "Talleyrand in Philadelphia, 1794–1796." *Pennsylvania Magazine of History and Biography*, XCI (July, 1967), 282–96.

Echeverria, Durand. *Mirage in the West: A History of the French Image of American Society to 1815.* Princeton: Princeton University Press, 1957.

Egan, Clifford L. "Additional Letters of John Adams Harper." *Historical New Hampshire*, XXXI (Spring–Summer, 1976), 52–55.

———. "Fracas in Savannah: National Exasperation in Microcosm, 1811." *Georgia Historical Quarterly*, LIX (Spring, 1970), 79–86.

———. "How Not to Write a Biography: A Critical Look at Fawn Brodie's *Thomas Jefferson.*" *Social Science Journal*, XIV (April, 1977), 129–36.

———. "On the Fringe of the Napoleonic Catastrophe: Joel Barlow's Letters from Central and Eastern Europe, 1812." *Early American Literature*, X (1975–1976), 251–72.

———. "The Path to War in 1812 Through the Eyes of a New Hampshire 'War Hawk.'" *Historical New Hampshire*, XXX (Fall, 1975), 147–77.

———. "Thomas Jefferson's Greatest Mistake: The Decision for Peace, 1807." Proceedings of The Citadel Conference on War and Diplomacy, 1977. Edited by David H. White and John W. Gordon. Charleston, S.C.: The Citadel, 1979.

———. "The United States, France and West Florida, 1803–1807." *Florida Historical Quarterly*, XLVII (January, 1969), 225–52.

———. "The Origins of the War of 1812: Three Decades of Historical Writing." *Military Affairs*, XXXVIII (April, 1974), 72–75.

Emery, William M. *Honorable Peleg Tallman, 1764–1841.* n.p.: n.p., 1935.

Ernouf, Baron. *Maret, Duc de Bassano.* Paris: G. Charpentier, 1878.

Feifer, Eliane. "Vergennes et Talleyrand." *Sciences Politiques*, LII (August, 1937), 239–52.

Fischer, David Hackett. *The Revolution of American Conservatism: The Federalist Party in the Era of Jeffersonian Democracy.* New York: Harper and Row, 1965.

Forbes, John D. "European Wars and Boston Trade, 1783–1815." *New England Quarterly*, XI (December, 1938), 709–30.

Fritz, Florence R. "Joel Barlow's Early Deistic Liberalism: A Study of Radical

Influences at Yale, 1774–1781." Paper read before the Connecticut Historical Society, April 6, 1937.

Fritz, Harry W. "The War Hawks of 1812: An Historical Reality." Paper read at the Annual Meeting of the Western Social Science Association, Denver, Colorado, May 1, 1975.

Fugier, André. *La révolution française et l'empire napoléonien.* Paris: Hachette, 1954.

Gaines, Edwin M. "The Chesapeake Affair: Virginians Mobilize to Defend National Honor." *Virginia Magazine of History and Biography,* LXIV (April, 1956), 131–42.

———. "George Cranfield Berkeley and the *Chesapeake-Leopard* Affair of 1807." In *America the Middle Period: Essays in Honor of Bernard Mayo.* Edited by John Boles. Charlottesville: University Press of Virginia, 1973.

Galpin, W. Freeman. "The American Grain Trade to the Spanish Peninsula, 1810–1814." *American Historical Review,* XXVIII (October, 1922), 24–44.

———. "The Grain Trade of Alexandria, Virginia, 1801–1815." *North Carolina Historical Review,* IV (October, 1927), 404–27.

Garçot, Maurice. *Le Duel Moreau-Napoléon.* Paris: Nouvelles Editions Latines, 1951.

Glover, Richard. *Britain at Bay: Defence Against Bonaparte, 1803–1814.* London and New York: Barnes and Noble, 1973.

———. "The French Fleet, 1807–1814: Britain's Problem and Madison's Opportunity." *Journal of Modern History,* XXXIX (September, 1967), 233–52.

Godechot, Jacques. *The Counter-Revolution: Doctrine and Action; 1789–1804.* New York: Howard Fertig, 1971.

———. *L'Europe et l'Amérique à l'epoque napoléonienne (1800–1815).* Paris: Presses Universitaires de France, 1967.

Goodman, Warren H. "The Origins of the War of 1812: A Survey of Changing Interpretations." *Mississippi Valley Historical Review,* XXVIII (September, 1941), 171–86.

Grand Dictionnaire Universel de XIXᵉSiècle. 17 vols. Paris: n.p., n.d.

Guice, C. Norman. "Trade Goods for Texas: An Incident in the History of the Jeffersonian Embargo." *Southwestern Historical Quarterly,* LX (April, 1957), 507–19.

Hammack, James Wallace, Jr. *Kentucky and the Second American Revolution.* Lexington: University Press of Kentucky, 1976.

Hammond, Bray. *Banks and Politics in America: From the Revolution to the Civil War.* Princeton: Princeton University Press, 1957.

Harastzi, Zoltan. *John Adams and the Prophets of Progress.* Cambridge: Harvard University Press, 1952.

Hatcher, William B. *Edward Livingston: Jeffersonian Republican and Jacksonian Democrat.* Baton Rouge: Louisiana State University Press, 1940.

Hatzenbuehler, Ronald L. "Party Unity and the Decision for War in the House of Representatives, 1812." *William and Mary Quarterly,* Series 3, XXIX (July, 1972), 366–90.

————. "To the Editor." *Pacific Historical Review*, XLV (November, 1976), 644–45.

————. "The War Hawks and the Question of Congressional Leadership in 1812." *Pacific Historical Review*, XLV (May, 1976), 1–22.

Heath, Phoebe Anne. *Napoleon I and the Origins of the Anglo-American War of 1812.* Toulouse: E Privat, 1929.

Hickey, Donald R. "Federalist Defense Policy in the Age of Jefferson, 1801–1812." *Military Affairs*, XLV (April, 1981), 63–70.

————. "To the Editor." *Pacific Historical Review*, XLV (November, 1976), 642–44.

Higham, Robin. "The Port of Boston and the Embargo of 1807–1809." *American Neptune*, XVI (July, 1956), 189–213.

Hill, Peter P. *William Vans Murray, Federalist Diplomat: The Shaping of Peace with France, 1797–1801.* Syracuse: Syracuse University Press, 1971.

Honeywell, Roy J. "President Jefferson and His Successor." *American Historical Review*, XLVI (October, 1940), 64–75.

Horsman, Reginald. *The Causes of the War of 1812.* Philadelphia: University of Pennsylvania Press, 1962.

Howard, Leon. "Joel Barlow and Napoleon." *Huntington Library Quarterly*, II (October, 1938), 37–51.

Hoyt, William D., Jr. "Self-Portrait: Eliza Custis, 1808." *Virginia Magazine of History and Biography*, LIII (April, 1945), 89–100.

Ivie, Robert L. "The Republican Dramatization of War in 1812." Paper read at the Annual Meeting of the Western Speech Communication Association, San Francisco, November, 1976.

Kaplan, Lawrence S. "France and Madison's Decision for War, 1812." *Mississippi Valley Historical Review*, L (March, 1964), 652–71.

————. "France and the War of 1812." *Journal of American History*, LVII (June, 1970), 36–47.

————. *Jefferson and France: An Essay on Politics and Political Ideas.* New Haven: Yale University Press, 1967.

————. "Jefferson and France: A Study in Political Opportunism." Ph.D. dissertation, Yale University, 1951.

————. "Jefferson, the Napoleonic Wars, and the Balance of Power." *William and Mary Quarterly*, Series 3, XIV (April, 1957), 196–217.

Kaufman, Martin. "War Sentiment in Western Pennsylvania: 1812." *Pennsylvania History*, XXI (October, 1964), 436–48.

Ketcham, Ralph. *James Madison: A Biography.* New York: Macmillan, 1971.

Labaree, Benjamin W. *Patriots and Partisans: The Merchants of Newburyport, 1764–1815.* Cambridge: Harvard University Press, 1962.

Lacour-Gayet, G. *Talleyrand.* 4 vols. Paris: Payot, 1928–1946.

Lacour-Gayet, Robert. "Napoléon et les Étas-Unis." *Revue d'histoire diplomatique.* LXXXIII (October–December, 1969), 289–302.

Lefebvre, Georges. *Napoleon: From Tilsit to Waterloo, 1807–1815.* New York: Columbia University Press, 1969.

Lemisch, Jesse. "Jack Tar in the Streets: Merchant Seamen in the Politics of Revolutionary America." *William and Mary Quarterly*, Series 3, XXV (July, 1968), 371–407.

Lent, Gregg L. "The American Revolution and the Law of Nations, 1776–1789." *Diplomatic History*, I (Winter, 1977), 20–34.

———. "John Adams and the Drafting of the Model Treaty Plan of 1776." *Diplomatic History*, II (Summer, 1978), 313–20.

Levy, Leonard W. *Jefferson and Civil Liberties*. Cambridge: Harvard University Press, 1963.

Lewis, Michael. *Napoleon and His British Captives*. London: George Allen and Unwin, 1967.

Lingelbach, W. E. "Historical Investigation and the Commercial History of the Napoleonic Era." *American Historical Review*, XIX (January, 1914), 257–81.

Long, David F. *Nothing Too Daring: A Biography of Commodore David Porter, 1780–1843*. Annapolis: United States Naval Institute, 1970.

Lyon, E. Wilson. *The Man Who Sold Louisiana: The Career of François Barbé-Marbois*. Norman: University of Oklahoma Press, 1942.

Madelin, Louis. *Histoire du consulat et de l'empire*. 16 vols. Paris: Hachette, 1937–1954.

———. *Talleyrand*. New York: Roy Publishers, 1948.

Mahan, Alfred Thayer. *Sea Power in Its Relations to the War of 1812*. 2 vols. Boston: Little, Brown, 1905.

Malone, Dumas, *et al.*, eds. *Dictionary of American Biography*. 22 vols. New York: Scribner's, 1925–1958.

———. *Jefferson the President: First Term, 1801–1805*. Boston: Little, Brown, 1970.

———. *Jefferson the President: Second Term, 1805–1809*. Boston: Little, Brown, 1974.

———. "Presidential Leadership and National Unity: The Jeffersonian Example." *Journal of Southern History*, XXXV (February, 1969), 3–17.

Mannix, Richard J. "The Embargo: Its Administration, Impact, and Enforcement." Ph.D. dissertation, New York University, 1975.

———. "Gallatin, Jefferson, and the Embargo of 1808." *Diplomatic History*, III (Spring, 1979), 151–72.

Masson, Frédéric. *Le département des affaires étrangères pendant la révolution, 1787–1804*. Paris: Plon, 1877.

Mayo, Bernard. *Henry Clay: Spokesman of the New West*. Boston: Houghton Mifflin, 1937.

McCaleb, Walter F. *New Light on Aaron Burr*. Austin: The Texas Quarterly Studies, 1963.

McColley, Robert. "Jefferson's Rivals: The Shifting Character of the Federalists." *Midcontinent American Studies Journal*, IX (Spring, 1968), 23–34.

McMaster, John Bach. *A History of the People of the United States from the Revolution to the Civil War*. 8 vols. New York: Appleton & Co., 1883–1913.

————. *The Life and Times of Stephen Girard, Mariner and Merchant.* 2 vols. Philadelphia and London: J. B. Lippincott, 1918.

Melvin, Frank E. *Napoleon's Navigation System: A Study in Trade Control During the Continental Blockade.* New York: D. Appleton and Co., 1919.

Miller, Victor Clyde. *Joel Barlow: Revolutionist, London, 1791–92.* Hamburg: Friederichsen de Gruyter, 1932.

Mohl, Raymond A. *Poverty in New York, 1783–1825.* New York: Oxford University Press, 1971.

Montor, Artaud de. *Histoire de la vie et des travaux politiques du comte d'Hauterive.* Paris: Librairie d'Adrien le Clerc et Cⁱᵉ, 1839.

Mooney, Chase C. *William H. Crawford, 1772–1834.* Lexington: University Press of Kentucky, 1974.

Moore, William Glenn. "Economic Coercion as a Policy of the United States, 1794–1805." Ph.D. dissertation, University of Alabama, 1960.

Morison, Samuel Eliot. *By Land and by Sea.* New York: Knopf, 1953.

Mott, Frank L. *Jefferson and the Press.* Baton Rouge: Louisiana State University Press, 1943.

Mudge, Eugene Tenbroeck. *The Social Philosophy of John Taylor of Caroline.* New York: Columbia University Press, 1939.

Muller, H. N. "Smuggling into Canada: How the Champlain Valley Defied Jefferson's Embargo." *Vermont History,* XXXVIII (Winter, 1970), 5–21.

Munroe, John A. *Federalist Delaware, 1775–1815.* New Brunswick: Rutgers University Press, 1954.

North, Douglass C. "Early National Income Estimates of the U[nited] S[tates]." *Economic Development and Cultural Change,* IX (April, 1961), 389–96.

Pancake, John S. "The 'Invisibles': A Chapter in the Opposition to President Madison." *Journal of Southern History,* XXI (February, 1955), 17–37.

Parker, Harold T. "The Formation of Napoleon's Personality: An Exploratory Essay." *French Historical Studies,* VII (Spring, 1971), 6–26.

Perkins, Bradford. *The First Rapprochement: England and the United States, 1795–1805.* Philadelphia: University of Pennsylvania Press, 1955.

————. *Prologue to War: England and the United States, 1805–1812.* Berkeley: University of California Press, 1961.

Peterson, Merrill D. *The Jefferson Image in the American Mind.* New York: Oxford University Press, 1962.

Phipps, Ramsay Weston. *The Armies of the First French Republic and the Rise of the Marshals of Napoleon I.* 5 vols. London: Oxford University Press, 1931.

Pratt, Julius W. "Aaron Burr and the Historians." *New York History,* XXVI (October, 1945), 447–70.

Prentiss, Hervey Putnam. "Pickering and the Embargo." *Essex Institute Historical Collections,* LXIX (April, 1933), 97–136.

Ragsdale, Hugh. "A Continental System in 1801: Paul I and Bonaparte." *Journal of Modern History,* XLII (March, 1970), 70–89.

Reinoehl, John H. "Post-Embargo Trade and Merchant Prosperity: Experience of the Crowninshield Family, 1809–1812." *Mississippi Valley Historical Review*, XLII (September, 1955), 229–49.

Rémond, René. *Les États-Unis devant l'opinion française*. 2 vols. Paris: Libraire Armand Colin, 1962.

Rubin, Israel. "New York State and the Long Embargo." Ph.D. dissertation, New York University, 1961.

Ruppenthal, Roland. "Denmark and the Continental System." *Journal of Modern History*, XV (March, 1943), 7–23.

Ryan, A. N. "The Defence of British Trade with the Baltic, 1808–1813." *English Historical Review*, LXXIV (July, 1959), 443–66.

Sapio, Victor A. *Pennsylvania and the War of 1812*. Lexington: University Press of Kentucky, 1970.

Saricks, Ambrose. *Pierre Samuel Du Pont de Nemours*. Lawrence: University of Kansas Press, 1965.

Schachner, Nathan. *Aaron Burr: A Biography*. New York: A. S. Barnes, 1937.

Seaburg, Carl, and Stanley Paterson. *Merchant Prince of Boston: Colonel T. H. Perkins, 1764–1854*. Cambridge: Harvard University Press, 1971.

Sears, Louis M. "Philadelphia and the Embargo, 1808." In American Historical Association *Annual Report, 1920*. Washington: Government Printing Office, 1925.

———. "Philadelphia and the Embargo of 1808." *Quarterly Journal of Economics*, XXXV (February, 1921), 354–59.

Shulim, Joseph I. "Thomas Jefferson Views Napoleon." *Virginia Magazine of History and Biography*, LX (April, 1952), 288–304.

Six, Georges. *Dictionnaire biographique des généraux & amiraux français de la révolution et l'empire (1792–1814)*. 2 vols. Paris: Bordas, 1934.

Skeen, C. Edward. *John Armstrong, Jr., 1758–1843: A Biography*. Syracuse: Syracuse University Press, 1981.

———. "Monroe and Armstrong: A Study in Political Rivalry." *New-York Historical Society Quarterly*, LVII (April, 1973), 121–47.

———. "Mr. Madison's Secretary of War." *Pennsylvania Magazine of History and Biography*, C (July, 1976), 336–55.

———. "The Newburgh Conspiracy Reconsidered." *William and Mary Quarterly*, Series 3, XXXI (April, 1974), 273–90.

Smelser, Marshall. *The Democratic Republic, 1801–1815*. New York: Harper and Row, 1968.

Smith, Jay D. "Commodore James Barron: Guilty as Charged?" *United States Naval Institute Proceedings*, XCIII (November, 1967), 79–85.

Smith, Theodore Clarke. "War Guilt in 1812." *Massachusetts Historical Society Proceedings*, LXIV (October, 1930–June, 1932), 319–45.

Smith, Walter Buckingham, and Arthur Harrison Cole. *Fluctuations in American Business, 1790–1860*. Cambridge: Harvard University Press, 1935.

Sorel, Albert. *L'Europe et la Révolution Française*. 8 vols. Paris: Librairie Plon, 1914.

Sparks, Jared. *The Life of Gouverneur Morris*. 3 vols. Boston: Gray and Bowen, 1832.

Spiller, Robert E. *The American in England During the First Half Century of Independence.* New York: Henry Holt, 1926.

Spivak, Burton. *Jefferson's English Crisis: Commerce, Embargo, and the Republican Revolution.* Charlottesville: University Press of Virginia, 1979.

————. "Republican Dreams and National Interest: The Jeffersonians and American Foreign Policy." *Society for Historians of American Foreign Relations Newsletter,* XII (June, 1981), 1–20.

Stagg, J. C. A. "James Madison and the Coercion of Great Britain: Canada, the West Indies, and the War of 1812." *William and Mary Quarterly,* Series 3, XXXVIII (January, 1981), 3–34.

————. "James Madison and the 'Malcontents': The Political Origins of the War of 1812." *William and Mary Quarterly,* Series 3, XXXIII (October, 1976), 557–85.

Steel, Anthony. "Impressment in the Monroe-Pinkney Negotiation, 1806–1807." *American Historical Review,* LVII (January, 1952), 352–69.

————. "More Light on the *Chesapeake.*" *Mariner's Mirror,* XXXIX (November, 1953), 243–65.

Stuart, Reginald C. "James Madison and the Militants: Republican Disunity and Replacing the Embargo." *Diplomatic History,* VI (Spring, 1982), 145–67.

Sullivan, William. *Familiar Letters on Public Characters, and Public Events: From the Peace of 1783, to the Peace of 1815.* Boston: Russell, Odiorne, and Metcalf, 1834.

Tansill, Charles C. *The United States and Santo Domingo, 1798–1873: A Chapter in Caribbean Diplomacy.* Baltimore: Johns Hopkins Press, 1938.

Tarlé, E. "L'Unité économique du continent européen sous Napoléon Iᵉʳ." *Revue Historique,* CLXVI (January–April, 1931), 239–55.

Taylor, George Rogers. "American Economic Growth Before 1840: An Exploratory Essay." *Journal of Economic History,* XXIV (December, 1964), 427–44.

Tolles, Frederick B. "What Instrument Did the French Minister's Secretary Play?" *William and Mary Quarterly,* Series 3, XI (October, 1954), 633–34.

Trent, William P., ed. *Mr. Irving's Notes and Journal of Travel in Europe, 1804–1805.* 3 vols. New York: The Grolier Club, 1920.

Turner, Lynn W. "Thomas Jefferson Through the Eyes of a New Hampshire Politician." *Mississippi Valley Historical Review,* XXX (September, 1943), 205–13.

————. *William Plumer of New Hampshire, 1759–1850.* Chapel Hill: University of North Carolina Press, 1962.

Tyler, Lyon Gardiner, ed. *Encyclopedia of Virginia Biography.* 5 vols. New York: Lewis Historical Publishing Co., 1915.

Walters, Raymond, Jr. *Albert Gallatin: Jeffersonian Financier and Diplomat.* New York: Macmillan, 1957.

Wehtje, Myron F. "Opposition in Virginia to the War of 1812." *Virginia Magazine of History and Biography,* LXXVII (January, 1970), 65–86.

Whitcomb, Edward A. *Napoleon's Diplomatic Service.* Durham, N.C.: Duke University Press, 1979.

White, Patrick C. T. *A Nation on Trial: America and the War of 1812*. New York: John Wiley, 1965.

Woodress, James. *A Yankee's Odyssey: The Life of Joel Barlow*. Philadelphia and New York: J. B. Lippincott, 1958.

Zimmerman, James Fulton. *Impressment of American Seamen*. New York: Columbia University Press, 1925.

Index

Adair, John, 59
Adams, Henry, 24*n*
Adams, John, 129, 137
Adams, John Quincy, 42, 77, 118*n*,
177*n*, 180, 189
Adams-Onís Treaty, 66
Address to the People of the United States,
135, 150, 151
"Advice to a Raven in Russia," 184
America, 119
Ames, Fisher, 72
Ames, Nathaniel, 72
Ammon, Harry, 24–25*n*
Anglophobia, 175
Anglo-American relations, 9–10, 73–75,
140, 147, 151–52, 174–75
Antiwar sentiment, 179
Armstrong, John: minister to France,
16–17; criticizes Federalists, 19; Berlin
decree, 29; West Florida negotiations,
50, 53–54; and Bowdoin, 58, 59, 61–
63; *New Jersey* claim, 58–59; supports
embargo, 76, Bayonne decree, 92–93*n*;
urges vigorous policy, 98, 110; influence of despatch, 98–99; and Coles
mission, 107; negotiations with d'Hauterive, 109–10, 111; on Madison and
Jefferson, 111*n*; on French policy
changes, 113–14; disliked by Napoleon, 114–15; assessment of, 114–15;
and Cadore letter, 121–22, 125; contrasted with Pinkney, 125; returns
home, 125; opinion about, 125–26,
127*n*, 128*n*; supports Russell, 126–28;
on trade with France, 141; and Burr's
proposal, 144; later career of, 190;
mentioned, 55, 61, 64, 70, 72, 110*n*,
142, 150, 154, 166, 187

Bachasson, Jean Baptiste, comte de Montalivet, 113, 121
Bacon, Ezekiel: and embargo, 93, 96*n*,
98–99; mentioned, 111

Baldwin, Clara, 153, 186
Baldwin, Simeon, 40*n*
Baltimore, U.S.S., 9
Bank of the United States, 5–6, 134
Baring, Sir Francis, 64
Barlow, Joel: and Parker, 64; and economic coercion, 72*n*; and embargo, 76;
career of, 128–32; assessment of, 128;
ideas about America, 130, 130*n*, 165;
named to French mission, 131–34; on
dying, 134*n*; skepticism of, 133–34,
153, 156; and Madison, 135*n*; seeks
settlement with France, 163–66, 168–
70, 173–74, 181–82; trip to Vilna,
182–85, 182*n*; death of, 185; mentioned, 17, 66, 104*n*, 109, 142, 146,
147, 153, 154, 171, 171*n*, 177, 189,
190
Barlow, Ruth: on reception in America,
130; life of, 186; mentioned, 128, 130,
131, 139, 153, 156, 171*n*, 184, 185,
187
Barlow, Thomas: trip to Vilna, 183–85;
later life, 190; mentioned, 153, 186,
187
Barnet, Isaac Cox, 76, 177–78*n*
Barney, Joshua, 174–75
Barron, James, 73
Bassano, duc de. *See* Maret, Hugues-
Bernard
Bassett, Burwell, 33
Battles: Ulm, 26, 67; Austerlitz, 26, 67;
Eylau, 26; Friedland, 26; Trafalgar, 26,
67; Aspern-Essling, 107; Wagram, 110;
Jena, 183; Tippecanoe, 166, 175
Bayard, James A., 189
Bayonne, 70
Belisarius, 119
Bigelow, Abijah, 172
Binns, John, 78, 174*n*
Bizardel, Yvon, 132*n*
Blockades: Fox's, 27–28; against Turkey,
73

Blumenthal, Henry, 163*n*
Bolkhovitinov, N. N., and S. I. Divil-'kouskii, 120*n*
Bonaparte, Jerome: marriage of, 39–40; mentioned, 36, 137
Bonaparte, Joseph, 23, 59
Bonaparte, Napoleon: and the United States, 24–25, 45; and commercial policy, 28–33; policy towards the United States, 33–34, 34*n*, 113–14, 165; and neutrals, 34, 122*n*; relations with subordinates, 34–55; and Turreau, 37, 137; anger at Jerome Bonaparte, 39–40; and West Florida, 46–47, 53, 66; and *Chesapeake-Leopard* affair, 75*n*; and embargo, 98; and Coles mission, 107–108; and Armstrong, 114–15, 115*n*; and license trade, 119; and Cadore letter, 121–24; and Champagny, 139; repeal of Berlin and Milan decrees, 139–40; and Russell, 143; absence from Paris, 156–57, 181–82; and Barlow, 163 and 163*n*; and Russia, 164, 168, 170, 177, 184; exile and death of, 190; mentioned, 1, 2, 17, 55, 56, 57, 59, 61, 106, 109*n*, 110, 120, 127, 128, 133, 138, 139, 145, 151, 152, 162, 166, 167, 179, 180
Bonnel, Ulane, 169*n*
Bordeaux, 32, 50, 70, 121
Bowdoin, James: mission of, 53; and Armstrong, 61, 65, 65*n*; death of, 189; mentioned, 17, 58, 59, 60, 61
Boston, H.M.S., 70
Bourne, Sylvanus, 111
Brent, Richard, 36*n*, 136
Brissot de Warville, Jean Pierre, 129
Brown, Roger, 149
Burr, Aaron: and Russell, 126, 144–45; overtures to French, 140n, 144; in France, 144–46
Burwell, William A., 102

Cabell, Joseph Carrington, 66*n*, 187
Cabot, George, 19
Cadore, duc de. *See* Champagny, Jean-Baptiste Nompère de
Cadore letter, 121–23, 125, 133, 151, 167

Caldwell, James, 180*n*
Cambacérès, Jean-Jacques Regis, Prince de, 181, 182
Campbell, Alexander, 179
Canada: vulnerability of, 74; as target, 76*n*, 180, 180*n*; trade with, 88–90, 89*n*
Canning, George, 105–106
Carnatic, H.M.S., 9
Cathalan, Stephen, Jr., 68
Cazenove, Théophile, 44, 64
Champagny, Jean Baptiste Nompère de, duc de Cadore: career of 44, 44*n*; on Sérurier, 138; replaced, 139; death of, 190; mentioned, 33–34, 107, 108, 110, 115, 121, 142, 166
Charles IV, 60, 61
Charleston, 121
Chasseboeuf, Constantin, comte de Volney, 43*n*
Chesapeake-Leopard affair, 65, 73, 74, 75, 76, 77, 106, 151
Claiborne, William Charles Coles, 66
Clarissa, 91
Clark, Daniel, 65*n*
Clay, Henry, 72, 178, 189
Clavière, Étienne, 129
Clinton, De Witt, 66, 150
Clinton, George, 59, 73, 134
Coleman, James, 70
Coles, Isaac: mission to France, 106–108, 110*n*; mentioned, 74*n*, 99
Colorado River (of Texas), 53, 54, 55
Columbiad, 131
Commerical restrictions. *See* Decrees; Blockades, Orders in council; License trade; Continental System
Congresses: Tenth, 107, 111–12; Twelfth, 147, 148, 149, 152, 153, 170–71, 176
Conlon, Mary Lou, 175*n*
Connecticut Wits, 129
Constitution, U.S.S., 133, 153, and 153*n*
Continental System, 31–32, 60, 113, 115, 120, 121, 122, 141, 164
Convention of Môrtefontaine, 10, 23, 24, 29, 30, 47, 133*n*, 162, 165, 166
Cook, Orchard, 56, 92
Cooper, Thomas, 20, 21

Correa de Serra, Joseph Francis, 187
Counseil du Commerce et des Manufactures,
    121
Crawford, William H.: on Parker, 64; and
    Warden-Lee clash, 187–88; as minis-
    ter, 188–89; later career, 189; men-
    tioned, 2, 128
Crillon, Edouard de, 171–72
Crowninshield, Jacob, 58, 73, 76–77
Crowninshield family, 119
Cunningham, Noble E., Jr., 54*n*
Curtis, Eliza, 138–39
Cutts, Charles, 141–42

Dalberg, duc de. *See* Emmerich
Dautremont, 62
Davenport, John, 172
de Staël, Madame, 25*n*, 177*n*
Decrees: Berlin, 28, 30, 76, 97, 108,
    109, 113, 121, 122, 124, 133, 137,
    139, 140, 142, 143, 144, 151, 152;
    Milan, 97, 108, 113, 121, 122, 124,
    133, 137, 139, 140, 142, 143, 144,
    151, 152; Bayonne, 97, 97*n*, 98, 108,
    153; Rambouillet, 115, 140, 153, 165;
    St. Cloud, 121, 169, 169*n*; Fontaine-
    bleau, 172
Decrès, Denis, 29, 98, 113, 121
Denmark, 25
Desha, Joseph, 148, 148*n*
Dey of Algiers, 130
Duane, William, 21, 150
Duer, William, 63, 129
Dundas, Robert Saunders, 2nd Viscount
    Melville, 176
Du Pont de Nemours, Samuel, 59
Du Pont, Victor Marie, 2, 4*n*
Durrell, Daniel, 78

Eaton, William, 72
Embargo (1807): adoption of, 76–78;
    violations of, 88–92; support of, 78,
    88, 92, 96*n*; opposition to, 93–94,
    96–97, 99–100; economic conse-
    quences of, 91*n*, 94–96; replaced, 101;
    mentioned, 5, 12, 105, 112
Embargo (1812), 172
Emmerich, duc de Dalberg, 170, 181–
    82

Empress of China, 63
Erskine, David M.: on embargo, 92, 97;
    on non-intercourse, 101*n*; accord with
    United States, 105–106; mentioned,
    42, 88, 109*n*, 110, 111, 115, 123
Escheverria, Durand, 132*n*
Essex, U.S.S., 151
Essex decision, 66, 67, 69
Europe, 2–3
Eustis, William, 127, 190

Factor, 167*n*
Fauchet, Jean Antoine Joseph, 35
Federalists: and France, 17–18, 110*n*; and
    Britain, 17–19, 19*n*; 106, 117–18,
    170–71, 176–77; weakening of, 18–
    19; criticism of, 20; on port clearance
    bill, 52; and West Florida, 56–58, 59;
    opposition to Republican policies, 77*n*,
    78, 88, 140–41; and Barlow, 132; and
    Monroe, 137; and Henry-Crillon affair,
    171–72
Federal Republican and Commercial Gazette,
    110*n*
Fischer, David Hackett, 19
Foster, Augustus John, 20, 36, 36*n*, 118,
    137, 138, 151, 152, 154, 156*n*,
    170–71, 174, 176–77, 177*n*, 180,
    180*n*
Fouché, Joseph, duc de Otranto, 113,
    144*n*, 144–45
Fox, Charles James, 27
France: commerce of, 30*n*, 32–33, 113,
    141, 153; and Russia, 31, 120; and
    Florida settlement, 46–47, 55, 66; and
    San Domingo, 51; bribery in diplomacy
    of, 53–54; European involvements,
    60–61, 107–108; and United States,
    70–71, 75–76, 97, 98, 120–24,
    139–40, 147, 151, 167, 173, 179–
    81, 188–89, 191; and license trade,
    118–19, 118*n*
Franco-American relations, 10, 33, 34,
    45, 105–106
Franco-American treaty of 1778, p. 23
French Revolution, 63, 129, 130
Fritz, Florence, 129*n*
Fulton, Robert, 130, 131, 131*n*, 134,
    153, 186

Gaëte, duc de. *See* Gaudin, Martin Michel Charles
Gales, Joseph, 138n, 149
Gallatin, Albert: and Republicans, 21–22, 134–35; and Turreau, 37; and d'Hauterive, 44, 110–11n; and Parker, 64; and embargo, 78; Henry case, 172n; mentioned, 45, 71n, 90, 104, 113, 116, 128, 150, 187, 189
Garnett, James Mercer, 173n
Gates, Horatio, 16
Gaudin, Martin Michel Charles, duc de Gaëte, 121
Gazette de France, 110
Genet, Edmond Charles, 35
Gerry, Elbridge, 21, 76, 139
Giles, William Branch, 21, 134–35, 150
Gilman, Nicholas, 112
Glover, Richard, 177n
Godoy, Manuel, 60, 62
Gore, Christopher, 117
Graham, John, 168n
Granger, Gideon, 171n
Great Britain: and the United States, 5, 9–10, 13, 27–28, 51, 51n, 75–76, 97, 105, 120, 166, 177; economic war with France, 26–28, 31–32, 118, 188n, 141; intervention in Iberian peninsula, 61; and impressment, 69–71; and American market, 77, 77n; and Berlin and Milan decrees, 123–24, 140, 151
Gregg, Andrew, 71, 72, 77, 93, 112
Griffith, Robert, 58
Grundy, Felix, 170
Guadalupe River, 54

Haley, Nathan, 162n, 170, 187
Hamburg, 119
Hamilton, Alexander, 8n, 129, 145
Hammond, Bray, 5n
Harper, John Adams, 148, 171n, 172, 173, 180n
Harrison, William Henry, 175
d'Hauterive, comte de. *See* de la Nautte, Alexander Maurice Blanc
Hay, George, 136n, 180
Heath, Phoebe, 140n, 169n

Hemings, Sally, 11
Henry, John, 171–72
Henry-Crillon affair, 171–72
Hillhouse, James, 56
Hind, 119
Holker, John, 63
Holland, 114
Horizon, 76, 108
Hornet, 59, 168, 171, 173
Hull, Isaac, 153
Humboldt, Baron Wilhelm von, 187

Impressment, 69–71, 69n, 70n, 73, 166, 175
Inchiquin, 41n
Irving, Washington, 2–4

Jackson, Andrew, 118n, 188, 191
Jackson, Francis James ("Copenhagen"), 19, 41n, 42, 104n, 106, 117, 117n, 118
Jackson, James, 77, 175n
Jay Treaty, 6, 9, 76
Jefferson, Thomas: attitude towards war, 1–2; and defense expenditures, 7; and balance of power, 9n; and impressment, 10, 70; and France, 10, 12–14; as controversial figure, 11; attitude towards Britain, 13, 50, 106, 106n; and commerce, 22; and peace, 22; and Moreau, 42; and Turreau, 42n; and West Florida, 46–48, 50, 54–55, 60; and San Domingo, 47, 51–52; and Spain, 55–56; and Armstrong, 59, 59n; and Parker, 64; and Bowdoin-Armstrong clash, 65; and commerical warfare, 71–72, 71–72, 76, 76n; and Monroe-Pinkney treaty, 71; and *Chesapeake-Leopard* affair, 74–76; and embargo, 77–78, 92–94, 93n, 116n; and Congress, 99–100, 112n; and Madison, 104, 188; and Barlow, 130; delays Livingston, 133n; supports war, 175n, 177n; defends Warden, 188, 188n; last years of, 189; mentioned, 62, 66, 104n, 106, 109, 112, 128, 135, 145, 151, 172, 173, 191
John Adams, 152

Johnson, Richard Mentor, 170
Jones, John Lane, 93, 93*n*
Josephine, Empress, 181
Junot, Andoche, 97

Labouchère, Pierre Cesar, 61, 62, 62*n*
Lafayette, marquis de. *See* Motier, Gilbert du
Latrobe, Benjamin, 168
League of Armed Neutrality, 34
Leavenworth, Mark, 184
Leclerc, Charles, 35
Lee, William, 2*n*, 13*n*, 32*n*, 114, 132*n*, 162, 162*n*, 165, 186–88, 190
Lefebvre, Georges, 169*n*
Le Havre, 70
Leib, Michael, 21, 150
Lettsom, John Coakley, 19
Lewis, Morgan, 60*n*
License trade, 30–31, 118–19, 121
Lincoln, Levi, 126
Little Belt, H.M.S., 143, 163
Livingston, Brockholst, 131–32
Livingston, Edward, 67*n*
Livingston, Robert L., 98*n*
Livingston, Robert R., 15–16, 47–48, 49, 53, 53*n*, 62, 64, 189
Logan, George, 57, 137
Lorient, 167*n*
L'Orient, 50, 70, 107
Louis XVIII, 190
Louisiana Purchase, 9, 10, 15, 18, 18*n*, 24, 25, 46–47, 50, 55, 59, 62*n*, 64, 165
Luther, Martin, 183

Macon, Nathaniel, 7*n*, 20–21, 52, 78, 99, 102, 116–17, 135*n*, 170, 173, 173*n*
Macon's Bill #1, 116
Macon's Bill #2, 75, 107, 112, 116–17, 121, 123, 124, 139
Madison, Dolley, 171, 186
Madison, James: and Jefferson, 14–15, 188*n*; and Republicans, 21–22, 150; and commerce, 22; and West Florida, 48, 54; and belligerents, 50, 97*n*, 140, 147, 173, 180; and San Domingo, 51,

52, 52*n*; protests impressment, 70; and embargo, 76; career of, 103; views of, 103–104, 104*n*, 148–49; policy of, 104; attitude in 1809, pp. 109, 111–12; as leader, 112–13, 148–49, 178; and Cadore letter, 122–24, 123*n*; and Armstrong, 125, 127–28; and Russell, 127–28; and Smith-Gallatin clash, 134–35; and non-importation, 139–40; and Burr's proposal, 145*n*; Annual Message of, 147; and Barlow's negotiations, 167–68, 173, 181; and grain trade, 167; and Henry-Crillon affair, 171–72; and ninety-day embargo, 172; delivers war message, 174; and Warden-Crawford struggle, 188*n*; death of, 189; mentioned, 7, 56, 62, 75, 98, 105, 106, 116, 117, 142, 152, 156, 175, 187
Manual of Parliamentary Practice, 36
Marbois, François de, 3, 4, 48, 49, 54, 61
Maret, Hugues-Bernard, duc de Bassano: and Barlow, 128, 163–64, 184; career of, 139; as foreign minister, 139, 143; and Burr, 145; and St. Cloud decree, 169; death of, 190; mentioned, 152, 156, 173, 181, 182, 183
Marie-Louise, 115
Marseilles, 32, 70, 121
Marshall, John, 131, 145
McMaster, John Bach, 47*n*, 148
McRae, Alexander, 17, 145, 145*n*
Melvin, Frank E., 119*n*
Meneval, Claude-Francois de, 29
Merry, Anthony, 36–37, 36*n*, 37*n*, 42, 71–72
Mirabeau, comte de. *See* Riquetti, Honoré Gabriel
Mississippi River, 46
Mississippi Territory, 46
Mitchell, John, 71*n*
Mobile Act, 48, 55
Mohl, Raymond A., 95*n*
Monroe, James: and Livingston, 15; on British attitude, 27; and West Florida, 48–50, 53; becomes secretary of state, 136–37; and Sérurier, 138*n*; and pol-

icy, 150–51; and Barlow's instructions, 153–54; writes editorial, 173; and Madison, 178; career of, 189; mentioned, 8, 54, 55, 64, 71, 75, 134, 142, 149, 150, 152, 156, 162n, 166, 168, 172, 175, 177, 180, 181, 190
Monroe-Pinkney treaty, 71, 72, 106, 136
Montalivet, comte de. *See* Bachasson, Jean Baptiste
Mooney, Chase C., 189n
Morales, Juan Ventura, 64n
Moreau, John Victor, 40, 42
Morier, John, 104n, 118, 137n, 140, 142n
Morris, Gouverneur, 8, 64
Morrow, Jeremiah, 179
Motier, Gilbert du, marquis de Lafayette, 63, 113, 128, 130
Mulford, Daniel, 69n
Murray, William Vans, 35

Nantes, 32, 50, 70, 121
Napoleon III, 191
National Convention, 129
National Intelligencer: denounces Fox's blockade, 28; on Pichegru, 40n; Jefferson's relationship with, 54n; supports embargo, 78; and attacks on shipping, 120; and criticism of Barlow, 130n; urges vigorous policy, 149–50; warns belligerents, 150n, 180–81; and St. Cloud decree, 169; and Britain, 173–74; mentioned, 10, 51, 54, 93, 138n, 176
de la Nautte, Alexander Maurice Blanc, comte d'Hauterive: career of, 44–45; and West Florida, 49; negotiations with Armstrong, 109–10, 111; death of, 191; mentioned, 54, 108, 110n, 113
Necker, Germaine. *See* de Staël, Madame
New York *Evening Post*, 70
Newburyport, 68–69, 68n
Newburyport *Herald*, 78
Nicholas, Wilson Cary, 21, 59, 59n, 101
Nicholson, Joseph, 100
Nicklin, Philip, 58
Niles, Hezekiah, 174–75
Niles' Weekly Register, 175n
Non-importation, 140–42

Non-intercourse, 93, 97, 100–101, 105, 107, 115, 116, 121, 122, 139, 148, 153
Notice Biographique sur le General Jackson, 188
Nova-Scotia Royal Gazette, 107n

Ohio Company, 129
Ohio General Assembly, 179
Oliver, Robert, 4
Olivers (of Baltimore), 100n
Orders in council: of June 3, 1803, p. 28; of January 7, 1807, p. 73; mentioned, 108, 120, 151, 152, 181
Otranto, duc de. *See* Fouché, Joseph
Otto, Louis Guillaume, 185

Pacte Maritime, 164n
Paine, Thomas, 72
Parker, Daniel: career of, 63–64, 189; and the Floridas, 64–65; on Franco-American relations, 110n, 168n; mentioned, 61, 62, 128, 129, 156, 181, 186, 190
Patterson, Elizabeth, 39–40, 137
Patterson, W. D., 32n
Peace of Amiens, 26
Perdido River, 46, 48
Perkins, Bradford, 33n, 78n, 148
Perkins, Thomas Handsayd, 3, 64, 74n
Perrin Du Lac, François Marie, 8n
Petry, Jean Baptiste, 62, 156, 164, 184, 185, 186
Pichegru, Charles, 40n
Pichon, Louis André, 13n, 35–36, 39, 51, 55, 56, 62, 191
Pickering, Timothy, 57, 111n, 132
Pinckney, Charles, 48, 49, 53, 55
Pinckney, Charles Cotesworth, 166
Pinkney, William, 71, 109, 125, 125n, 142, 144n, 151, 165n
Pitkin, Timothy, 172
Playfair, William, 132n
Plumer, William, 5n, 12n, 21, 36–37, 41, 72, 93n, 103, 163n, 175
Poindexter, George, 77, 142, 148, 170
Pope, John, 179, 179n
Port clearance bill (1805), 50–52
Port clearance bill (1806), 57

Porter, Peter B., 172
Portugal, 25, 60
Preble, Francis Anica, 190
President, U.S.S., 143, 163
Prevost, Sir George, 89

Quasi-War, 10, 15, 23, 58, 76, 130
Quids, 20
Quincy, Josiah, 142n, 172

Randolph, John (of Roanoke), 15, 20, 56, 58, 59, 72, 150
Reid, Thomas, 176
Republicans: factions, 20–22, 128, 150, 164; and Berlin decree, 72; and Smith-Gallatin feud, 134–35; and non-importation, 141–42; support for war, 178
Revenge, 77
Rhea, John, 100
Ribera y Lazaun, Eugenio Izquierdo de, 64
Riquetti, Honoré Gabriel, comte de Mirabeau, 43n
Rio Bravo (Grande) River, 54, 55
Roberts, Jonathan, 19
Rodman, John, 106
Rodney, Caesar A., 21
Root, Erastus, 5
Rule of 1756, p. 67
Russell, Jonathan: and French mission, 25, 142–43, 144n; career of, 126–27, 189; solicits ministerial post, 127–28; and Barlow, 132–33, 133n, 164n; and Monroe, 137n; and Burr, 144–45; and St. Cloud decree, 169; mentioned, 15, 64, 119, 168, 181, 187
Russia, 120, 177

Sage, Ebenezer, 112, 131n, 135n, 170, 180n
Saltonstall, Leverett, 102n
San Domingo (Haiti), 37, 50–51, 58
Savannah, 152–53
Scioto Associates, 129
Scott, Sir William, 118n
Sérurier, Louis-Barbé-Charles, comte, 123n, 132, 133, 134, 137–39, 138n, 139n, 140, 143, 147n, 151–52, 171n, 173, 191

Sevier, John, 145n
Short, William, 21, 60, 62, 64, 118–19, 150
Silliman, Benjamin, 176n
Skipwith, Fulwar, 15, 49n, 59–60, 60n, 62, 66, 66n, 98n, 126, 164n, 190
Smilie, John, 71n
Smith, John Cotton, 137n
Smith, John Spear, 162, 162n, 164, 169
Smith, Robert: and municipal regulations, 123; dismissal of, 134; feud with Gallatin, 135; later life, 135, 150; mentioned, 21, 104, 122, 125, 131, 136, 137, 143, 144, 151
Smith, Samuel: and French mission, 16; on Armstrong, 17, 58; and foreign policy, 21–22, 150; and Macon's Bill #1, 116; and Russell, 127, 127n; on Barlow, 132; feud with Gallatin, 134; on Monroe's appointment, 136n; mentioned, 56, 104, 110, 115
Smith, Samuel Harrison, 93
Spain, 46–47, 48, 49, 50, 53–55, 60, 61
Spivak, Burton, 68n, 71n, 75n
Stagg, J. C. A., 150n
Stephen, James, 167
Stewart, Robert, Viscount Castlereagh, 176
Stoddert, Benjamin, 104n
Story, Joseph, 96, 98, 99
Sullivan, James, 62
Sullivan, James (Governor), 90–91
Sumter, Thomas, 64
Swan, James, 62

Taggart, Samuel, 52, 58n, 103
Talleyrand-Périgord, Charles Maurice de, 35, 43–44, 44n, 46, 48–49, 53–54, 53n, 59, 62, 64, 98, 190
Tallmadge, Benjamin, 170–71, 172
Tallman, Peleg, 148
Tansill, Charles Callan, 47
Taylor, John (of Caroline), 20–21, 180
Taylor, John (Representative), 116
Tazewell, Littleton Waller, 136, 136n
Third Coalition, 26
Thompson, Benjamin, Count Rumford, 63, 185

Thornton, Edward, 6, 10n, 13, 15n, 70
"Timoleon," 54
Treaty of Ghent, 189
Triangular war, 100, 180
Trianon tariff, 122
Tucker, Beverly, 18n
Turreau de Garambouville, Louis Marie: conduct of, 35–37; naming of as minister, 38–39; as diplomat, 39, 42; and Bonaparte-Patterson marriage, 39–40; and Moreau, 40; and United States, 40–41, 110n; on *Chesapeake-Leopard* affair, 75; on French policy, 98; return to France, 136; death of, 190; mentioned, 53, 55, 56, 58n, 72, 104n, 105, 109, 138, 143, 156
Turreau, Madame, 37

United States: chooses neutrality, 1–2; strength of, 1, 6–7; reasons for neutrality, 2–9; contrasted with Europe, 3–5; and foreign commerce, 6; view of war in, 7; and balance of power, 8–9; "rapprochement" with Britain, 10

Varnum, Joseph B., 77, 93
Vaux, Robert, 92n
Vermont, 88–89
Villeneuve, Admiral Pierre, 26
Vision of Columbus, 129, 131

War Hawks, 104, 149, 150, 178, 178n
War in Disguise; or the Frauds of the Neutral Flags, 67, 68

War of 1812: causation, 9, 71, 101, 104, 123, 147, 148, 149–52, 166, 172, 174–75, 177–78, 178n, 180, 180n
War sentiment, 100, 115–16, 141, 148–51, 170–71, 174–77, 178, 180–81
Ward, Samuel, 4, 6
Warden, David Bailie: dismissal of, 126; and Russell, 126n; assists Barlow, 162; and Lee, 162, 186–88; and Crawford, 188n; mentioned, 15, 17, 31, 145, 153, 166, 190
Washington, George, 7–8, 7n, 8n, 9, 43, 63, 129, 171
Washington, Martha, 138
Waterhouse, Benjamin, 19
West Florida: and Franco-American relations, 46–47; purchase of, 53; speculative interest in, 64–65; takeover of, 65–66; mentioned, 12, 14, 17, 34, 53, 57, 63, 74, 140
West Indies, 57n
Whole Truth, The, 127
Wilkinson, General James, 91
Willett, Marinus, 95
Williams, Jonathan, 74
Winchester, David, 141n
Wirt, William, 175
Wolcott, Alexander, 156
Worthington, Thomas, 179

XYZ Affair, 35, 52, 53, 166

Yazoo scandal, 56